TERRORISM AND THE NEW WORLD DISORDER

Edited by

Richard H. Ward
And
Cindy S. Moors

Office of International Criminal Justice

Printed in the United States of America

ISBN: 0-942511-85-9

TABLE OF CONTENTS

PART ONE: TRENDS

TRANSNATIONAL THREATS
Phil Williams..1

THE CHANGING FACE OF CONFLICT IN THE NEW WORLD DISORDER
Andrew S. Riddile..41

INFRASTRUCTURE AT RISK FROM TERRORIST THREAT
Sean Hill..51

PART TWO: INTELLIGENCE AND INFORMATION

INTELLIGENCE, TERRORISM, AND THE NEW WORLD DISORDER
Scott McHugh..57

INTELLIGENCE AND LAW ENFORCEMENT: A CANADIAN PERSPECTIVE
Dr. G. David Smith..61

INTELLIGENCE AND TERRORISM: LOCAL LAW ENFORCEMENT PERSPECTIVE-CHICAGO TERRORIST TASK FORCE
Terry Hillard..65

INTELLIGENCE AND TERRORISM: A CANADIAN PERSPECTIVE
Wendy Nicol..71

PART THREE: THREATS

TIMOTHY JAMES MCVEIGH AND THE OKLAHOMA CITY BOMBING CASE STUDY
Lawrence W. Myers..77

AVIATION SECURITY AND THE CURRENT TERRORIST THREAT
Frank J. Donahue..113

THE CONVERGENCE OF TERRORISM AND DRUG CRIMES
Marc Steven Colen..119

HIGH NOON IN NORTHERN IRELAND
Paul Clare..129

SINGLE-ISSUE GROUPS
Dr. G. David Smith..151

THE RETURN OF THE LEFT WING
Wendy Nicol..165

ETHNO-RELIGIOUS VIOLENCE: ISLAMIC TERRORISM
Dr. Frank Tachau..171

ORGANIZED TERRORISM & MAFIA CRIMINALITY
Giacomo Barletta..173

PART FOUR: RESPONSES

BIOLOGICAL TERRORISM: THE THREAT & THE RESPONSE
Frank McDonald..183

TACTICAL RESPONSES TO TERRORISM
Rod Paschall..191

TERRORISM AND LOCAL LAW ENFORCEMENT: NEW COMPLEXITY, NEW FEARS
Matt L. Rodriguez..215

INDEX..219

PART ONE:
TRENDS

TRANSNATIONAL THREATS

Phil Williams

Microbes are often more dangerous to one's health and well being than more visible threats. They are also more pervasive, more difficult to detect, more difficult to avoid, and more difficult to counter. Security threats in the post-Cold War world have many of the same qualities. While there are still potential dangers from states that deploy large-scale military power, threats to U.S. security are no longer restricted to such states.

Such threats come in many different guises, extend well beyond military power, emanate from a growing variety of actors, are no longer linked inexorably to territory and, paradoxically, stem in part from developments that traditionally have been regarded as positive and benign in their effects. Globalization, in particular, a development that has long been hailed by liberal institutionalists as holding out the promise to transcend the parochial power struggles of a Hobbesian world, has provided new opportunities for the emergence of transnational threats. Such threats are the theme of this chapter, with particular attention given to the activities of transnational criminal organizations (TCOs), a term that is used to encompass drug trafficking organizations and transnational terrorist groups.

The major paradox of the Cold War world was that security rested upon threats that would have been disastrous to implement. In some respects power and wealth may be a source of weakness rather than strength and sophistication, particularly in technology, a source of vulnerability rather than protection. The new world has seen not so much a multiplication of potential targets--these have always been there--but an increase in both the attractiveness of many targets and in the capacity of "sovereign free actors" to exploit or destroy them.

The structured chess and poker analogies of nuclear deterrence have given way to a world in which there are fewer rules, and in which norms of behavior and conventions of restraint are no longer compelling. If a dominant theme of Cold War competition was the game of chicken, the dominant theme of the post-Cold War era is cacophony. There are many games being played simultaneously, overlapping with and impinging on one another. The playing field has become more fluid and less definable, the areas for offensive and defensive operations more problematic, and the players more varied and less predictable. Moreover, it is not always clear whether particular actions are intended to exploit or to destroy. Counterfeiting of the dollar, for example, can be either a deliberate effort to undermine the stability and integrity of the United States currency or simply an illicit way of obtaining greater wealth.

In considering the threats posed by TCOs and by transnational terrorist organizations, it is tempting to conclude that there is a blurring between the two kinds of groups. After all, transnational criminal organizations, such as the Italian Mafia and the Colombian cartels, have used terrorist attacks against the home state in an attempt to deter or disrupt vigorous law enforcement campaigns and generally maintain an environment conducive to a continuation of their criminal activities. And with the end of the Cold War, proxy factions in civil wars can no longer count on support from superpower patrons, while there has also been a decline in state sponsorship for terrorism. In these circumstances, terrorist organizations, insurgency groups, and participants in ethnic conflicts are turning to criminal activities in order to obtain funding to continue their political and military struggles.

Not surprisingly, there are growing links between criminal and terrorist organizations, both operate in the same murky world, and on occasion, see mutual benefit in deals involving weapons for illicit products or services. At times, there are natural synergies; in other instances, the alliances are forged out of necessity. Peruvian drug traffickers and Shining Path guerrillas, for example, have worked together, while in Colombia the cartels have had an ambivalent but nevertheless continuing relationship with groups such as the FARC and M-19. Whether forged out of a convenience or necessity, such links and synergies enhance the capacity of both criminal and terrorist organizations and make the threats they pose even more formidable.

Important as these tendencies are, they point to an overlapping of activities and a mixture of cooperative and conflicting relationships between the two kinds of organizations rather than towards convergence.

After all, terrorist and criminal organizations have very different objectives--political change in the former case and the accumulation of wealth in the latter. For terrorist groups, violence is not simply fundamental to their activities but is their raison d'être. For transnational criminal organizations, violence is an instrument that is often used selectively, rarely used indiscriminately, and is generally eschewed in favor of the other major instrument of transnational organized crime--corruption.

Transnational criminal organizations prefer to work within the existing system as long as this is malleable, in-so-far as they have political objectives. These are aimed against specific law enforcement policies rather than designed to overthrow the existing power structure. Co-option is generally the preferable alternative. Only where this has not worked, or where the state authorities are deemed to have reneged on their side of the bargain, do those criminal organizations resort to terror tactics.

Terrorist groups, in contrast, pursue political objectives aimed at the overthrow of the national or international status quo. For terrorist groups, the aim is political. Criminal activity such as drug or arms trafficking is simply a means to an end. If one kind of organization wants money to facilitate its terror activities, while the other uses terror to protect its business activities, they both use the same infrastructure of globalization and are both able to exploit the crisis of authority and legitimacy that has taken place in many states.

Nevertheless, divergent aims and priorities represent a potential source of tension between the two kinds of groups. Transnational criminal organizations want profit and the continued ability to exploit the financial and other systems that could increasingly become the target for destruction or disruption by terrorist organizations. Acknowledging the differences between terrorist and criminal organizations, therefore, is crucial. In both cases, however, it is essential to understand the reasons for their emergence, their future directions, and what can be done about them. Accordingly, this chapter sets out to answer several broad questions:

- Why have transnational threats emerged?
- What forces, trends, and developments are likely to shape their future direction?
- What are the major trends in transnational threats?
- What, if anything, can be done about these threats?

Explaining the emergence of transnational threats is relatively easy. Transnational crime has grown out of the economic interdependence that has for so long been regarded by liberal commentators as a stabilizing and pacifying influence in international relations. The same developments that have encouraged the growth of justifiable economic activity have also helped to promote illicit activity. As the dark side of interdependence, transnational organized crimes profess major challenges to national and international security. At the same time war, instability, and the crisis of state authority that exists in large parts of the world feed transnational organized crime, like transnational terrorist activity.

There are new opportunities for transnational crime and terrorism; new markets for illicit products; continued incentives to engage in these activities; a growing capacity for exploitation and disruption; and, if not an absence of countervailing pressures, at least a very patchy implementation of policies designed to prevent and control criminal and terrorist activities and mitigate the consequences of their actions. In effect the emergence of the global village has been accompanied by a loss of authority by the traditional guardians. The elders of the village (governments) no longer have the power to determine and enforce the rules of village life or the capacity to control the activities that take place.

The domain of state authority has contracted significantly as a result of long term secular trends that are impossible to reverse. Simultaneously and connected in part to this, there has been a loss of legitimization and authority at the national level in many states. This does not mean that the state system has lost its hold. In some cases of civil strife there has been an almost complete failure of the state and a reversal to tribalism and ethnicity as the basis for political action. But the conflict still centers on the form the state should take, in terms of either it's territorial or ethnic composition. Yet in some states, at least there is also a growing sense of alienation towards government authority per se. This is evident even in the United States where it has been a major factor in the rise of militias.

Accompanying these developments at the national level has been the process of globalization, a process that has led many corporate executives to embrace the idea of a borderless world and the twilight of national sovereignty. Transnational operations in the new global market have become a central characteristic of the modern corporation. But the very things that have made it possible to move goods, people, and money through the global economy have also facilitated the movement of "dirty money" and contract killers as well as the transportation of drugs, arms, and illegal aliens. Just as borders no longer provide an impediment to lawful business activity, they are no longer a barrier to illicit activities.

In short, globalization has provided new opportunities and capabilities for transnational criminal organizations and transnational terrorist organizations. Ironically, if globalization has reduced the importance of borders and undermined traditional conceptions of national sovereignty as impediments to criminal and terrorist activities, borders and the formalities of sovereignty continue to impede efforts by governments to respond effectively to such activities. While transnational criminals and terrorist groups operate in what is in effect a borderless world, law enforcement still operates in a bordered world--even if the borders themselves are often contested.

The twin processes of globalization and the crisis of state authority have produced a fundamental challenge to global governance, and will continue to do so. If globalization has become a dominant motif during the last quarter of the twentieth century, there is no evidence that the processes involved have run their course. Indeed, globalization is more likely to intensify rather than abate as we move into the next millennium. Moreover, since globalization has resulted in new economic and social interdependencies, efforts at reversal would have serious debilitating consequences for legitimate trade and financial flows.

Similarly, the crisis of state authority and the inability of many states to meet the needs and demands of their citizens will continue to have profound implications for the future development of transnational threats. These highly diverse developments not only make it impossible to eliminate conditions that facilitate the activities of transnational terrorist and criminal organizations, but have also resulted in a new form of geopolitics.

While traditional geopolitical competition based on power and territory is unlikely to disappear, it is accompanied by a new form of geopolitics based on very different factors and actors. The geopolitics of transnational threats differs in many respects from traditional geopolitics, in which control of natural resources and critical geographical areas was central. Yet like its predecessor, the new geopolitics rests on a series of interlocking and complimentary features of global politics and economics that helps to explain not only the growth of transnational threats but also why they are likely to intensify rather than abate.

Although the term "globalization" has long been used, it was only with the demise of the Soviet Union and the breakdown of barriers between the East and West that the process became truly global. The following analysis identifies several crucial components of this process and considers their implications for both the present and the future of transnational threats.

To a greater extent than ever before, the free movement of people, information, and ideas has become truly global. This trend is likely to intensify. At one level it is very simple. Air traffic, in particular, has provided the easy mobility that facilitates international business meetings, international vacations, and travel on a scale that is unprecedented. Among the countries that account for particularly large numbers of passengers arriving in the United States by air are France, Germany, Britain, Mexico, and Canada. Also significant are the Bahamas, the Dominican Republic, and Jamaica--all countries that have increasing links to the drug trafficking industry. There is nothing to indicate that the upward trend in mobility is likely to be reversed over the next ten to fifteen years. On the contrary, one of the most significant results of the collapse of the Soviet Union has been the emergence of new air routes to and from regions such as Central Asia that were previously inaccessible. Direct connections, for example, now exist between Tashkent and New York with a brief stop in Amsterdam. This allows new business linkages, but also facilitates the movement of drug traffickers from areas of production to the large consumer markets in Western Europe and the United States.

The other and more complex aspect of mobility of people is migration. Migration is far from a new phenomenon, and has long been propelled by the desire to escape poverty and carve out a better life. The extent of migration has never been as great as it is today, however, with some estimates claiming that there are now about 100 million migrants worldwide.

Sarah Spencer has distinguished factors that facilitate migration, factors that encourage it, and factors that necessitate it. One of the most important facilitating and encouraging factors has been transnational social networks that "tie potential immigrants to actual residents in the receiving countries, whether through families, information dispersion, or labor recruitment." The necessitating factors include famine, conflict, and repression.

There has been a vast explosion in the number of refugees in the world from 4.6 million in 1978 to over 18 million (with 6 million in

Africa and 5 million in the Middle East) by 1993. Unless the political and economic upheavals of the post-Cold War world abate significantly, the refugee problem is likely to increase. So too is migration. The difficulty, however, is that the developed countries that are the targets for migrants have unemployment problems that have reduced the demand for outside labor, creating a disconnection between supply and demand. One result of this is that those who are unable to acquire legal access to a target state may well try to enter the country illegally. Indeed, the same pressures that generate legal migration also create "unlawful flows of migrants and a boom industry for traffickers in people."

Immigration into the United States during the 1980's reached its highest level since the 1900's with over 7 million people entering the country and another 4.5 million joining them between 1991 and 1994. Western Europe has also had a major inflow both from the South and from the East although the massive exodus from Eastern Europe predicted by many observers has not taken place. In addition to the legal migrants, of course, there are also the illegal immigrants, over one million of who were apprehended by the United States border patrol in 1994.

Many demographic analyses suggest that migration, driven in a large part by economic necessity, will continue. Between 1991 and 2025 the global workforce will increase by around 1.48 billion people, of which 1.4 billion will be in the developing world. With over 40 million would-be workers entering the job market every year in the developing world and finding that jobs are simply not available, the potential for increased migration and diasporas is enormous. If developed states fail to increase immigration, illegal immigration will increase enormously. All of this has important implications for transnational criminal and terrorist organizations and activities.

Most migrants, of course, are law-abiding citizens. Yet among those who emigrate, there are inevitably members of criminal organizations who bring with them their criminal skills, knowledge, affiliations, and contacts. Chinese, Nigerian, Italian and Russian diasporas have all contained significant criminal elements. This should not be surprising when criminal organizations come under pressure in their home state either from law enforcement or as a result of internecine warfare. One response of some members is to migrate to areas and states where the risks are lower and conditions are generally more congenial.

The Sicilian diaspora of the 1960's and 1970's to places as diverse as Australia, Venezuela, and Germany is a good example.

Eventually this became a major asset as La Cosa Nostra increasingly became involved in transnational activities. The Contrera family in Venezuela became a key factor linking Italian organized crime and cocaine supplies from Latin America. Similarly, during the 1970's and 1980's, some of those allowed to emigrate from the Soviet Union were criminals. This provided a foundation for criminal activities in the United States and Israel that subsequent Russian émigré groups were able to consolidate and extend.

Greater mobility has increased the capacity of criminal organizations and their individual members to elude national criminal jurisdictions where they are high priority targets. The increase in business, personal, and leisure travel as well as the increase in migration, exacerbates the difficulties confronting governments in their efforts to monitor and control access to an exit from their national territory. There is likely to be a marked intensification of alien smuggling. Current estimates suggest that around 100,000 Chinese illegally enter the United States every year. The trends described above suggest that there will be growing diversification in the nationality of illegal immigrants as well as continued increases in their number. The corollary of course is the consolidation and extension of human commodity trafficking and increased profits to those that organize and facilitate illegal entry into the United States and other developed countries.

Air transport has provided unprecedented opportunity for individuals or groups to enter a country, commit a crime or series of crimes or engage in terrorist activity, and then depart before they are caught. Contract killers can be brought in to Brighton Beach from Yekaterinburg, fulfill their contract, and depart again before the crime has even been discovered.

The ethnic networks resulting from diasporas provide links with the home bases of criminal and terrorist organizations. These networks are an important resource for many transnational criminal organizations. They provide cover, recruits, and transnational linkages that facilitate criminal activity. And because immigrant communities are difficult for law enforcement to penetrate, they provide a built-in security mechanism. Ethnic networks make it difficult for governments to distinguish between external and internal threats posed by transnational criminal and terrorist organizations.

One of the major components and underpinnings of globalization has been the vast growth of international trade, a process greatly facilitated by the free trade system set up after World War II. The lowering of tariffs, the creation of free trade arrangements, and the gradual integration of the former Soviet bloc into the global trading system have all encouraged steep increases in global trade during the 1990's. This growth is reflected in many indices, including the use of dry cargo containers. Between 1990 and 1994, for example the availability of cargo containers jumped from 5,874,084 to 8,339,432.

There has also been an increase in the amount of world sea-borne trade. Apart from a temporary downturn in the mid-1980's resulting from lower demand for crude oil, there has been a constant increase in the amount of sea-borne trade. Forecasts through to 2005 suggest that this upward trend will continue. Once again, this provides an environment that is highly conducive to the activities of transnational criminal organizations and, to a lesser extent, terrorist organizations. There are several ways in which criminals and terrorists benefit from continued increases in global trade:

- The opportunities to embed illicit goods in licit ones are multiplying.
- Problems of inspection and monitoring are becoming even more formidable. The United States typically inspects about four percent of the containers coming into the country. As container trade continues to grow, inspections will pose even less of a barrier to smuggling.
- The number of targets for terrorist activity is increasing.
- The opportunities for smuggling weapons of mass destruction into the United States are increasing significantly.
- The number of opportunities for financial maritime fraud is increasing.
- The number of opportunities to use false invoicing for imports to the United States and Western Europe is increasing, thereby providing greater opportunities for money-laundering and the repatriation of profits from illicit activities.

While the global trading system was the initial manifestation of globalization, its importance has, if anything, been overtaken by the development of the global financial system. A major component of the new geopolitics is the financial infrastructure--a system that links countries, banks and other financial institutions such as brokerage houses and stock markets, currencies and investment portfolios in a global exchange mechanism that operates 24 hours a day. Reflecting the revolution in communications and information technologies, this system is reliant on what Joel Kurtzman has termed "megabyte money." As he notes, most money now appears as symbols on computer screens and is best understood as a network which includes all the world's markets--stocks, bonds, futures, currency, interest rate, options, etc. If money has in some respects been transformed, it retains its fungibility and can be moved from continent to continent and owner to owner, through a global system of electronic transfers that incorporates clearing mechanisms such as Chips, Swift, and Fedwire.

One of the other major characteristics of this system is that it is not under state or government control. As Kurtzman has noted, the financial economy is akin to an electronic commons that is owned by the people using it. "While its ultra-high-tech infrastructure straddles the globe and moves several trillion dollars a day between the major and minor 'nodes' on the network, it is largely unregulated."

To some extent governments and central banks have themselves to blame for this situation. As Helmut Schmidt once observed, central banks "did not see that they were losing their grip over the markets when they allowed commercial banks to establish offshore affiliates...they are not really cooperating closely enough to prevent the internationalization of financial flows without an international controlling agency. Nowadays you have one worldwide stock exchange. Nobody is controlling it. You have one worldwide money market. Nobody is controlling it."

If this situation arose in part through a lack of both foresight and oversight, once the process of deregulation had started, governments tended to embrace it as synonymous with enhanced competitiveness. The result has been described as a "competition in laxity." Yet even without government connivance, major change was inevitable, facilitated by technology and driven in part by the massive increase in the number of transactions and the move from an investment economy to a transaction economy, or what Susan Strange termed as "casino capitalism."

The increased volume of financial business has not been matched by the development of regulatory measures. And the situation may be getting even worse. The increase in the number of monetary instruments, the increased number of financial transactions (such as futures and derivatives, that are not necessarily linked directly to real products), the growing use of cyber-money and smart cards, new banking methods (such as correspondent banking), and the use of representative offices and foreign branches all make control even more difficult. If the system as a whole is impossible to control, the lack of control is not uniform.

The global banking system can be divided into three main sectors: a relatively well regulated zone in which there is strict regulation against money-laundering; the offshore banking havens that place a premium on secrecy; and the unregulated zone in countries of the former Soviet Union and parts of the developing world where appropriate norms, procedures, and conventions have not yet been established.

Passas has argued that "the combination of the internationalization and deregulation of banking in the 1980's effectively furnished both legitimate corporations and criminals with a protective shield of secrecy that undermines control efforts." While this is correct so far as it goes, it does not convey the whole picture. The privatization of former communist economies and the introduction of a commercial banking sector have added another massive obstacle in efforts to establish a global anti-money-laundering regime. As banks in Russia are integrated into the global financial system, they bring with them those elements of organized crime that exert direct control or indirect influence over their activities.

Another problem is that divergent levels of regulation ensure that efforts to prevent the global financial system from being used for money-laundering and other illicit transactions have little impact. They simply push money-laundering activities from areas where they are illegal to countries where the origin or source of money is irrelevant. This is not surprising. For both developing economies and economies in transition, capital flight tends to be more of a problem than laundering the proceeds of illicit activity. Incoming money tends to be welcomed as foreign investment--whatever its source. Even if legislation against money-laundering is enacted, it will not necessarily be implemented vigorously. In sum, unless there is universal adherence to norms of financial transparency and general adoption and implementation of laws and regulations directed against money-laundering, laundering activities simply relocate from one venue to another.

In one sense the problems that come from possible criminal exploitation of the global financial system are simply a subset of the much larger problem of state control and regulation of a vast array of transnational financial activities. Even so, it is possible to identify several ways those transnational criminal organizations, drug trafficking, and terrorist organizations can exploit the global financial system.

- The system has many points of access and makes it possible to trade anonymously, to move money rapidly and easily, and to obscure the origin and ownership of money making. Thereby, it is impossible to differentiate between dirty and clean money. Indeed, the mobility of capital parallels that of the transnational criminals themselves and could not be better suited to the activities of transnational organized crime. Megabyte money is enormously difficult to track and to control, while the creation of new stock exchanges combined with the growing popularity of future options and derivatives makes effective policing impossible. Hot money has simply become too hot to catch.
- The offshore banking sector provides attractive opportunities for the transfer and secretion of funds in places where they are relatively safe from identification and seizure by law enforcement. Some of the new trading schemes encourage a risk-taking mentality that often goes hand in hand with disregard for regulation. As Jessica Matthews has noted, the global financial system is a "space without rules" that is "made to order for those who operate without them." A system in which Nicolas Leeson can operate without supervision is a system that is easily exploited by the successors of Meyer Lansky.
- The integration of Russian banks into the global system carries with it very considerable dangers since, according to many reports, between 40 and 80 percent of these banks are under the control of organized crime. There are increased opportunities for repatriation of profits from illicit activities. Much of what is popularly termed money-laundering is not so much about disguising or cleaning money as it is about repatriating it to the home state of the criminal organization, where it can be used with impunity. In many cases the home state does not inquire as to the source of the money.
- The global nature of the system and the anonymity it affords makes it easier to provide financing for criminal or terrorist groups active in host states. As cyber-money and smart cards become increasingly popular, they are likely to be fully exploited by criminal organizations for money-laundering and other activities.

- The global financial system with its major nodes in "global cites" provides an attractive target for terrorist activity. Because the system is global and highly reliant on electronic networks, it probably has some redundancies built in. Nevertheless, terrorists, by coordinating strikes in several different locations, might be able to do serious damage to the functioning of the system and create a financial crisis of unprecedented gravity.
- The global financial system provides a myriad of new opportunities for the mixing of crime and terrorism in ways that manage to send a political message while also being very lucrative. Purchases of future options for foreign countries' wheat crops prior to biological attacks on the United States wheat crops could allow those involved to get rich and get even. Such initiatives are essentially hybrid activities that do not fall neatly into traditional categories of crime or terrorism, but are feasible contingencies and should be treated very seriously.
- The global financial system offers opportunities to increase corruption of government officials, thereby ensuring the maintenance of safe home bases for transnational criminal organizations.

A fourth dimension of the new geopolitics is the emergence of global cities, i.e. cities that have large cosmopolitan populations connected to one another by advanced telecommunications, that form the major and minor nodes of the global financial and trading systems, and that provide transportation links both to one another and to the national hinterlands they serve. Some of these cities are national capitals, while a small number have also become mega-cities with over 10 million inhabitants. Many of these cities are hosts to an influx of people coming from rural areas in search of economic opportunity.

In practice, aspirations are rarely fulfilled and most new urban dwellers find that they have merely traded a life of rural destitution for one of urban destitution. As Wally N'Dow, head of the Habitat 11 Conference has noted, there are now more than 600 million people officially homeless or living in life-threatening urban conditions. More than one billion lack sanitation. "A low-grade civil war is fought every day in the world's urban centers. Many cities are collapsing. We risk a complete breakdown in cities. People feel alienated." Nor are conditions likely to improve in the near future as the number of mega-cities increases from 14 in the mid-1990's to over 25 by 2015.

This is an urban environment in which survival takes precedence over the rule of law, in which alienation and anger are rife, and in which localized street gangs become the dominant form of social organization. The most ruthless and efficient of these gangs are likely to develop into more significant and powerful criminal organizations. For some individuals, solace and bonding will be found not in crime but in forms of political, social, and economic activism that could all too easily become transformed into new forms of economic-based terrorism. In other words, the rise of global cities has several consequences for transnational threats:

- Such cities are excellent incubators for criminal and terrorist groups. They provide anonymity and encourage the kinds of survival skills and bonding mechanisms that underpin all successful criminal enterprises.
- Urban youth provides an excellent recruitment pool for existing transnational criminal organizations.
- Mega-cities are likely to be a breeding ground for a new radicalism that is rooted in the desire for revenge or simply a fervent wish to destroy what one cannot hope to have.
- Such cities provide excellent opportunities for the establishment of links among criminal organizations and between criminal and terrorist organizations. Cities like Rio de Janeiro have already witnessed the development of a kind of criminal cosmopolitanism in which criminals of various nationalities work side by side, a form of cooperation that often endures and extends beyond the city and ultimately beyond national borders.

Another component of the new geopolitics is the development of global information and communication systems that are linked to--and complement--the global financial and transportation systems. Although it is possible to talk about the emergence of a global information system, it is, however, a system in which some countries are much more advanced than others are.

In developing countries and countries in transition, the level of computerization is still relatively low. However, in post-modem states such as Japan, Western Europe, and the United States, sophisticated computer and information systems have become key components of the economy. Moreover, as corporations and governments have downsized, they have turned to technology for greater efficiencies at lower costs. As one Rand Corporation report noted, "there is a powerful commercial imperative to ensure that the emerging system of cyberspace networks operate with increased efficiency so that inventories of any data and/or material commodity can be exploited with less need for the maintenance of large inventories that compensate for uncertainties about supply and demand." The result has been considerable increases in both sophistication and dependence. Technology has been embraced enthusiastically and with little attention to inadvertent vulnerabilities that might result.

As David Gompert has noted, reliance on information technology has grown much faster than our grasp of the vulnerabilities inherent in the networks, systems, and core technologies that knit the nation together. Furthermore if anything, the trends are accelerating rather than slowing down. The Rand report cited above highlighted several dimensions of this continuing technological momentum. Some of which are the cellular revolution, the expansion of the Internet and the World Wide Web, increased connectivity among computers, the growth of electronic commerce, the growth in activist use of the National Information Infrastructure (NII) and the Global Information Infrastructure (GII), and the increased reliance of the Department of Defense on the commercial switched telephone and public data systems.

At the national level the information infrastructure is used to control oil and gas pipelines, electric power grids, transportation systems, banking transactions, and the health care system, as well as, many commercial enterprises. Consequently, this infrastructure is a very tempting target. This is particularly true of the Department of Defense. According to a General Accounting Office report in the spring of 1996, the Department of Defense uses over 2.1 million computers, 10,000 local networks, 100 long-distance networks, 200 command centers, and 16 central computer processing facilities (or MegaCenters). There are over 2 million Defense computer users and another two million non-Defense users that do business with the Department.

Not surprisingly, this system has certain vulnerabilities. Preventing and sometimes detecting intrusions has proved highly problematic. Only about 1 in 500 attacks are detected and reported even though there are around 250,000 attempted intrusions per year. Those attacks that have been detected have involved the theft, alteration, or destruction of data and software systems (GAO). Commercial systems almost certainly have similar problems, although assessing the extent of these is difficult as corporations seek to avoid publicity that might encourage copycat attacks.

In short, the new global and national information infrastructures represent a new set of vulnerabilities that can be exploited by transnational criminal organizations, as well as, by individuals. Indeed, it is in the area of information technology that there is perhaps the greatest diffusion and democratization of threats to security and a decoupling of the traditional linkages between territorial integrity and security.

In the past, threats to national security have generally been associated with large accumulations of power and resources, and efforts at territorial aggrandizement. National security has required a capacity, either through one's own efforts or through a shrewd policy of coalition building, to defend against such aggrandizement by other states. Physical invasion of territory or physical destruction of resources and wealth along with the coercive power that came from the capacity for such actions were the major threats. They have not disappeared and it would be foolish to suggest that they are a thing of the past.

But there now exists a new set of vulnerabilities that are wholly independent of territory or physical resources. Ironically, these vulnerabilities are also asymmetrical: the greater the level of sophistication, the greater the vulnerability. As societies become more dependent upon linked communication and information systems, the possibility that these systems will be compromised or disrupted becomes more salient, and the resulting consequences more catastrophic. The disruption of the systems that facilitate national and global financial transactions, stock markets, air traffic control, the collection of taxes, the operation of social security, let alone key components of the military, intelligence, and law enforcement infrastructures, all could have far reaching effects on the ability of society and government to function effectively.

Moreover, the capacity to engage in actions that produce catastrophic disruptions in the national and global information infrastructures is also becoming more widespread. What one journalist has termed the "democratization of high technology" has been accompanied by a new form of individual empowerment, the positive side of which is the growth of computer literacy and the negative side is the emergence of the hacker/cracker subculture.

One Rand report made the same point in a different way when emphasizing the low entry costs to engage in offensive strategies in cyberspace, "The price to develop a high performance Information Warfare capability is low and is available to a wide range of participants. Unlike previous high-performance weapon technologies, new potential information warfare weapons can be developed by skilled individuals or groups residing anywhere within the GII."

One person with a computer, a modem, and the requisite knowledge and skills has the capacity to wreak considerable havoc on national and global information systems--even those that have security mechanisms and fire walls. Furthermore, there are multiple opportunities for the hacker to protect his anonymity through a process that is the cyberspace equivalent of the establishment of front companies. Most hacking has simply involved efforts by the hackers to display their skills. Yet as this form of individual empowerment becomes more closely linked to transnational criminal organizations or terrorists, the potential vulnerabilities loom very large:

- We should expect a growing convergence between organized crime and white-collar crime as criminal organizations use the information infrastructure as the mechanism for both old and new forms of financial fraud.
- If transnational criminal organizations will look to use the global information system primarily for new avenues for financial gain, they will also have the capability to inflict major damage on the system. National and global information systems open up not only new opportunities for fraud and embezzlement, but also for disruption and extortion. To the extent transnational criminal organizations feel threatened by law enforcement efforts, they might engage in disruptive activities of this kind. Alternatively, exhibiting a capacity to damage crucial nodes in the information and communications infrastructure could in itself enhance the coercive power of these groups. Vulnerabilities in national and global information infrastructures provide transnational criminals with new forms of bargaining power.
- The growth of information technology and the speed and ease with which information can be knotted provides greater opportunities for theft of data and intellectual property, and make such activities almost impossible to prevent or control.

- There are increased nodes of vulnerability especially at the points where the virtual and the real meet. Tampering with data and software in the virtual system could have major repercussions in the physical world, involving such things as disruption of air traffic control systems, tampering with automated computer controlled pharmaceutical or food production, and interfering with financial transactions. Although such activities are often described as cyber-terrorism, this is a misnomer in that the consequences are not limited to the world of cyberspace, but are felt in very telling ways in the physical world. It is simply that there are new instruments through which terrorists can attack society.
- The dependence on information systems also provides some opportunities for terrorist activities that can damage a target government but that do not necessarily kill innocent civilians. As Arquilla and Ronfeldt note, the advantage of this is that it avoids the opprobrium that otherwise can seriously damage the cause of the terrorist, and therefore, could provide the best of all worlds. At the same time, the extent to which such actions become a source of publicity is uncertain.
- There are novel opportunities for extortion. Criminal organizations can use threats to computer and information systems in order to extort large payments from companies that find it preferable to pay up rather than lose their capacity to operate effectively in a very competitive business environment. In Britain, it was reported in early June 1996 that a number of companies, banks and trading houses had paid over 600 million dollars to avoid having their computer systems shut down or disrupted. Although the accuracy of these reports was challenged, this is almost certainly a trend for the future. And unless potential targets of "cyber-extortion" manage to reduce their vulnerability, they are likely to continue at the mercy of those that have developed a capacity to inflict serious damage on what has in effect, become the central nervous system of corporations and financial institutions. Three characteristics of these threats stand out: the perpetrator would prefer acquiescence of the target to implementation

of the threat; they are anonymous, and the objective is financial gain.

- Another consequence of the growth of information systems and their vulnerability is that it will become even more difficult to differentiate between an accident and an act of terror. A shutdown in the system and the loss of data may result from an internal problem or an external attack. In some cases it may be impossible to determine the cause. Closely related to this is the possibility that there will be a significant time lag between the attack. Ties that bind criminal organizations are also based on more extensive social mechanisms such as common ethnicity, shared experience (e.g. in prison, or in street gangs), or even in the Chinese case, the notion of *suanshi*, or reciprocal obligation, that can span generations and continents. These binding mechanisms create a basis for trust and make it difficult for law enforcement to penetrate or infiltrate the organizations. Network organizations also have the advantage that they are fluid, highly adaptable, and resistant to disruption. They have a degree of resilience that other forms of organization lack. The network is an ideal form for maintaining organizational integrity because networks are characterized by considerable redundancy and linkages can be maintained through a variety of different connections. If some of the connections are broken, they can be replaced--enabling the organization to reconstitute itself without great difficulty. Furthermore, even if the periphery of a network is infiltrated, the core can still be insulated. This is partly because of what is termed "loose coupling." In organizations or systems where the components are tightly coupled, disturbance or dislocation in one component can create a damaging chain reaction. In contrast, as Perrow notes, "loose coupling gives time, resources, and alternative paths to cope with the disturbance and limits its impact."

The value of network structures is increasingly being recognized in the commercial and industrial world where some businesses are finding that alternatives to traditional hierarchy are both more efficient and more effective in terms of innovation and the achievement of goals. Transnational criminal organizations, however, have been in this position for some time and have instinctively developed a form of organization that offers distinct advantages over any other--advantages that are increasing as a result of the information and communications revolutions. Indeed, there are several implications of the growing importance of transnational network structures that need to be identified:

- The possibility of new forms of cooperation among criminal organizations. As Arquilla and Ronfledt have noted in a brilliant study entitled *The Advent of Netwar*, the network form of organization is becoming a new source of power, especially "for actors who have previously had to operate in isolation from each other and who could or would not coalesce into a hierarchical design." Criminal organizations that jealously guard their own prerogatives and independence and that would find merger unacceptable are both able and willing to engage in extensive cooperation through networks.
- Criminal organizations tend to extend their influence into the licit sectors of the economy, society, and government by extending their network using coercion, co-option or corruption as necessary. This serves to prevent or undermine law enforcement activities. The difficulty for those trying to attack networks are that it is often unclear how extensive the network is, let alone where the crucial nodes and linkages are located.
- Terrorist groups are also becoming increasingly reliant on network structures. Again, as Arquilla and Ronfeldt note, "many revolutionary and terrorist organizations are adopting networked command structures that are segmented and polycephalolis (i.e. having a number of commanders who are positioned at various nodes but who are able to exert strategic control over the whole network)." This makes them even more difficult to counter.

The growth of global information systems has gone hand in hand with the development of global communications. At its most obvious, the spread of telecommunications, fax machines, electronic mailboxes, and the like has opened up many more opportunities for cross border contacts and the development of more extensive networks. In some ways this has served to establish and entrench the dominance of Western popular culture in many parts of the world; but it has also helped to create global markets for licit and illicit products alike.

If global communications have created more homogenous markets, however, they have not dispelled inequalities among potential consumers. In fact, the globalization of communications has served to highlight and accentuate social and economic inequalities. As the Commission on Global Governance has noted, "the number of absolute poor, the truly destitute, was estimated by the World Bank at 1.3 billion in 1993, and is probably still growing. One-fifth of the world lives in countries, mainly in Africa and Latin America, where living standards actually fell in the 1980's. Several indicators of aggregate poverty--1.5 billion lack access to safe water and 2 billion lack safe sanitation, more than 1 billion are illiterate, including half of all rural women-are no less chilling than a quarter-century ago" (Commission on Global Governance).

The difference is that those who live in abject poverty are becoming increasingly aware that everyone does not share their predicament. One result of this is that the poor segments of the population are less likely to passively accept their fate. There are several implications of all this:

- The imperative to design global marketing strategies is as relevant to those who trade in illicit products as for those who provide illicit goods and services. For example, illicit drugs have become truly global products. In the last few years new forms of drug use have spread to areas such as South Africa and the former Soviet Union, where substance abuse was traditionally a much more restricted activity.
- There is a market for drugs even in the poorest segments of the population where narcotics provide an escape from the harsh realities of day to day existence.
- The other result of the growing awareness of inequalities is likely to be the desire either to become wealthy--by whatever means necessary--or to strike out in retaliation at those who possess the wealth and are seen as exploitative. In short, the global communications revolution is also likely to enhance the recruitment process for both criminal and terrorist organizations.
- There are massive target audiences for acts of violence, something recognized as long ago as the Palestinian attack at the Munich Olympics. But that is no longer dependent on the global spotlight being in one place. In light of the global communications revolution terrorism is no longer

merely theater, it is now global theater. And terrorists themselves can create the stage rather than relying on a pre-existing stage.

It is clear from all this that one of the most pervasive consequences of globalization is the contracting domain of state authority. States can no longer determine what and who crosses their borders, can no longer control transnational markets, and can no longer prevent the growth of parallel economies. If all this represents an attack on state authority and sovereignty from above, it has been accompanied by an attack on state legitimacy from below.

The demise of the nation state has been long predicted, but states retain their position as the dominant organizing device for political life. At the same time, in many states there has been a reduction in both internal cohesion and the capacity to govern. For most of the twentieth century strong authoritarian or totalitarian structures were a major force in political life. The dominant theme of the 1990's--and one that is likely to continue--is the collapse of totalitarian forms of government in the former Soviet Union and their tacit abandonment elsewhere. While this was widely hailed as a victory for both democracy and market economies, it has also brought with it a collapse of social controls that has had all sorts of unforeseen consequences, and that has become central to the new geopolitics.

In the new geopolitics, the crucial variable is not power so much as authority, or rather the lack of it. Criminal organizations flourish in those countries where authority has been eroded (or never properly established) and the state is weak. Such organizations not only thrive on political weakness and instability but also exacerbate the consequences of the breakdown of authority structures that occurred in an increasing number of states during the 1980's and the first half of the 1990's. The era of the failed nation-state is also the era in which organized crime has become a major problem both domestically and across national borders.

One of the crucial factors, for example, in the emergence of organized crime and drug trafficking in many of the countries of Eastern Europe and the former Soviet Union is the weakness of the new states. Few states in transition have effective criminal justice systems to assist in the struggle against organized crime. They have no legislation that allows them to target criminal organizations as such, or that facilitates witness protection schemes, asset forfeiture, and electronic surveillance, all of which are essential in efforts to combat organized crime. Furthermore in many of these states, banking regulations are notably lax, thereby providing an attractive environment for money-laundering both by indigenous criminal organizations and by groups from elsewhere.

Weak state capacity, however, goes beyond the absence of appropriate legislation. Massive social and economic dislocation, hyperinflation, unemployment, a limited tax base, and a multiplicity of demands on the state have all contributed to the under-funding of law enforcement, which typically has poor transportation, limited communications systems and relatively unsophisticated computer equipment. These trends have also removed the social safety nets that existed before the collapse of communism. The result has been erosion of social controls at the time when they were most needed.

Perhaps nowhere have such developments been more obvious and more alarming than in Russia's diminution of control over its inventory of nuclear materials. At the same time, poor economic conditions and the lack of a regulatory framework for the transition to capitalism has encouraged the development of a culture in which everything is for sale. The result has been a process of nuclear material leakage from Russia that is likely to continue for some time, and that could be exploited by both criminal and terrorist organizations.

Even where the state has the capacity to take effective action against organized crime, a government may acquiesce in criminal activities either because there is recognition that these activities provide certain benefits to the state or because portions of the population benefit from them. Indeed, transnational criminal organizations often portray themselves as positive forces in society and the economy, providing jobs that would otherwise be unavailable, and offering services that the government has failed to provide.

Some groups are highly paternalistic. The Japanese Yakuza's provision of food parcels and other assistance during the Kobe earthquake was not really out of the norm. Pablo Escobar had a housing program called "Medellin without slums," while the drug lords of Rio de Janeiro occasionally provide food and hospital transportation for the inhabitants of the favelas. As well as making it possible to obtain counter-intelligence that is useful when governments and law enforcement agencies do go on the offensive, such actions tend to create a degree of public sympathy for criminal organization that makes such offensives by governments less likely.

This is not to ignore the alienation of the population that occurs when transnational criminal organizations embark on offensives of violence against the state authorities. Short of this, however, the degree of tolerance for organized crime compounds the difficulties faced by many governments.

Corruption offers another way in which transnational criminal organizations can nullify or disarm the home state. When individuals or groups within government benefit directly as a result of the continuation of the criminal activities, then their desire to prevent those activities and destroy the organizations that engage in them is likely to be minimal. Indeed, as Shelley notes, "the extensive penetration of such groups into the state sector has immunized most transnational groups from the law enforcement controls of their home countries." Such corruption can reach a level where there is a virtual partnership between the criminal organization and the government that embrace one another in a symbiotic relationship.

In sum, criminal organizations can prosper in a safe home base that may be based on the weakness of government (lack of capacity to do anything about the criminal organizations), the acquiescence of government (lack of will to do anything about it), on corruption, or collusion. In the last two of these the distinguishing feature is simply the extent of the corruption. In the collusive state, the government has gone beyond the recipient of benefits provided by the criminal organization to become a partner in criminal enterprise. Collusion of this kind is based on mutual convenience and shared greed.

Another form of collusion is that between government and terrorist organizations. In these cases, however, collusion is based less on expediency and more on common values and a shared antipathy to the major target of terrorist action. Terrorist groups, of course, have long operated from sanctuaries provided by states that have sponsored and supported their activities. If much terrorist activity has traditionally been an extension of state policy, we are also likely to see the emergence of terrorist groups based in states that are not necessarily sympathetic to their activities but that are unable to do anything about them.

Acting from a "sanctuary" or safe haven, criminal and terrorist organizations are able to extend their criminal activities into other countries, often developing important regional networks and sometimes extending their operations globally. The irony is that whatever the internal condition of the state, so long as it retains nominal control over its territorial base, it is recognized as a sovereign entity by others. Weakness, acquiescence, and corruption are not in themselves a justification for external intervention in a state system in which respect for sovereignty remains one of the most important norms (although one that was frequently violated on grounds of national security during the Cold War).

National sovereignty is almost invariably exploited by criminal organizations in an effort to ensure that the home base remains safe from foreign law enforcement activities. As they try to prevent the emergence of a strong home state and to protect themselves from domestic law enforcement, criminal organizations use national sovereignty as a barrier to the law enforcement agencies of other states, even while they themselves are routinely violating the sovereignty of these other states in pursuit of profit and access to markets. Indeed, borders are important for criminal organizations only because they represent different levels of risk and demarcate different markets. In almost every other way they are irrelevant. The implications of all of this are:

- Transnational criminal organizations have a variety of home bases where the risks they face are low and which act as sanctuaries from which they can engage in criminal activities with impunity.
- The number of sanctuaries has increased significantly through the 1980's because of the weakness, acquiescence, or corruption of states.
- Terrorist organizations have a slightly less congenial environment but can usually find a few acquiescent or collusive governments that will provide protection and support. Increasingly they are also likely to take advantage of the weakness of specific states in establishing the home base for their activities.
- The use of corruption and the development of collusive relationships exemplify the growing sophistication of criminal organizations that are concerned not only with increasing their profits but also with preventing and controlling the risks they face from law enforcement.
- The collapse of the Soviet Union brought a new set of opportunities for criminal organizations to acquire and sell not only state property and strategic metals and minerals, but also armaments and even, on occasion, nuclear materials. It will be some time before the new opportunities are blocked by the re-establishment of effective control mechanisms.

The other major development at the national level has been not simply the loss of state authority but the disintegration of some states into warring factions. Even during the Cold War the majority of wars took place within national boundaries. Since its end, this tendency has become more pronounced. Between 1989 and 1992, there were 82 armed conflicts in which more than 1,000 people were killed. Of these conflicts, 79 were internal.

The tendencies towards fragmentation are in many ways the complete antithesis of those towards globalization. Yet they pose an equally profound challenge to nation-states--albeit from within rather than without. Barker notes "retribalization of large swaths of humankind by war and bloodshed" offer good business opportunities for criminal organizations while also providing the kind of environment in which the losers resort to terrorist activity as a way of continuing their struggle.

Ethnic conflicts offer numerous opportunities for trafficking in arms. Indeed, arms for drug deals sometimes characterize them, as ethnic groups seek ways of acquiring the means to continue the armed struggle. This has been an important feature of the war in Yugoslavia and has been replicated elsewhere. Linkages between the warring parties and criminal organizations willing to take the risks of dealing with them tend to be mutually beneficial. In some cases, however, the criminal organizations are cut out as the participants in conflict engage in criminal activities of their own, a phenomenon one journalist has described as "fighters-turned-felons." This phenomenon seems likely to grow as ethnic factions, insurgency movements, and terrorist groups all find it more difficult to obtain state sponsorship for their activities. Criminal endeavors provide a substitute that enables them to finance and sustain their political struggles.

This has been reflected in the large number of Tamils who have been arrested in Europe and North America for drug trafficking. Close relationships have also been forged between criminal organizations and revolutionary or guerrilla movements. Ideological antipathies have been no barrier to alliances of convenience. When in Peru a few years ago, El Vaticano, one of the country's most prominent drug traffickers, was sentenced to imprisonment. This was not for his drug trafficking but rather for his cooperation with the Shining Path guerrillas.

This is not to deny that, on occasion, political instability and military conflict poses problems for criminal organizations. Traffickers bringing heroin to Western Europe from Southwest Asia, for example, have had to find alternatives to the Balkan route as a result of the conflict in Yugoslavia. However, for the most part, criminal organizations flourish amidst such conditions--as is evident in the two states that are the largest producers of opium, Burma and Afghanistan, both of which are torn by ethnic and tribal conflict and are home to major drug trafficking organizations.

It is difficult, therefore, to avoid the conclusion that "whatever form they take--guerrillas going criminal or finding Mafia allies or Mafia profiting from war--the links between war and crime are growing stronger in the 1990's." In the short term, not only do these links add to the profits that accrue to transnational organized crime, they also tend to perpetuate conflicts, encourage terrorism, and make an enduring peace more elusive. They may also encourage the emergence of new forms of hybrid organizations that are part criminal organization, part terrorist, and part mercenary, who provide specialized forms of violence against either competitors or government forces. Ethnic conflicts, therefore, have significant implications for transnational criminal and terrorist activities:

- They provide incentives to engage in criminal activity in order to fund political struggles.
- They create and perpetuate hatreds that transcend national boundaries and the immediate locale of the conflict. That can lead to an extension of terrorist activities.
- They provide a large cadre of well-trained specialists in violence with the knowledge and expertise that can be directed against governments or used by criminal organizations as they engage in struggles for dominance with each other. The growing professionalization of violence makes these groups even more formidable adversaries for governments.

Indeed, the implication of this analysis is that governments will find themselves facing criminal organizations that are not only sophisticated in the use of corruption and techniques of co-option, but that they will also have the capacity to initiate a level of violence going well beyond that perpetrated by traditional organized crime groups.

One of the implications of the proceeding analysis is that there is enormous scope for a much more diversified terrorist threat, in terms of the groups themselves, the instruments they use and the target sets available. As terrorist groups become more varied, they are also likely to be less predictable. Terrorist groups that are the product of some kind of national independence movement (e.g.. the Basque ETA and the Irish Republican Army) are likely to continue their struggle in the future. So too are Middle Eastern terrorist groups whose activity is directed against the state of Israel and its supporters.

While these latter groups are not synonymous with radical Islamic organizations, they do overlap with them. The groups themselves are highly fluid, subject to both fractionalization and factionalization. Increasingly groups whose allegiance to a political cause is less clear, whose targets are less obvious, and who are far less predictable are joining them. There are two kinds of groups in particular that seem likely to become an increasingly important part of the terrorist scene.

The first set of groups are those that are likely to arise from continued poverty and despair in the developing world. With their predicament accentuated by a global media that can hardly avoid highlighting the gap between the 'haves' and the 'have-nots', the increased radicalization of the poor, especially in Africa, may well be unavoidable. Ironically without the Marxist alternative that promised a form of economic redemption, the main motive could be the desire to highlight their plight and to ensure that greater efforts are made to alleviate it. At the same time, the desire for simple revenge on those who are seen as the exploiters could also become a powerful impulse. In turn, this could lead to the emergence of terrorist groups whose targets are the symbols of wealth and power, such as the key institutions of the global financial system or transnational corporations whose offices and personnel symbolize the kind of wealth that members of the indigenous population can hardly imagine, let alone attain. Kidnappings of personnel, bombings of banks, and attacks on corporate offices are likely to become even more common occurrences than they are at present as the politically disaffected are joined in the terrorist ranks by the economically deprived.

A second kind of terrorist group that could become much more common is the transnational cult group, particularly in the remainder of the 1990's and the early years of the next millennium. The difficulty with these groups is that they are unpredictable, the targets of their activity are not always obvious, and their rationale is difficult for outsiders--including intelligence agencies--to understand. The capacity to predict and forestall their activities therefore will be problematic at best. Such groups will often have low visibility, only being recognized as a problem after they have initiated a terrorist campaign. They will also tend to have radicalized nihilist, and somewhat bizarre philosophies that are closer to the ramblings of Charles Manson than to the more familiar tenets of radical Marxism or radical Islam.

Aum Shinrikyo has some of these characteristics and, in some respects, could be the prototype for the transnational terrorist threat of the twenty-first century (Senate Permanent Committee on Investigations). There are several characteristics of the Aum that may be difficult for other groups to emulate: its membership (40 to 60,000 worldwide, with 3 times as many members in Russia as Japan); its assets of over 1.3 billion dollars; the extent to which it infiltrated key sections of government, industry, law enforcement, and the military; and its transnational reach, which included extensive activities in Russia, the United States and Australia.

Nevertheless, Aum Shinrikyo's efforts to recruit scientists to develop weapons of mass destruction, the production of chemical weapons, (sarin, phosgene and sodium cyanide), as well as its efforts to develop biological weapons (anthrax and botulism) and to acquire exotic but deadly viruses (such as Ebola) all provide what could unfortunately be a foretaste of things to come. As Bruce Hoffman has noted, Aum Shinrikyo's willingness to inflict large-scale civilian casualties crossed a threshold that can never be reinstated. Even though Aum Shinrikyo was unsuccessful in its efforts to create a catalytic conflict between the United States and Japan, it has certainly been a pioneer. Where Aum Shimrikyo has led, others may be only too willing to follow. The real danger will arise if these groups are like Aum Shinrikyo in their ability to operate effectively beyond the radar screens of most intelligence services and thereby obtain strategic surprise.

Matching the diversification of terrorist groups is an increase in terrorist targets. One of the consequences of the triumph of democracy is that there are more and more states that are reluctant to impinge upon fundamental freedoms of their citizens in the name of protecting national security. The result is the predominance of soft targets that continue to be readily accessible. As suggested above, the information infrastructure provides both a set of targets and a set of channels for striking at these targets.

One of the intriguing results of this is the increased opportunity for separation between a terrorist action and its consequences. Tampering with air traffic control systems could cause as much destruction as several bombs placed aboard airliners, but could be achieved at a distance, and with a very low risk that the perpetrators would be captured. By threatening airline safety and disrupting schedules, such actions could also create havoc with the conduct of business. It is not inconceivable that these measures could be part of a carefully orchestrated assault on the national and global information infrastructures, including the global financial system.

Equally important could be the shift in terrorist methods. The loss of life to terrorism has thus far been relatively small. This could change in the future as terrorist groups exploit not only the vulnerability of information systems, but also the availability of the components and materials for weapons of mass destruction. The ease with which weapons of mass destruction can be manufactured should not be exaggerated. In spite of its wealth and all its efforts, Aum Shinrikyo failed to develop biological weapons or to deploy a chemical weapon system with high lethality. Nevertheless too much comfort should not be taken from this.

Radioactive material smuggling from Russia is extensive. That there have been very few cases involving weapons grade material is a comfort to those who are concerned only about proliferation, but does not mean that even some of the lower grade materials could not create widespread death and destruction if used in conjunction with conventional explosives. The availability of radioactive materials provides opportunities for the creation of crude but effective radiological weapons. It is worth emphasizing that Aum Shinrikyo's failure was in the delivery not in the chemical weapon itself.

Nor is it wholly inconceivable that transnational terrorist groups from the developing world will be able to use rare but highly virulent diseases such as the Ebola virus as crude biological weapons. Biological toxins are also widely used in research and are not as stringently controlled as might be expected, even in the United States. The degree of control in developing nations may be even lower.

One of the most telling developments of the 1990's for transnational criminal organizations has been the emergence of a variety of countries as safe havens. Unless present trends are reversed, the number of sanctuaries for criminal organizations is likely to increase. Acquiescence is likely to be transformed to active support and collusion, especially in poorer countries. Such countries are likely at best to tolerate, and at worst to welcome criminal organizations so long as these organizations provide benefits to the economy--whether in terms of providing criminal capital as a substitute for foreign direct investment or as an economic multiplier. One of the problems with efforts to deal with national criminal organizations is that these organizations are not an unmitigated evil and in some states are regarded with tolerance and occasionally even affection.

Hand-in-hand with the spread of safe havens, there is likely to be a growing diversity of criminal organizations. There are several dimensions to this. One is that successful criminal enterprises encourage emulation. This helps to explain for example, why many Ghanaians have followed Nigerians into drug trafficking, so much so that in Britain the problem is referred to not as Nigerian but as West African.

Another problem is that as one kind of ethnic group become more entrenched, secure and successful in its activities, it will look for mules, couriers, or other rank and file members who do not fit law enforcement profiles. The growing diversity of groups will pose considerable problems, as such groups are likely to be not only outside the experience of domestic law enforcement, but also outside that of much of the national security and intelligence community. Dealing with unknown quantities adds enormously to the fragility and frustrations of predictive assessments.

The growing diversity of groups is likely to be matched by a growing diversity of the products traded by transnational criminal organizations. These products will include any licit goods where tax differentials across borders make smuggling very attractive (cigarettes); goods that are prohibited but for which there is demand (drugs and CFCs); goods for which demand greatly exceeds supply (organs for transplant surgery); and goods which promise high levels of profits (materials and components for weapons of mass destruction).

There is also likely to be a consolidation and a gradual blurring of different kinds of crime and of the organizations perpetrating them. Organized crime and white collar crimes are becoming increasingly difficult to distinguish as Russian criminal organizations, for example, engage in elaborate schemes for financial fraud. Similarly, actions that have traditionally been associated with terrorism could also become the hallmark of certain organized crime groups. Conversely, terrorists could use extortion as a means of obtaining funding. All this suggests another closely related trend towards an increase in the level of violence threatened or implemented by transnational criminal organizations. Large-scale violence, for example, has been predominantly the province of terrorist organizations, et in the future; the threat of large-scale violence as an instrument of extortion could become more pervasive.

The availability of the capabilities to engage in such threats is already apparent. The implication of all this is that criminal organizations could increasingly obtain access to destructive capabilities that could be used for extortion against states, cities or corporations.

Providing credibility will simply require that those being extorted find evidence that the organization really does have the material to inflict considerable harm. Similarly, criminal organizations, by acquiring the expertise of skilled hackers, may be able to threaten, to disrupt, or to corrupt major communications and information systems, as well as, to obtain access to bank and corporate funds.

Another trend that could prove equally disturbing, if less dramatics is that criminal organizations may well move from corruption and co-option of political elites to more direct control of political power. Bolivia in the early 1980's provides an example of a state being governed for a short time by what was, in effect, a "narcocracy." The pattern for the future is likely to involve not only more cases of this, but also more enduring rule by criminal organizations, albeit with a veneer of respectability and legitimacy. The rise of the "outlaw state" will pose considerable difficulties for efforts by the international community to create regulatory regimes or norms of behavior to deal with transnational organized crime.

Efforts to achieve a global money-laundering regime currently encounter major difficulties but will be even more problematic where criminals control governments and prevent them from joining such efforts. An even more disturbing scenario is one in which several powerful states fall under criminal domination and take concerted action to obstruct efforts by the international community to initiate more vigorous measures against transnational organized crime. Should this occur, it is not inconceivable that one of the main fissures in international politics would be that between "outlaw states" and law-abiding states. The clash would be not one of civilizations, but between criminal cultures and those who uphold the rule of law.

As well as moving to more direct control of political power, transnational organized crime could move from infiltration to control of licit businesses. This has certainly happened already in certain economic sectors (the construction industry and waste disposal are very obvious examples) and in certain cities and regions, but could become much more widespread. There are signs of this in Russia where organized crime has taken control of large sectors of the economy, including a significant portion of the banking industry. This endows criminal organizations with advantages that go beyond those they currently enjoy. When one controls or owns the bank, for example, it is not necessary to worry about suspicious transaction reports, even if there is legislation mandating such transactions. Such developments can all too easily take on their own momentum. Control of some businesses might be extended into other areas through the use of coercion for competitive advantage. The implication of all this is that BCCI could not be a footnote to the 1980's so much as a model for the twenty first century, although one in which the barriers to external investigation and control are more difficult for law enforcement to overcome.

It is also likely that there will be a consolidation of strategic alliances among criminal organizations. The late 1980's and early 1990's witnessed several meetings between various bosses of the criminal worlds. Characterizations of these as "criminal summits," leading to the emergence of Global criminal syndicates tended to inflate the threat posed by these meetings. Nevertheless, it is clear that criminal groups are engaging in cooperation at both strategic and tactical levels. Many of their alliances are on-off, but others tend to be more sustained and to involve an expectation of future cooperation. The real cooperation comes not at so-called summit meetings but at the level of practical criminal operations.

It has recently been reported, for example, that both Colombian drug traffickers and Russian criminal organizations are increasingly prevalent in Aruba. As one official noted, "the drug barons flourish, thanks to corrupt public servants and politicians, including on Aruba and the Netherlands Antilles. Each time you see the same pattern. Where the Colombians appear with their cocaine, they bribe government functionaries and politicians at every level. The latest development is that the Russian Mafia has also established itself in the Caribbean area in order to do business directly with the Colombians" (WNC). This is to be expected. The efforts of law enforcement provide a continued incentive for criminal organizations to cooperate. Just as strategic alliances have become more pervasive and entrenched in the lawful business world so they are likely to become an even more central feature of the operations of transnational criminal organizations.

Another trend is towards greater sophistication. This is likely to be reflected in the growing use of specialists by transnational criminal organizations. This has been particularly evident in the use of specialists for money-laundering and the employment of mercenaries or military veterans for security. In the future criminal organizations are likely to recruit information technology specialists. Such people are likely to become as important for criminal enterprises as they have become for licit businesses and will provide new offensive options.

Equal attention is likely to be given to defend against law enforcement and hostile governments. Some criminal organizations have already developed sophisticated three-pronged strategies that allow them to prevent, control, and absorb the risks they confront from law enforcement. Maintaining a congenial environment through corruption is obviously the best ways of preventing risk. Yet attention is also given to defensive measures that rely on good counterintelligence obtained through infiltration of government and law enforcement agencies.

Criminal organizations have also developed ways of protecting their assets and minimizing the penalties that the members incur when they are brought to justice. This multi-tiered approach may not always be sufficient to prevent inroads against a particular organization, but it certainly complicates the task of law enforcement. On the basis of all this, it is possible to devise a worst case scenario for the years 2005 to 2010. The main features of which are:

- Growth in number of safe havens for transnational criminal groups and terrorism organization that, in more and more cases, and is based not on weakness or acquiescence but on corruption and collusion.
- An increased number of money-laundering centers that are resistant to efforts to impose control and regulation and see this as an effort by the "haves" to ensure that the proceeds of crime do not come to the "have-nots."
- Increased linkages among criminal organizations themselves and between them and terrorist organizations which serve to make criminal organizations more violent and terrorist organizations more criminal.
- Increased capacity of both criminal and terrorist organizations to exploit technological vulnerabilities especially in information infrastructures for both violence and extortion.
- A further breakdown of the inhibitions against the use of weapons of mass destruction by terrorist organizations.
- A further erosion of the capacity of intelligence organizations to penetrate or monitor criminal and terrorist organizations and their activities. This results in more strategic surprises.
- The consolidation of symbiotic relations that are virtually impossible to unpackage and that sabotage efforts to provide global regimes against terrorist and criminal organizations and their activities.

- More and more licit businesses driven out by "unfair" competition from the illicit and more and more industries that are dominated by criminal organizations.
- A Russia in which the dictatorship of the Communist Party has been replaced by a democratic front government that has minimal impact on a state apparatus in which symbiotic linkages with criminal organizations are pervasive.
- A growing supply of synthetic drugs that are more powerful than heroin and opium and that make use of the surplus technological expertise available throughout the former Soviet Union.

There are other dimensions that could easily be added, but this gives a flavor of the kind of situation that could very easily develop if present trends go unchecked. While some components of this worst case situation could prove unavoidable, others could be prevented by effective counteractions. The worst case is not inevitable.

In efforts to level the playing field against transnational organized crime and transnational terrorist groups, it is essential to adopt a holistic approach. Organized crime and terrorism are not merely law and order problems and cannot be dealt with simply by increasing the amount of resources devoted to law enforcement. A holistic approach must incorporate efforts to modify the environment in which criminal and terrorist organizations emerge and flourish, attacks on the integrity and viability of the organizations themselves, efforts to inhibit their activities by removing or reducing the markets for illicit products whether drugs or protection services, and the confiscation of their assets.

The environmental modification has several pillars: re-establishing strong and legitimate government where it is weak or acquiescent, transparency where there is corruption and collusion, and effective criminal justice systems where they do not yet exist. This requires that criminal justice assistance has a much higher priority and become the post-Cold War equivalent of military assistance during the Cold War years. Such actions would increase the level of risk faced by transnational criminal organizations and would remove safe havens from which they can conduct their criminal enterprises. Only when the level of risk faced by criminal organizations is higher and more evenly distributed will it be possible to go beyond forcing their relocation and to make real inroads against them.

At the same time, it is necessary to identify and remove perverse incentives for criminal activities. In Russia, for example, prohibitive taxation rates encourage widespread tax evasion by businesses. Information about these businesses is often obtained by criminal organizations through the banks. And when the businesses are approached, they are both vulnerable to extortion and willing to pay criminal taxes that are less than government taxation.

Creating an environment that is less conducive to the growth of criminal and terrorist organizations also requires that 'sustainable development' becomes more than a catch-phrase and that efforts are made to mitigate some of the worst consequences of urban poverty. Without systematic efforts in this direction, getting rich through crime and getting even through terrorism are likely to become dominant aims of more and more people in developing countries.

Another, and more controversial, approach is to encourage the legitimization of both criminal and terrorist groups. This is an approach that is not always palatable, but one that could have some payoffs. It requires recognizing that at least some terrorist groups might have a real basis for some of their grievances, and doing something to remove these grievances, while simultaneously encouraging the participation and legitimization of the group in some kind of peace process.

As for criminal organizations, amnesties for members who are willing to leave the illicit business could encourage the process of legitimization that has helped to weaken the Mafia in the United States. When Lee Iacocca replaced Lucky Luciano as the role model for Italians in the United States, the Mafia lost the basis for continued dominance of the criminal world. This process was accelerated, of course, by the successes of the FBI and by the growing challenge from other ethnic criminal organizations. Nevertheless, it provides a model that might be worth considering, especially in relation to Russia where criminal groups often display real entrepreneurship.

Both this alternative and those policies designed to create an environment less conducive to the growth of criminal and terrorist organizations are not measures that will have immediate or short-term impact. In the meantime, it is necessary to pay attention both to defensive or control measures and to steps that can be taken to mitigate the consequences of criminal or terrorist actions. Priority should be given to protecting the national and global information infrastructure, as well as, urgent steps to minimize the vulnerabilities of those systems that are particularly attractive as terrorist targets or as targets for criminal extortion. It is necessary to develop a much greater rapid response capability to contain those that occur anyway and to establish enough redundancy to mitigate the consequences of system disruption. A similar mix of prevention, control, and mitigation should be devised to ensure the integrity of financial institutions and other businesses that are likely to be prime targets for organized crime. In some cases this requires more and better regulation. In others, a process of deregulation and greater competition might be more effective.

In terms of efforts to control terrorist and criminal organizations, it is essential to go beyond strict hierarchical or bureaucratic solutions and develop new networks that are as flexible as the organizations they are trying to counter and that combine various forms of expertise. For example, the Center for Disease Control could become as important as the Pentagon in responding to certain kinds of threat to United States security. Exploiting synergies and developing capacities for rapid response are critical to effectiveness against terrorist and criminal organizations. Networks should be both multi-jurisdictional and transnational in scope.

In terms of intelligence, the need is partly to cast the net wider and try to avoid situations where new groups like Aum Shinrikyo can achieve a form of strategic surprise. Less obvious groups need to be monitored and particular attention given to the destitute areas of mega-cities that are likely to generate the terrorists of the future. As far as transnational criminal organizations are concerned attention needs to be given to devising models that build on the current level of understanding of these groups. Attention needs to be given to their origin and development. This is crucial to providing preventive measures and devising reversal strategies to rollback the process of development. As Peter Lipsha notes, it is also necessary to identify the major triggers that enable criminal groups to advance from predatory to parasitic organizations and ultimately to develop symbiotic relationships with government officials.

As well as looking at the context within which the groups operate, attention needs to be given to their network structures, in an attempt to identify key nodes of communication and vulnerability that, if destroyed, would have a major impact on the capacity of the network to function. Another fruitful area is the decision process of these groups and in particular the information on which they base their profit-making and risk management strategies. Obtaining this would offer new opportunities to provide misinformation that could lull criminal organizations into a false sense of security or encourage them to take actions that would prove damaging.

More attention also needs to be given to patterns of activity especially the ways in which criminal organizations circumvent law enforcement efforts. What tends to happen in many cases is that law enforcement creates a form of displacement in which criminal activities are simply relocated to areas of lower risk. During the first half of the 1990's, for example, Uzbekistan introduced tough measures against the cultivation and trafficking of drugs. The result was simply to drive these activities across the border into Tajikistan where the government and law enforcement agencies were much weaker. By predicting displacement efforts it might be possible to forestall them and use a more effective "squeeze strategy" against transnational criminal organizations.

Even with such initiatives, the obstacles to effective national and international responses to transnational organized crime and terrorism are formidable. A more favorable future requires a coordinated international approach incorporating agreement on goals, agreement on means or instruments, and effective implementation involving extensive and dense cooperation among states and law enforcement agencies. It requires far greater inter-operability, if not complete harmonization among legal systems (especially in relation to extradition mutual legal assistance), the creation of public private partnerships that create more serious barriers to the infiltration of organized crime into licit business and industry, and the elimination of safe havens or sanctuaries for transnational organized crime. It also requires education campaigns to reduce demand for illicit products, thereby removing the markets that much organized crime requires.

Greater use could also be made of technology to combat organized crime, terrorism, and drug trafficking. Even with innovations in all these areas, however, there are limits to what can be achieved. Transnational organized crime, terrorism, and drug trafficking cannot be eliminated. Reducing them to "acceptable levels" where they no longer pose a threat to security and can be treated as law and order problems is perhaps the most that can be achieved. And even this is a daunting task.

Phil Williams *is Director of the University of Pittsburgh's Ridgway Center for International Security Studies and Professor in the Graduate School of Public and International Affairs at the University. He has taught at the Universities of Aberdeen and Southampton and has published extensively in the field of international security, including Security in Korea: War, Stalemate and Negotiation. During the last five years his research has focused on transnational organized crime and drug trafficking. Dr. Williams is the editor of Transnational Organized Crime. He is currently preparing a major book on transnational organized crime and is co-editing a volume on drug-trafficking and national security.*

THE CHANGING FACE OF CONFLICT IN THE NEW WORLD DISORDER

Andrew S. Riddile

Recent research shows that the information revolution, with all of its benefits, has a down side: it enables a new kind of terrorism. As a matter of fact, information technology has changed the face of a broad range of conflict. This chapter will explore perspectives of this phenomenon at senior levels of government and industry.

While serving as a Fellow at the Rand Corporation in Washington, DC. I teamed up with two very savvy Rand researchers, named Roger Molander and Peter Wilson, to put together a series of table-top exercises for senior government and industry leaders. The exercises were based on a methodology know as "The Day After..." which was developed by my colleagues at Rand. The object of the exercise was not just to create plausible and challenging crisis scenarios as an exercise for senior decision-makers, but to help them develop policies to minimize the prospect that such crises could occur, or, if they did, to mitigate their consequences. We called this exercise, "The Day After ... in Cyberspace." We hoped to learn what senior government and industry officials see as the features and issues associated with what have been called, for better or worse, information warfare.

The exercise was developed over a six-month period, using a series of different sets of participants. The series began with a small group of Rand researchers in Washington and progressed to include four-star military officers and deputy secretary-level officials representing departments and agencies from across the Executive Branch. Senior industry executives from large information-systems companies were included throughout the series once it emerged from early testing. Eventually, over 170 people participated. They brought with them significant experience in national security and military affairs. Some of them were experts in information warfare. They represented various levels of industry, academia, the analytic and research communities, the intelligence community, national security policy makers, and the military services. As the development of the exercise progressed, we adjusted the scenario to clarify understanding of the features and implications of information warfare and to examine the emerging policy-related issues. The objectives of the exercise were to help us explore the features and issues of information warfare, to help the participants sharpen their focus on both information warfare and the implications for national security, and to take steps toward development of strategy and policy that is still missing.

The information revolution has changed the character of the full range of conflict, from crime through terrorism to warfare. The United States is the most advanced nation in the world in cyberspace, but the dilemma for our leadership, including the Secretary of Defense, is that the U.S. may also be the nation most vulnerable--at least in some areas. Take the military itself. Nearly everything it does, from designing weapons and guiding missiles to paying, training, equipping, and mobilizing troops, depends upon computer-driven civilian networks. And the military has no legal or political authority in peacetime to protect civilian information networks from hackers, saboteurs or terrorists.

As we move from petty crime to global war, we see clear distinctions in intensity of action, warning, domestic-to-foreign involvement, private-to-government involvement, and level-of-government involvement. In the good old days, there were clear distinctions between stealing an apple from the grocer on the comer and global nuclear war. Distinctions were clear in a number of ways. The intensity of the attack on the grocer was distinctly different than that which we expected from ICBMs coming at us from over the North Pole. The grocer got little warning, if any, before his apple disappeared; but we could see global war coming weeks, months, even years before the bombs started dropping. The misdemeanors and felonies that disturb us most were those committed down the street in our cities and towns; the closer to home, the more troublesome. Wars, on the other hand, usually happened when foreign nations misbehaved overseas. As the value of the target increases, the probability that the matter involves the authorities and the government also increases. And as the value of the target increases, the level of government involvement increases; that is to say, conversely, neither the President nor Congress cares much about the apple. This is not a perfect representation, but it is helpful, especially when we see what has changed. The distinctions are now seriously bluffed and, in some cases, even gone. Information technology and current government and industry practice make possible attacks against U.S. strategic targets by the apple thief with his newly-acquired Macintosh computer (pun intended). Not only that, he can do so without getting caught, much less without giving any warning. And, he can do it from a corner in Baghdad as well as from down the street.

There are at least two general factors that result in rapidly increasing vulnerabilities and issues associated with the kind of problem we are talking about. The first factor is the proliferation of information technology with low-cost computing and computer networking. A second factor adds significantly to vulnerabilities and issues. That is the rush toward other kinds of precision solutions to problems requiring efficiency or utility, doing more with less. The general downsizing across government and industry requires increased efficiency. And government and industry also require the increased utility of advanced technology.

Efficiencies are often, but not always, technologically based. Just-in-time techniques for reducing inventories and lightening logistical loads are used to increase efficiency. Infrastructure consolidation, the use of commercial off-the-shelf technology, and outsourcing are other examples of efficiencies. Examples of efficient and high-utility weapons systems are precision-guided munitions. The former Director of Central Intelligence John Deutch, in his testimony before the Investigations Subcommittee for the Committee on Governmental Affairs said, "The electron is the ultimate precision-guided weapon."

All of these examples achieve increased efficiency and/or utility. But they also increase infrastructure vulnerability wherever they are used. With increased use of information technology and precision solutions, we become dependent upon them and then we become vulnerable.

The confluence of the wild proliferation of information technology and precision solutions in the context of the 1996 post-Cold War, uncertain and dangerous world presents the United States with a very different set of problems under the concept of information warfare.

The United States has substantial information-based resources, including complex management systems and infrastructures involving the control of: electric power, money flow, air traffic, oil and gas, and other information-dependent systems. If and when potential adversaries, state-sponsored forces or non-state terrorists attempt to damage these systems using information warfare techniques, this kind of conflict inevitably takes on a strategic aspect. This fact, when combined with the features of information warfare, present a situation that calls for our nation's attention at the highest levels. Imagine strategic terrorism. It is possible now.

My definition of information warfare-terrorism-crime is invoked when an adversary, as either a means of attack or a target of attack uses information technology or a precision solution, or both. That means to me, for example, that when the Islamic radical uses a gasoline-based car bomb to destroy a mated pair of public network switches located in Chicago's Loop, he is using an information warfare technique against a U.S. strategic infrastructure.

What kind of stuff are we talking about here? What does this stuff do? How much damage? How much blood? Just how bad can this be? Several years ago, this last question appeared on the cover of *TIME Magazine*. The cover featured a helmeted soldier with bolts of radio frequency energy reflected off his goggles. The background depicted conflagration and destruction. The article was hyped, but I quote it here to show that when telephone service stops, when funds transfer systems are disrupted, when refineries explode and regional power goes out, when military mobilization is disrupted, when trains collide and airplanes crash, when Americans die, and when U.S. senior leaders don't know who is responsible, the result can be bad.

How bad is it? As participants were immersed in the scenario, they expressed a wide and telling range of perspectives on the gravity of this threat. The participants came into the exercise at various points on the range of perspectives. Some toward the top confidently stated that this is nothing new, not a problem, and certainly not worth spending another nickel on. Others, toward the bottom, publicly expressed relief that the infrastructure of America has not yet been devastated by one or more of the thousands of information warfare attacks it has already suffered. There were 250,000 attacks of varying significance on computer networks last year. We keep hearing about an "information warfare Pearl Harbor."

One of the top requirements for the scenario was plausibility. We took great care to protect the plausibility of projections into the future. Forecasts of capabilities were straight-lined and based on serious research. As the participants progressed through the scenario and emerged a few hours later, the consensus perspective of the information warfare threat invariably moved downward along this graph. When the participants finished the exercise, nearly all had moved down along this range.

What is new and different about information warfare? Those well-established aspects that fall in the area of what the military calls command and control, or electronic-warfare, in the context of the battlefield. These aspects are not new to U.S. military strategy and our military establishment is exceptionally good at developing doctrine and conducting operations in this area. But what we found from our exercise series is a newer, emerging, and far more ominous facet of information warfare. This facet includes a wider range of potential adversaries with the same selection of weapons, ranging from digits to dynamite. When these new actors point their weapons toward information-dependent infrastructures in the United States, such as the public switched network or financial or air traffic control systems, information war takes on another dimension. It takes on a strategic dimension.

Shown another way and at the risk of overstating the point, a complete description of modem information warfare ranges from well-understood, tactical command-and-control warfare to what is newer, a more penetrating kind of conflict that reaches the center of the U.S. homeland. Information warfare threatens the U.S. as sanctuary. The newer aspects of this kind of warfare (or terrorism) are strategic in nature.

As we watched the exercise participants struggle with the scenario, it became apparent that different aspects of information warfare are in competition. That is to say, participants naturally dealt most easily with what they knew best. Information-based conflict in the region (electronic warfare in regional war like Desert Storm) presented minor challenges. But when the information war campaign was brought to the U.S. and allies' heartland, the regional war became almost irrelevant. Attention was spread from one or two traditional campaign areas (or theaters) "over there" to four fronts, including "here."

When responding to information warfare, our military strategy can no longer focus on just support to and operations in regional war. We must also examine implications on U.S. strategic infrastructures that depend upon information. The features of information conflict as we analyzed the play of the exercise starting with:

- Low entry cost. Anybody with an $800 personal computer, a six-pack of beer and a pizza can attack.
- Blurred traditional boundaries. Distinctions that once made thinking and acting on threats fairly easy and predictable are largely gone.

- Perception management. An effective information attack would rely heavily on deception.
- Strategic intelligence. The intelligence resources in our police departments and the intelligence resources of the federal government are short on clues. Today they hardly know what we are talking about.
- Tactical warning and attack assessment. This may be the hardest part: warning when an attack is underway and what is under attack. This kind of terrorism can be done with no warning leaving no evidence.
- Building and sustaining coalitions. How can we rely on the Canadians or the British, or the New Yorkers, when they are just as vulnerable as we are?
- The United States is vulnerable. Securing American public support for Desert Storm was a cake walk. We are now talking about warfare or terrorism that reaches into our homes. The attack is no longer over there. It is not even on the far South Side. It is right here!

It seems to me that there are features of terrorism that line up very well with the features of information warfare. Terrorism is the power of the weaker against the stronger. The terrorist is usually under-resourced relative to the victim. Terrorism (as distinguished from sabotage) is usually directed at the innocent and involves a certain measure of cowardice. And the common objective of terrorism is psychological in nature. The low entry cost, lack of intelligence, lack of warning and attack assessment, psychological impact, effectiveness against very high-value targets and potential anonymity must all be attractive to those who would terrorize.

Unlike traditional weapon technologies, development of information-based techniques does not require sizable financial resources or state sponsorship. Information systems expertise and access to important networks may be the only necessities. Interconnected networks may be subject to attack and disruption not just by states but also by non-state actors, including dispersed groups, and even individuals. Potential adversaries could also possess a wide range of capabilities. Thus, the threat to U.S. interests could be multiplied substantially and will continue to change as ever more complex systems are developed and the requisite expertise is ever more widely diffused.

Given the networking and wide array of possible opponents, weapons, and strategies, once-clear distinctions have become blurred.

The traditional role distinction between domestic law enforcement, on the one hand, and national security and intelligence entities, on the other, is far more complicated. Another consequence of this blurring is the disappearance of clear distinctions between different levels of anti-state activity, ranging from crime to warfare. A domestic attack may be crime. A foreign attack may be war. Either may be terrorism. But now what is domestic? What is foreign? What is crime? What is war? Who is in charge of the attack? And who is in charge of the defense and counterattack?

Opportunities for information warfare agents to manipulate information that is key to public perceptions may increase. Political action groups and other non-government organizations can utilize the Internet to galvanize political support, as the Zapitistas in Chiapas, Mexico have been able to do. The possibility arises that the very "facts" of an event can be manipulated via multimedia techniques and then be widely disseminated. Conversely, it may be more difficult to build and maintain domestic support for controversial political actions.

Traditional intelligence-gathering and analysis methods may be of limited use in meeting the intelligence challenge. Collection targets are difficult to identify; allocation of intelligence resources is difficult because of the rapidly changing nature of the threat; and vulnerabilities and target sets are not, as yet, well understood. The U.S. will have difficulty identifying potential adversaries, their intentions, and their capabilities.

This feature of conflict presents fundamentally new problems in a cyber-space environment. A basic problem is distinguishing between attacks and other events, such as accidents, system failures, or hacking by thrill seekers. The main consequence of this feature is that the U.S. may not even know when an attack is underway, who is attacking, or how the attack is being conducted. I believe that this problem will be one of the toughest to solve. Imagine the terrorist striking at the speed of light and leaving no evidence.

In a series of follow-on infrastructure exercises, we saw this feature, combined with the lack of strategic intelligence, present a situation almost intolerable to the exercise participants. The factor of ambiguity with regard to who is carrying out a strategic attack on the United States can result in bizarre decision making. Inaction and even consideration of surrender are results we sometimes observed.

In a regional or global crisis, the maintenance of coalitions with our allies is going to be more difficult. And, the very different information systems the various levels and kinds of domestic law enforcement agencies depend on are susceptible to digital diddling, making cooperation between agencies a tougher thing to do.

Potential battlefields are anywhere networked systems allow access. The U.S. economy will increasingly rely on complex, interconnected network control systems for such necessities as oil and gas pipelines, electric power grids, and so on. The vulnerability of these systems is poorly understood. Most of our generals and admirals do not understand that strategic targets within the U.S. are just as vulnerable to attack as battlefield command systems; nor do they understand the implications of this. But, neither do our state governors, our mayors or our police chiefs. As a matter of fact, the American public in general pretty much does not understand how vulnerable the U.S. national infrastructures are: our telecommunications and information systems sector, our electric power system, our transportation system, banking and finance, gas and oil storage and distribution, water supply systems, emergency services, and continuity of government operations.

So what are we going to do about all this? I have described to you a very difficult problem facing the United States. But is the sky falling? Heck, no! Solutions to this problem begin here. We need to understand better the threat and our vulnerabilities. We need to establish effective indications and warning, attack assessment, and damage assessment capabilities. Nothing particularly effective can be done without unprecedented cooperation between private industry and the various levels of government. A public education program should be implemented. And our national security and military strategies must incorporate information warfare as a fundamental consideration. Virtually all participants agreed upon these recommendations.

One of the first steps necessary toward development of strategies offering effective information warfare defense is a risk assessment. Those most lucrative U.S. infrastructures that form likely strategic targets must be identified and the weapons effects on them must be understood. United States national security strategy must look closely at the implication information warfare may have on emergency preparedness. The problem of missing presidential policy should be corrected as soon as possible. Our military leadership needs to understand and plan for the impact of strategic information war on national security and force projection. Lastly, the question of a federal-government role in preparing the nation against this threat is a difficult one. There must be very close cooperation with private industry and there must be aggressive leadership from the White House.

In 1996, the President signed an executive order entitled, "Critical Infrastructure Protection." This executive order was a Janet Reno initiative and it established a Commission tasked to identify, assess, and recommend solutions to everything previously listed. The executive order also established an Infrastructure Protection Task Force within the Department of Justice to coordinate existing protection efforts. The executive order is weakest where it involves private industry. The vast majority of strategic targets in the U.S. today belong to the private sector. Industry's role should go beyond representation by an Advisory Committee to the Commission.

Senator Sam Nunn has chaired hearings on U.S. infrastructure vulnerability to information-based attack before the Senate Governmental Affairs Permanent Subcommittee on Investigations. Also in an amendment to the Defense Authorization Act of 1996 (now public law), Senator Kyl wrote a requirement for the President to report to Congress his outline of a plan to provide indications and warning of strategic attack against the national information infrastructure.

In his testimony, Senator Kyl said that today, there is no defense against invasion of our society's nerve centers. Our military has little ability and no authority to defend against such strategic attacks, while over 100 countries are working on information warfare techniques. No department, no agency, or individual of the U.S. government has responsibility for the mission of protecting the nation against this strategic threat.

***Andrew S. Riddile** is Senior Program Manager at National Security Research, Inc., affiliated with the National Institute of Public Policy. He is responsible for national-level strategic security policy analysis and operations, especially in the areas of strategic information warfare and national infrastructure protection. Mr. Riddile served as Presidential Emergency Plans Officer in the White House Military Office during the Reagan Administration and as coordinator for development of all presidential aircraft and command and control matters. He served as the first Director of the President's Emergency Operations Center in the White House and also served for three years as Senior Military Advisor to Vice President Dan Quayle. During his 26-year naval career, he became the only person ever authorized to wear the Presidential Service Badge, Vice Presidential Service Badge, Office of Secretary of Defense Identification Badge, and the Joint Chiefs of Staff Identification Badge.*

INFRASTRUCTURE AT RISK FROM TERRORIST THREAT

Sean Hill

A recent report of the President's Commission on Critical Infrastructure Protection (PCCIP), formed by President Bill Clinton on July 15, 1996, has concluded that the United States is not well prepared to cope with attacks mounted by terrorist groups or others who have the capability of disrupting key government and private facilities.

Although the Cold War is over, the United States should not become less vigilant, notes the report, citing the terrorist bombings of a U.S. barracks in Saudi Arabia, the World Trade Center in New York City, and the federal building in Oklahoma City as examples of recent violence aimed at destroying the infrastructure of the U.S.

The Commission defined five sectors, examined their vulnerabilities, and looked for ways to improve their structures. The five sectors are:

1. Information and Communications,
2. Banking and Finance,
3. Energy, including Electrical Power, Oil and Gas,
4. Physical Distribution, and
5. Vital Human Services.

A comprehensive paper outlines recommendations prepared on each sector.

The Commission was a compilation of leaders from federal departments and agencies and from the private sector. The Commission was divided into three Committees:

1. Advisory Committee of industry leaders appointed by the President;
2. The Steering Committee, including the Commission's Chairman and four top government officials to supervise the activities of
3. The Principal's Committee, the main body

composed of Cabinet Officers, heads of agencies, and senior White House staff members.

The study found consistent increases in the dependence of three critical infrastructures: electrical energy, communication, and computers. The growing complexity of energy and communication systems increases the chances of small problems that cause catastrophic events. The blackout of ninety-five percent of the beepers and cellular phones in May due to the loss of a satellite is a prime example of how essential parts of society such as businesses, hospitals, transportation, and the military are relying on high technology communications.

The increasing threat of cyber-terrorism is another reason to search for better ways to protect the national infrastructure. The increasing use of computers by the public has resulted in more than half of the homes having at least one computer. The majority of these households are connected to the Internet. The skills to be a cyber-terrorist can be learned in schools at a young age, and the devices are in the family living room. Although explosives and other terrorist tactics continue to be a major threat, so-called cyber-terrorists represent a growing concern. Government officials recently reported on an effort by the Black Tigers of Eelam, a faction of the Tamil Tigers, to disrupt embassies by simply overloading systems with thousands of e-mail messages (known as spamming).

The Commission also emphasized how the diversity of threats can cause disruption at any time, from anywhere and for a myriad of reasons. The reasoning is not likely to be discerned until the identity of the perpetrator is known.

Errors and omissions by humans still cause the major portion of disturbances not explained by natural events and accidents. Too many people with authorized access, referred to as insiders, to sensitive areas can also be harmful. The remaining categories are familiar to most people: recreational hackers, criminal financial activity, industrial espionage, terrorism, national intelligence, and information warfare. The greatest challenge remains to define and write laws for each of these categories. The study concludes that there is a lack of awareness by the general public and a failure to maintain a national focus on infrastructure protection.

Cyber-crime continues to pose the biggest threat because the act can have no detectable preparation, can be conducted anywhere in the world, and last only a few seconds so the identity and location of the attacker is virtually impossible to find. The lack of definite laws and investigative authority is reinforced by the Commission's statement, "With the existing rules, you may have to solve the crime before you can decide who has the authority to investigate it." The study states that the responsibility for infrastructure protection and assurance cannot be decided by who the attacker is or where the attacks stem but must be shared cooperatively among all industry and government leaders. The need for programs on awareness and education of vulnerabilities is also stressed.

Establishing proper information sharing networks between government agencies and private industry to prepare risk management assessments is also vital. This will speed up communication if one of the infrastructures is under attack and will therefore expedite a solution. The examination and reconsideration of laws related to technology will help promote this idea and also allow leaders and operators of infrastructures to take better precautions. Not least in importance is the need for greater security and the administration of numerous simulations to understand the capabilities of closely inter-dependent infrastructures. A national organization structure was also proposed to gain a better understanding of how these recommendations should be implemented.

Sector coordinators will aid in information sharing and policy. Lead agencies within the federal government will be assigned to serve as liaison from the government to each sector. A National Infrastructure Assurance Council comprised of industry CEOs, Cabinet Secretaries, and state and local government representatives will give policy advice. An Information Sharing and Analysis Center will distinguish an attack from an accidental event. The Infrastructure Support Office will house the majority of the national staff responsible for management and implementing the recommendations. The Office of National Infrastructure Assurance will be the top policy making body and will work closely with the National Security Council and the National Economic Council.

The growth of the Information Age requires numerous partnerships between private industry and government agencies to ensure the security of our infrastructures. Technology is increasing faster than laws can be established to control it. New security measurements must be continuously generated to promote the safety of the economy and society. The strength of the military, friendly neighbors, and vast oceans cannot stop the destruction caused by a few keystrokes.

Five public meetings in major cities were held as well as numerous meetings with professionals, academics, and Congressional members associated with one or many of the sectors, two simulations were also conducted with participants from every infrastructure and all levels of government.

Sean Hill is a research analyst at the Office of International Criminal Justice at the University of Illinois at Chicago, with responsibility for terrorist groups. He has conducted research in China, Vietnam, England, Australia and the Middle East. Mr. Hill served in the Marine Corps in the area of special operations as part of an anti-terrorism unit.

PART TWO: INTELLIGENCE AND INFORMATION

INTELLIGENCE, TERRORISM, AND THE NEW WORLD DISORDER

Scott McHugh

Pan Am 103, the Olympic bombing, the World Trade Center, Saudi Arabia, Oklahoma City, and Beirut--the list of terrorist attacks grows longer and the number of causalities continues to climb. A terrorist attack can rapidly and violently destroy hundreds of innocent people, and unless the U.S. begins to focus on the "front end" of the terrorism problem, the number of destroyed lives will continue to grow. To level the playing field and give law enforcement and security the tools required to neutralize this threat to national security, the U.S. must implement a terrorism intelligence analysis system capable of attacking the problem from a proactive and preventive organizational dynamics perspective. The United States has the finest post-incident investigative agencies and process in the world, but it has largely ignored terrorism from a pre-incident analysis and preventive security perspective. Consequently terrorists have had a free hand to pick and choose targets of opportunity with relative impunity.

Terrorists have succeeded in America because U.S. law enforcement is always one step behind the terrorist with respect to intelligence collection and analysis, and security counter-measures. When a terrorist attack occurs today, vast numbers of forces are mobilized to investigate the crime using advanced and sophisticated investigative and forensic methods that have been superbly successful in identifying the perpetrators of terrorist attacks. As a by-product of the post incident investigation, new intelligence about the terrorists' methods are gleaned and passed to the security countermeasures professionals who proceed to develop and implement security processes to defeat similar future attacks. The problem with this system is that the terrorists are always one attack ahead of the law enforcement and security professionals, and as a result of this advantage, are frequently successful. This advantage can be neutralized by refocusing our government's counter-terrorist information collection, management, and analysis methods and integrating threat analysis with threat based security countermeasures tailored to law enforcement interdiction operations.

To date, law enforcement and security professionals have constructed anti-terrorist security countermeasures from a "one size fits all" perspective, i.e., all terrorist groups are alike, and the techniques used to deter one bomber will work against all bombers. Unfortunately, that approach does not work well since each terrorist group is as different as one individual is from another. Terrorists have organizational strengths, weaknesses, likes, dislikes, prejudices, experiences, and capabilities which, if understood, provides an opportunity for the U.S. to prevent rather than react to terrorism.

Terrorists, like any other structured organization, have signature traits that can be analyzed to understand group-operating processes. Studying group structure and operational patterns will identify terrorist capabilities, as well as, their weaknesses and vulnerabilities to governmental interdiction or interruption. This method, known as Indications and Warnings (I&W) analysis has been successfully used in the counter-narcotics and the military areas for years. I&W seeks to understand how terrorist groups function and implement their operational goals and information to identify pre-incident indicators of future activity. Through the identification of pre-incident indicators, analysts can reasonably predict future targeting activity and provide a guide for law enforcement and security professionals in the creation of threat based security procedures tailored to group capabilities and target vulnerabilities. This interaction between threat intelligence and security minimizes the use of "one size fits all" static security measures that are easily defeated by today's sophisticated and talented terrorists.

To put a practical face on I&W analysis, consider that every recent post incident investigation of a terrorist attack has revealed observable and identifiable pre-incident indicators that intelligence should have, and in most cases, did detect in advance. However, the pre-incident indicators were never viewed as important because the analysts did not know or understand the significance of the information with respect to individual terrorist group dynamics and potential target vulnerabilities. Consequently, the information not acted upon and the opportunity to deflect, deter, or neutralize the threat, was lost because of a simple lack of knowledge.

I&W analysis also seeks to identify group vulnerabilities and weaknesses that can be exploited by law enforcement to interdict or interrupt a planned terrorist attack. The knowledge gained through I&W analysis will enable the U.S. to become more proactive and preventative in its counter-terrorist operations by using arrest, security-countermeasures, psychological operations, logistical interruption or any of dozens of methods to interrupt terrorist plans.

The U.S. government needs to be prepared to face a sophisticated, deadly foe that understands America and is prepared to exploit the current systems' weaknesses. The defeat of terrorism will require the merging of post incident investigations and prosecutions with a more preventive based National Terrorism Indications and Warnings Analysis process. A National Terrorism I&W system using open source information collected from state, local, and federal law enforcement and security agencies will provide a systematized means of attack warning and the information necessary to neutralize a terrorist attack before it starts.

The future effectiveness of U.S. counter-terrorist operations can be improved upon by discarding the current reactive approach to terrorism and replacing it with the means to prevent terrorist operations. To reduce the level of success achieved by terrorists, U.S. counter-terrorism policy must be amended to include an integrated indications and warnings analysis program whereby intelligence, law enforcement, and security at all levels of government function together seamlessly. The first step in establishing this amended policy is the creation of a national I&W information processing and analysis system to attack and defeat the problem using knowledge gained by studying terrorism from an organizational structure perspective. Unless terrorism is attacked from the front end of the problem, it will continue to successfully kill American citizen with impunity.

Scott McHugh *is the Director of Intelligence Research and Analysis at Orion Scientific Systems, Inc. He recently retired after twenty years as a Special Agent and Special Agent In Charge with the U.S. Department of State's Bureau of Diplomatic Security. His permanent assignments included Algiers, Beirut, Khartoum, Moscow, and Rome. Mr. McHugh's other assignments included teaching counter-terrorism operations and physical security courses and managing the State Department's Anti-Terrorism Assistance Training Center in Arizona.*

INTELLIGENCE AND LAW ENFORCEMENT: A CANADIAN PERSPECTIVE

Dr. G. David Smith

The functions of security intelligence and law enforcement at the federal level in Canada are centered in two agencies within the Ministry of the Solictor General Canada. Law enforcement is the purview of the Royal Canadian Mounted Police (RCMP), the famed "Mounties". Responsibility for security intelligence is vested in the Canadian Security Intelligence Service (CSIS), formed in 1984 with the passage of the Canadian Security Intelligence Act.

The CSIS is a domestic internal security intelligence agency. It does not have law enforcement powers. As described by its mandate, the purpose of the Service fundamentally is to gather information and to inform the government of Canada. Unlike the CIA, for instance, the CSIS does not operate abroad. The Service does maintain security Liaison Officers (SLO) in certain countries; the United States and the UK for instance, but the role of the SLO is just that--liaison. The CSIS also has established Memorandums of Understanding (MOUs) with a number of foreign security and intelligence agencies. The individual MOU's facilitate the sharing of information and data between the Service and the foreign agencies, but the CSIS remains purely a domestic service.

As shown below, the mandate of the Service, as contained in Section 12 of the CSIS Act, is:

> *"To COLLECT, by investigation or otherwise, to the extent that it is strictly necessary, and ANALYSE and RETAIN information and intelligence respecting activities that may on reasonable grounds be suspected of constituting threats to the security of Canada and, in relation thereto shall REPORT to and ADVISE the Government of Canada."*

Threats to the Security of Canada are described in Section 2 of the CSIS Act as:

- Espionage and sabotage;
- Clandestine foreign influenced activities;
- Politically motivated violence; and
- Destruction or overthrow of the constitutionally established system of government in Canada.

The CSIS was formed from the Security Service Branch of the RCMP in 1984, partly as a result of concerns that a national law enforcement agency should not have both policing and intelligence powers. Both agencies continue to work closely together, however, as described in more detail in the chapter by Wendy Nicol. Each agency maintains Liaison Officers (LOs) in the other's headquarters for example, and CSIS provides on-going threat assessment data to the RCMP to allow for appropriate levels of VIP protection.

The Service also works closely with other government departments and agencies in a similar fashion--with Customs and Immigration, to warn of possible movement of terrorists or contraband; with Foreign Affairs (the Canadian "State Department") to permit appropriate protective actions abroad; with Defense to warn of threats to military equipment, personnel or installations. As mentioned earlier, the CSIS also provides parallel exchanges with foreign security and intelligence agencies--in that regard, while the Service develops much of its own information, it does make use of input from relationships with foreign services.

Again, as described by Wendy Nicol, the Service provides information to the RCMP on a formally agreed basis. But that information is intended to form the basis for the RCMP to develop its own investigative and enforcement activity, if the RCMP so wishes. CSIS members and sources do not participate in court cases. It is a major concern that the Service protects its sources from exposure--a fundamental principle for an intelligence agency.

However, that does hot mean CSIS can run rampant--it is probably the most carefully scrutinized intelligence service in the world. The CSIS has an internal Inspector General (IG) reporting directly to the Director of the Service--who, incidentally, can serve a maximum of two 5-year terms. As well, the service has an oversight committee, the Security Intelligence Review Committee (SIRC), responsible for the review of all Service activities. The committee has government-appointed members, including representatives of major political parties, as well as a permanent staff. It reports to the government in a public document each year.

The Service obtains intelligence material in various ways and by use of various investigative methods: from open source material, from other government departments and agencies, through interviews with individuals, through sharing arrangements with foreign services, and by surveillance and technical means. To conduct any intrusive investigative techniques such as telephone interception, it is necessary that the Service obtain a very stringently examined federal court warrant on each occasion.

The CSIS maintains very effective cooperative exchanges with the RCMP and other federal departments, as well as foreign services. The Service has a number of methods of disseminating intelligence: regular operational traffic and threat assessments, short intelligence briefs for perishable data which must get to senior officials, reports on specific subjects such as the activities of terrorist groups, as well as more lengthy studies involving strategic assessments. The majority of the material produced by the Service is classified, although the CSIS does publish an open source document known as *COMMENTARY,* which examines a broad range of issues considered real or emerging threats to the security of Canada.

Dr. G. David Smith *is the Deputy Director-General - Strategic and Emerging Issues for the Canadian Security Intelligence Service (CSIS). He has been with the Ministry of the Solicitor General for Canada and the CSIS since 1987. Dr. Smith was the Chief of Staff for Canada's Federal Counter-Terrorism Task Force from 1988-89. A career armored cavalry officer with service in North America, Europe, the Middle East, Cyprus, and Vietnam; Smith retired with the rank of Lieutenant Colonel.*

INTELLIGENCE AND TERRORISM:
LOCAL LAW ENFORCEMENT PERSPECTIVE – CHICAGO TERRORIST TASK FORCE

Terry Hillard

The Chicago Police Department, the Illinois State Police (ISP), and the Chicago division of the FBI created the Chicago Terrorist Task Force (CTTF) during late 1981. It was initially formed to respond to the threat posed by the Puerto Rican terrorist group *Fuerzas Armadas de Liberacion Nacional Puertorriquena* (FALN).

At that time the FALN had perpetrated approximately 100 actual bombing/incendiary attacks, various armed robberies, and three violent armed takeovers of occupied buildings. The group's bombing attacks had resulted in millions of dollars in damages, five deaths, and scores of injuries. Targets included the Chicago Police Department headquarters, the City-County building in downtown Chicago (twice), the 40th precinct of the New York Police Department, and the New York Police Academy. Numerous large corporations and financial institutions located in downtown Chicago and New York were also among the group's targets.

The CTTF was founded by necessity. In 1980-1981 the three agencies actively investigating the FALN in Chicago (the FBI, CPD and Illinois State Police) were constantly encountering each other during the course of investigations. In some instances the actions of one agency were accidentally disrupting that of another agency (i.e. one agency's discreet surveillance of a subject might be disrupted by an overt interview of that subject by another agency). Compounding the situation was that none of the agencies involved had enough manpower committed to conduct truly productive investigations against such a formidable target. Sharing of information existed, but was quite limited. Consequently, duplication of effort was more the rule than the exception. Therefore, another advantage that resulted from the creation of the CTTF was the resultant sharing of techniques and authorities. A prime example of this was the ability of the CPD and ISP to share in the fruits of electronic coverage's which are not normally available to them. Conversely, the federal agencies were able to benefit from the state/local agency's much better access to city/state records. All of these problems were eliminated when the CTTF was created, and success was had by all as a consequence. Obviously, all of the problems that caused the CTTF to be established in 1981 could re-emerge if the CTTF ceased to exist.

Of the CPD compliment of 12 investigators, two are sergeants who, along with the FBI's SSA, are in charge of the daily operations of the CTTF. The sergeants regularly brief the commander of the CPD intelligence division on CTTF operations, and the FBI SSA has regular contact with the commander as well. The FBI SSA and the ASAC hold quarterly briefings with certain ranking members of the CPD, who possess appropriate security clearances.

The United States Secret Service has two special agents on the CTTF. One USSS special agent is designated "senior" at all times and he provides regular briefings to his SSA. The FBI SSA periodically provides briefings to the USSS SSA.

The Bureau of Alcohol, Tobacco and Firearms joined the CTTF in January 1995. The single ATF Special Agent working on the CTTF regularly briefs his SSA. In the future, the FBI SSA will confer with the ATF SSA.

The success of the CTTF in 1983 led to an increase in manpower and responsibility. The member agencies came to regard the CTTF as their response to the entire field of domestic terrorism. During 1984, the CTTF was assigned to handle all domestic terrorist investigations, regardless of the group or philosophy involved. By 1985, the task force expanded its responsibilities to include international terrorist investigations and assumed primary responsibility for any criminal violation occurring in Chicago wherein terrorists were involved. Their successes of in the mid-1980's also caused the member agencies to expand coverage to include all terrorist investigations including domestic and international matters. In the early 1990's the CTTF had become deeply involved in investigating major international terrorist organizations that had a presence in the Chicago area. In summary, the CTTF is regarded by the community as being a highly effective, professional entity that has provided a very necessary service to Illinois and to the City of Chicago. It represents the member agencies primary response to political terrorism.

Although the CTTF is targeted at terrorism investigations, periodically it ventures into related areas of community concern. In 1992, a series of bomb threats and two arsons so totally disrupted the activities of a major Chicago hospital that the United States Attorney's Office requested that the CTTF become involved. Within several weeks, the CTTF identified the perpetrator and was able to literally catch the man in the act of making a bomb threat. The offender was convicted of 37 counts in federal court. In another incident, the Chicago police department requested CTTF assistance in solving the firebombing of two Korean-owned grocery stores located in a black neighborhood.

Unlike some countries, the United States and the State of Illinois do not have statutes that make it a criminal offense to be a "terrorist" or to hold membership in any particular terrorist group. Instead, it is the illegal activities by terrorists that enable local law enforcement agencies to investigate them. Virtually any violent political attack perpetrated by a terrorist group constitutes a federal, state, and/or local violation. Most of the actions taken by a terrorist group to enable them to function also constitutes federal, state, and/or local violations (i.e., robberies, burglaries, and thefts done to raise funds, the acquisition of weapons and explosives, and the use of false identification to rent and purchase vehicles, equipment and safe-houses).

During the first five years that the CTTF existed, the federal government did not reimburse local law enforcement officers for their overtime. Given the fact that the City of Chicago and the Illinois State Police (who were members of the CTTF at the time) were suffering budgetary problems, it was often not possible for these agencies to give their officers overtime during certain periods of time. As a result the officers could not continue working after they had completed their basic work hours. (Chicago City-Union contract agreements make it very difficult for an officer to "voluntarily" work overtime without receiving compensation).

Another alternative allows for the officer working overtime to receive "compensatory time off" in exchange. However, this means that the CTTF loses the services of that officer at some other time during the year. The advent of the reimbursed overtime allowed for all CTTF employees, regardless of agency, to work the same hours and to, therefore, work side-by-side on CTTF investigations. The Illinois State Police left the CTTF in 1991 due to severe budgetary cutbacks. The CPD budget is still limited and it is doubtful that the CPD would be able to compensate their officers on the CTTF for the overtime that they are currently working.

All records pertaining to CPD overtime are recorded and monitored by CPD supervisors (sergeants). The time and attendance clerk of the CPD is custodian of these attendance records. A CPD lieutenant reviews and certifies all overtime claimed by each CTTF police officer. He then forwards these records to the director of finance of the CPD who makes an official request to the Chicago division of the FBI for reimbursement. An FBI special agent accountant reviews the CGPD request and forwards them to FBI headquarters for payment.

The CTTF regularly works closely with various other federal and local agencies. Depending upon the nature of the case being investigated, an Immigration and Naturalization Service special agent is assigned to the CTTF on a part-time basis and regularly works with the CTTF on matters of interest. Close relationships also exist with the U.S. Passport Office, Illinois State Police and various entities within the CPD--particularly with the bomb squad and certain districts where active investigations are underway.

As I mentioned previously, the Chicago Terrorist Task Force was created in 1981 in response to the threat being posed by the Puerto Rican FALN terrorist organization that had perpetrated numerous bombings and assorted criminal violations in the Chicago-land area as well as in other parts of the country. These attacks included bombings that targeted the mayor of Chicago, the Chicago police department, and major Chicago-area banks and corporate entities. By mid-1983 the CTTF had successfully apprehended the members of a clandestine "cell" of the FALN, as that cell was making final preparations for July 4th bomb attacks in Chicago.

The CTTF instituted a variety of investigative techniques, including surveillance and electronic coverage. A break in the case determined that the Libyans had offered the El Rukn street gang a large sum of money in exchange for perpetrating terrorist attacks in the United States on behalf of Libya.

The mission of the CTTF is to respond to all terrorist threats, both domestic and international, that occur within the Chicago area. The CTTF also investigates all criminal activities perpetrated by terrorist groups to garner the funds, weapons and equipment that they need to function. The CTTF consists of 12 CPD officers, 23 FBI agents and one FBI supervisory special agent. In response to the rapid increase in domestic terrorism, coupled with the increased public awareness of the dangers inherent from fringe elements of both domestic and foreign violent groups, the Chicago Terrorist Task Force is now divided into two groups: International and Domestic. This new breakdown allows a more concentrated effort in investigations. Each group has its own analyst as well as clerk. The grouping seeks to maximize the efficient flow of information, especially in the domestic realm, an area having the most impact on the host-city and state.

Terry Hillard *is currently the Superintendent of Police and a former Chief of Detectives for the Chicago Police Department. A thirty-one year veteran of the CPD, he has served at the Training Academy, in the Executive Protection Detail, and as Commanding Officer in the Narcotics Section, District Commander and Deputy Chief of Patrol. Chief Hillard also spent six years on Chicago's FBI Terrorism Task Force as the Surveillance Coordinator. He has participated in national and international seminars, conferences and training programs on terrorism, including many at the FBI training academy at Quantico.*

INTELLIGENCE AND TERRORISM: A CANADIAN PERSPECTIVE

Wendy Nicol

Intelligence, very simply, is communication. It is the issue of managed information. It starts out as raw information and it is the knowledge of the investigators and the analysts, which turns it into intelligence. Intelligence has been called a form of knowledge that is more than information and less than established fact. It is raw information that is collected, analyzed, and interpreted for meaning. There are two basic types of intelligence, tactical and strategic. Tactical is that which is immediately useable, it is collated and analyzed to some degree but it is usually information from a specific case or investigation which is to be used in the short term. Strategic intelligence is usually more complex, it often takes the tactical and goes further. It may have a different purpose, it usually has a different audience, but it is an educated, speculative outlook.

The sources of information vary greatly, from a phone call or a cultivated informant to an intelligence agency or the local newspaper. Terrorism, in its simplest definition, is organized crime with a more complex motivation from what we usually think of as organized crime. Whether it is money or ideology, the motivating factors eventually become immaterial except as they pertain to the ability to obtain resources and evade detection or arrest.

The Royal Canadian Mounted Police (RCMP), as with most police forces, have a large number of intelligence sources. For national security and criminal extremism/terrorism issues a major source, particularly on foreign-based criminal extremists is the Canadian Security Intelligence Service (CSIS). In addition we have our own sources which are developed independently of the service. The RCMP is a national police force but we also function as the provincial police in eight of ten provinces and the two territories and in some instances we are also providing municipal policing services. This enables us to gather intelligence from diverse sources. A drug investigator looking at smuggling by a Middle East based group, for example, may find extremist ties, or an officer investigating aboriginal street gangs may find connections in the native sovereignty movement.

The force generally, and our directorate specifically, has developed a number of initiatives to facilitate intelligence gathering. These include a new criminal intelligence officers course which is primarily for officers who investigate organized crime, but which has implications for those investigating criminal extremism. The course focuses on not just evidence gathering for the purposes of laying charges but also on probing for more information and trying to determine how that information pertains to other investigations and the storing of that information for use in future investigations.

Our hands are somewhat tied when compared to police forces in other countries. We cannot investigate groups associated with ideological beliefs. Membership in these groups almost always overlaps with legitimate, legal, political activities and dissension and our focus must be on individual criminal activity. The CSIS is able to follow all behavior which is a security concern, although it may not yet be in the criminal milieu. Obviously group involvement and association is of interest to us. It forms the backbone of our undercover concerns and helps us determine targets and tactics.

The Criminal Intelligence Directorate was formed eight years ago with the commitment to, and in recognition of, the importance of intelligence. We need to communicate. Most criminal extremists are travelers, whether from a foreign or a domestic base and a piece of intelligence is of no use to an investigator in Vancouver if the investigator in Montreal has it and does not know about the Vancouver investigation. We have a major secure databank that supports our program and where documents are uploaded throughout investigations. Other national data banks allow communication between investigators across the country.

Communication forms the core of our intelligence needs and is crucial to the gathering, analysis, and dissemination of information/intelligence. The need goes across the scale with improved internal communications with less guarding of personal subject areas to more sharing nationally and internationally. The sharing must be international to be effective with security and reliability. The more we share, the more problems we have with security. But information without sharing is useless. Therein lies our dilemma.

***Wendy Nicol** joined the Royal Canadian Mounted Police eight years ago and is a Strategic Intelligence Analyst in the Criminal Extremism Analysis Section of the Criminal Intelligence Directorate. Ms. Nicol has degrees in journalism and sociology, with a major in criminology. Before joining the RCMP, she was a reporter and editor at a number of major Canadian daily newspapers.*

PART THREE: THREATS

TIMOTHY JAMES MCVEIGH AND THE OKLAHOMA CITY BOMBING CASE STUDY

Lawrence W. Myers

After seven months of biographical research into the life and times of Oklahoma City bombing suspect Timothy James McVeigh, culminating in an interview with him in December 1995, the author made the following observations:

1. On at least a half dozen occasions in the seven year period prior to his arrest on April 19, 1995, McVeigh's personal contacts with law enforcement could have likely resulted in the prevention of the Oklahoma City bombing if agents and officers had coordinated their intelligence product and identified a pattern of escalation which was clearly evident with this offender for more than two years prior to the blast.

2. In our civil libertarian society, although intervention would have probably not incapacitated this suspect, certain actions could have resulted in at least placing McVeigh under surveillance for what he clearly indicated to a number of friends and family members he intended to do. Indeed, the argument can be made that a simple authorized mail cover alone could have prevented McVeigh's alleged involvement in the Oklahoma City Bombing.

3. The elements of ideological escalation indicated in Timothy McVeigh's adult life are clear. His incredible outward facade of normalcy, which continues to this day, is evidence of the intensity of his self-indoctrination and clarifies the threat the emerging

radical right political movement can pose to other individuals from similar backgrounds who possess rage at their government, but no other evident predisposition to offend. The case perhaps represents a model for political terrorism in the United States in the 1990's.

4. Once again, several reports of a suspected bomber testing improvised explosive devices (IED's) went unnoticed or were inadequately investigated by law enforcement. Bomb data personnel agree this chronic pattern of failure must be immediately corrected.

Ideological Escalation Model – Timothy James McVeigh

Ideological Predisposition to Violence and Terrorism
1995 February-Kingman Bombing, April-Oklahoma City Bombing
Action 3-"War Mobilization"
1995 "Final Arrangements", Haircut, Boots, Always Armed
Action 2-"Subversive"
1994 Explosives Theft, Moore Burglary, Constant Travel
Action-"Voluntary Non-Compliance"
1994 Failure to File Income Tax, Chip Removal, Fake ID and Aliases

FINAL STAGE

"Dissident"
1994 Gun Shows, Roger Moore, United Nations Facility
Paranoid Delusions
1994 Methamphetamine, Bill Cooper, James Nichols
Delusions of Grandeur
1994 CIA Letters to Jennifer, Mark Lane Book
Recruitment-Rejection
1994 Friends Refuse Contacts, Family Concerned
Collapse of Social Net
1993 Former Fellow Soldiers Ignore, Press Conspiracy
Self Indoctrination
1993 Linda Thompson Video-"Waco: the Big Lie"
"Government Historically Wrong"
Conspiracies or Demographics Are the Cause
"Government Intentionally Wrong"
1993 Ad in Spotlight, Short-wave Radio

ESCALATION STAGE

"Government Always Wrong"
1993 Gays in Military, Waco, Spotlight
"Government Usually Wrong"

1992 Race War Letter to Editor, Randy Weaver, Bill Clinton
"Government Sometimes Wrong"
1991 Gulf War, LA Riots, SF Failure, Discharge
"Country And Government Are Separate"
1988 Gun Culture, Survivalism, Turner Diaries
"My County-Right or Wrong"
1983 Grenada, Buffalo Bills Football, Middle School Hockey

NORMAL STAGE

Subject Begins with Middle American Predisposition to Patriotism, Strong Belief System, Adolescent Militancy

Biographical Summary:
"Start With an Interventionist Personality"

The young man thought he was going to die that night. The single car crash occurred along a lonely stretch of I-70 near the Illinois-Indiana border. He was ejected from his vehicle through the windshield and was laying unconscious in the grass in the median. He woke up screaming in pain. His mangled red Chevy Blazer was crushed and upside down just off the interstate surrounded in shattered fragments of glass and steel.

The concussion caused his eyes to be slightly out of focus. He watched an eighteen-wheel truck pull over as he lay staring into the dense cold fog. Two men began shouting and searching around what was left of his vehicle with flashlights. Though he was less than fifty yards away in the grass, they could not see him. Bleeding profusely from an open fractured leg and unable to move, he was helpless. The rumbling diesel truck engine and road noise muffled his pleas for help.

American soldiers are trained to scan the darkness with their pupils darting rapidly back and forth across the horizon. When properly applied, this simple training technique greatly enhances the night vision ability of the human eye. The soldier traveling east on I-70 who came upon the scene that night was extremely well trained. He immediately saw the man down in the median and looked for a place to park.

The crash victim continued to panic when the Chevy Spectrum Turbo did not look like it was going to stop. The driver slowed down for a moment and then appeared to go on. Then a car door slammed, heavy boot steps came in his direction, and the soldier was at his side. He set a large shoulder bag down in the grass and began to unzip one of the pockets. He told the injured man he was going to be all right as he inspected the shattered bones of his leg, which were protruding through his clothes. He then applied a compress wound dressing to slow down the bleeding.

The victim recalls the soldier was confident, quiet, and efficient. To centralize his circulation, he elevated the man's undamaged limbs and warned him to be calm to avoid going into shock. He checked his pulse and flashed a small penlight across his pupils. The man, who only a moment earlier was convinced he was going to die, shivered in the dark and started laughing. He told the tall young stranger he was never going to buy another Chevy Blazer again. The soldier smiled as he rolled up the victim's right sleeve and pushed in the needle to start a saline IV into his veins. "You've lost a lot of blood and you risk going into shock. This is an IV to help stabilize you and keep your fluids going. Relax. You'll be fine," he told him. He placed the clear plastic IV bag under the man's hip and checked his pulse again.

In the distance, an ambulance siren screamed over the sound of the truck engines as Timothy James McVeigh quickly packed up his Army-issue trauma kit and disappeared into the night. The responding EMS crew told the state police officer who arrived at the accident minutes later that they had never come upon such a potentially deadly crash to find a severely injured man relaxed and laughing, neatly bandaged with an IV dangling from his arm. Noted as a "random act of kindness", the local newspaper speculated about the mysterious Samaritan who had stopped to stabilize a crash victim and then headed down the highway without a word.

Develop an Improvisational Mindset

Early the next morning, when McVeigh finished his 1200-mile drive and was back home with his family in Pendleton, New York, he was more than just a little worried. Having just graduated the 46-hour medical aid course at Fort Riley and personally signing for his Combat Lifesaver Pack, he knew it was against regulations to take the kit off base. He could replace the bandages, but he was now missing a saline IV bag and needed to find another one, fast. His four-day weekend was almost half over.

Tim said he knew the man he found bleeding to death on the interstate probably felt lucky a passing stranger was equipped to help him. As a professional soldier, he generally believed that luck was opportunity meeting preparation. Everyone acquainted with Sergeant Tim McVeigh can recall with absolute certainty that he was the most prepared individual they ever met.

That same day, McVeigh called a friend who worked as a volunteer at his hometown Emergency Medical Service and arranged to replace the IV bag. He never spoke of the incident again.

"An attention-seeking loner with a grudge against the government and a psychotic hatred for humanity" is the fictional profile the FBI has leaked, and the news media has used, to describe McVeigh. From a historical perspective, most Americans probably hope such a description is true.

The public generally demands that anyone charged with mass murder be described as identifiably different than the rest of us. To place some sort of logic to the act McVeigh stands accused of, it is almost comforting to conclude that the key suspect in the worst terrorist attack in

United States history is a cruel and calculating offender with a deficit of social skills and a dysfunctional sense of decency. The media campaign against him has been impressive. Based on often-fabricated representations about who and what he is, Tim McVeigh has indeed already been tried and convicted in the court of public opinion.

The record, however, tends to dispel many of the myths about the life of this 27 year-old war hero. He has no prior criminal record or affiliation with any known extremist group.

Gradually Expose Subject to Indoctrination

Less than a year before his arrest, for example, in the Summer of 1994, after *The Spotlight* ran a story about UN troops and vehicles near Gulf Port, Mississippi. McVeigh personally drove to the alleged "UN staging area," hopped the fence, and inspected the facility where a local businessman had a contract to modify old Soviet and east bloc vehicles for United Nations humanitarian work. McVeigh noted the lack of weapons mounts and armor on the vehicles, checked out the company involved, and reported observations to anyone who would care to listen as he traveled the gun show circuit.

Meeting McVeigh face to face confirms he is neither a monster nor a mad man. After months of requests, McVeigh granted me a face to face interview. It became obvious during the hour-long discussion that Timothy McVeigh is neither a monster nor a madman. He is, however, a man with strong convictions and a deep sense of honor. What he stands accused of, combined with an outward facade of normalcy and an almost frail humanity, is more disturbing than anything fabricated in the press to present us with assurances to our illusions.

The interview was specifically biographical. Because the U.S. Attorney's office was collecting every printed word about the Oklahoma City bombing for possible use in court, they entered thousands of news-clippings into evidence, it was agreed beforehand that McVeigh would not be quoted directly and that the charges against him were not to be a topic of discussion. McVeigh's attorney, Stephen Jones, was present for the tape-recorded interview.

White Adult Male, Intelligent, Middle-Class, Some College, Military Training

A tall athletic young man with a muscular neck, broad shoulders and huge hands, Timothy James McVeigh resembles a first-year college basketball player. According to the United States Army, he also fits the "physical characteristic profile" of the ideal Special Operations soldier. Contrary to the muscle-bound Rambo image portrayed in the media and the movies, the average Army Ranger or Special Forces "Green Beret" is generally lanky and lean with minimal body mass and not an ounce of fat. This highly intelligent breed of elite warrior is built for speed and endurance. Trained and developed to quietly carry heavy loads over long distances, and to fight more with his mind than with bulky muscle, America's best commandos and paratroopers more resemble Tim McVeigh than Sylvester Stallone or Arnold Schwarzenegger.

Like many combat veterans, a part of McVeigh will probably always be in the Army. The very physical and absolute nature of military indoctrination tends to stay with a young man, sometimes forever. He preferred to keep his sandy blond hair cropped short. He responds to questions from strangers with "sir" and he maintains his body in top condition through almost constant exercise, despite his highly restrictive circumstances. Tim is not permitted outdoors or to work out in a gym. He stays surprisingly fit with a calisthenics regimen of push-ups and sit-ups in his solitary cell.

McVeigh has never smoked or overindulged in alcohol. Even as a single soldier living in the boredom of a barracks, fellow soldiers say he generally avoided the legendary binge drinking associated with the life of an infantryman. His clear eyes, bright teeth, and ruddy pink complexion are indicative of a life of healthy living. He could probably still pass the grueling Army Special Forces Physical Fitness test.

An Identifiably Voracious Appetite for Alternative Information

The pages of newsprint he handles every day darken his long slender fingertips. For most of his life, McVeigh has had an incredible appetite for information. He reads almost every page of the *Dallas Morning News* and the *Washington Times* along with a large bundle of letters he receives from around the world each afternoon. He also has a Bible and several books in his cell. McVeigh is not permitted to watch television. Other than almost daily visits from his legal team, his only contacts with the outside world are the printed material he receives and occasionally listening with headphones to a radio mounted in the wall of his cell. When propagation conditions are good, he tries to tune in the Chuck Harder Show broadcast each night on KTOK, an AM news talk radio station out of Oklahoma City that seldom comes in very well at El Reno. He also reads Harder's *"For the People"* newsletter and several other alternative publications, including the *New American,* a monthly national newsmagazine published by the John Birch Society in Appleton, Wisconsin. Although it has evolved into the most popular military periodical among current and former American infantrymen, after *Soldier of Fortune* caustically attacked the patriot community last summer, this publication has not been welcome in McVeigh's cell.

Aside from the *Spotlight,* McVeigh says he read, or at least was familiar with, a lot of alternative media publications, including Jack McLamb's *Aid and Abet* newsletter and Bo Gritz's *Center for Action* newsletter, as well as others. He also recalled getting and reading with interest the first two copies of *The Resister,* a newsletter originating from Fort Bragg, North Carolina that purports to be from the "Special Forces Underground." He said he got his first copy of the controversial military publication from *Soldier of Fortune* and the next edition at a gun show.

The government was expected to assert he was somehow "indoctrinated" into the radical right with all of these publications. McVeigh smiled at the notion. He observed the fact that he may have seen or read some of the alternative or fringe printed material, widely available at gun shows across the country, is by no means an indication that he believed in what they said or even read them in their entirety.

Considering what he would face in the coming months, the first impression one gets of McVeigh was his astonishing good humor. He responded to questions like a young man with a bright future and endless optimism. He smiles easily and often. He lacks the far away stare of a war veteran. His sapphire blue eyes are intelligent and expressive and, when speaking, he looks directly into your eyes without a trace of fear or suspicion.

Uncharacteristic Image of Rage

Some people who know Tim McVeigh did not even recognize the man dressed in an orange jumpsuit being paraded by the FBI out of the Noble County Jail on April 21, 1995. "The man I saw on TV looked mean and hard," said Robert Nichols, Terry Nichols' father. "The young man who came to my house for Thanksgiving a couple years ago never looked like that. He did not have it in his character to look mean".

When the FBI interviewed the elder Nichols and he was shown a news photo of McVeigh in chains, he denied ever having met him. He passed a polygraph to that effect the following day. Until his son James assured him it was the same Tim McVeigh, he would not believe it.

With a long oval face and high cheekbones, McVeigh's features are reflective of his Irish and western-European ancestry. Although he fought aggressively in Iraq and survived the desert war without a scratch, the cartilage of his nose is just slightly disfigured from where it was broken while attempting to break up a fight between a member of his squad and a civilian in the parking lot of a bar outside Fort Riley, Kansas.

Our conversation opened up with the incident along the interstate. McVeigh was impressed and somewhat surprised with the intensity of research conducted on his life. He had mentioned his intervention at the accident scene to only two or three people in the past five years. His attorney was not even aware of it.

McVeigh recalled the wreck, which occurred around April 1990, and said at the time he was in a hurry to get home and at first was not going to stop at the accident scene. But when he noticed the injured man lying in the grass with no emergency medical personnel around, he felt obligated to check on him. He declined to be more specific about the accident or to name the EMS worker in his hometown who had replaced his Army issue saline IV bag. His friend evidently broke his agency's rules to help McVeigh replace the medical package.

Although only anecdotal, this single incident tends to dispel the notion that McVeigh is a sociopath loner out to seek attention. The fact that he chose to stop, render aid, and then leave the scene once medical help arrived suggests a personality that did not need or want the world to know he had probably just saved a man's life.

The son and grandson of union auto workers, and a product of small town America, McVeigh was known to make the 1,200-mile trek to his home in upstate New York from Fort Riley, Kansas every chance he could. According to Staff Sgt. Albert Warnement, his direct supervisor at Fort Riley from 1988 to 1990, McVeigh would rush home to Pendleton on the four-day holiday weekends routinely given to U.S. military personnel and on every annual leave.

An Acquired Lack of Respect for Authority

Tim is also known to drive fast. He smiled sheepishly as he admitted that making the trip in about 16 hours required him to habitually and carefully exceed the speed limit in the Chevy Spectrum Turbo he bought new with money he saved as an armored car guard after high school. He would travel Interstate I-70 from Ft. Riley all the way to Indianapolis before heading northeast to the Canada-New York border town of Pendleton, NY, just outside of Buffalo.

Aside from the incident at Ft. Riley, where he tried to stop a fellow soldier from being attacked, and his actions on the interstate, McVeigh's protective and interventionist personality is reflected in several other anecdotes throughout his life.

Develop Existing Predisposition to Militancy and the Gun Culture

McVeigh recalled the most important and influential book of his youth was *To Ride, Shoot Straight, and Speak the Truth* by Jeff Cooper. The text, written by America's foremost authority on the .45 ACP pistol, describes the personal responsibility an American has to protect and defend himself, his family, and his country. The conservative, tough-on-crime textbook has become a classic in law enforcement circles. The tradition of individualism and the principles of personal protection are outlined in the 384-page hardcover work. The content and tone of the Cooper book is quite cogently stated in the advertisement in the Paladin Press catalog, "Knowledge of personal weapons and the skill in their use are necessary attributes of any man who calls himself free."

McVeigh took an interest in computers, advanced science, and mathematics early in his high school years. He also learned the importance of self-reliance. Using the Cooper book and the writings of personal defense author Massod Ayoob as reference works, McVeigh acquired a $C0_2$ powered 177 caliber pellet gun to train himself in the proper handling of a pistol. The Daisy Powerline Model 92 fires pellets at about 400 feet per second, has a rifled steel barrel, and is an exact size replica of the Baretta 92S, the 9mm sidearm of the United States military. Tim said he practiced carefully with the pistol and was soon able to put all his shots into a small target in his backyard. He developed good gun handling skills with the Powerline, including an apparently natural ability to rapidly fire the pistol accurately in double action mode. His friends were indeed impressed with his ability to control the weapon as he rapidly emptied it into tin cans 25 yards away.

One of McVeigh's first handguns, purchased a few years later, was a Taurus Model PT-92AF 9mm automatic pistol, an exact replica of the $C0_2$ pistol he had become so proficient at handling. McVeigh was issued his first concealed carry permit on April 23, 1987, his 19th birthday.

McVeigh grew up around firearms. His grandfather, Ed, gave him a .22 rifle when he was in his early teens. Tim was very close to his grandfather who also gave him his first shotgun when he was about 14. Ed McVeigh died in October 1994 and Tim traveled across the United States to attend the funeral. The neighbors across the street from the McVeigh's were also enamored with the gun culture, according to Tim's father, Bill, who observed that his son accompanied the family when they went shooting on weekends. This exposure evidently assisted Tim in acquiring the gun culture mindset that was not particularly present in his own household, nor was this manifested in his normal social circles.

Many news reports suggest McVeigh was involved in the "paramilitary survivalist" culture while in high school. He denies any such contact, and close friends confirm that McVeigh associated exclusively with honor students and intellectuals in school. As Justin Gertner, who has known McVeigh since they were in the second grade recalls, there was a small clique of students at Starpoint Central High School who wore camouflage fatigues and played war games, but McVeigh never had any known contact or interest with them. "He hung around with the intelligently elite at Starpoint," Gertner said in a telephone interview. "Tim was in the Regent's program in our school for advanced placement students who planned on attending college. He also created and ran our community computer bulletin board system. He was very good with computers and was known as the 'Wanderer' on the BBS system. He helped just about everyone around here with his or her Commodore 64. I never went out with any of the military types in our school. I was shocked when he was arrested. I thought he would end up going to a prestigious college and become an engineer. I never imagined he, of all the people I knew in high school, would end up in jail for anything."

The "Tendency to Mobilize"

A generic interest in basic survivalism is, however, not unusual in McVeigh's hometown. The people of rural upstate New York are conservative and self-reliant by necessity. The harsh northern winters of the area, located only a few miles from the Canadian border, requires citizens to have plenty of firewood or fuel in case of power outages. Heavy snowfalls can reach fifteen feet and roads can be impassable for days. Most households stock-up with several weeks' supply of food and water in preparation for being shut in.

Being prepared to deal with such adversity is something Tim's father noted about his son when he began storing water in the basement of their home in his early teens. Similar to the habits of his grandfather, being ready to weather a storm is something Tim McVeigh quite naturally elevated to.

Tim said he first began acquiring guns as a potential investment against inflation. He had already bought about nine acres of land with his savings by the time he reached his 20th birthday, and he also maintained a steady bank account and a Visa card almost immediately after graduating high school. James Nichols, Terry Nichols' brother, observed that McVeigh was one of the thriftiest young men he has ever met. "Tim did not like to go out to eat or drink because it cost money. He saved his pennies very carefully," Nichols stated in an interview.

McVeigh's father and grandfather taught him to be very frugal with a dollar. He also evidently learned the intrinsic value of saving things other than money. McVeigh recalled he also collected rare comic books in his youth after learning of their high investment value. He said the hobby of collecting firearms was something he picked up from his grandfather for the same reason. The notion that he was completely enamored with the gun culture is simply not true, he said. McVeigh describes guns simply as tools and pointed out that most of the acquisitions of firearms in his life have been for their future value.

The potential investment value of old rifles and shotguns are based on a shrewd eye for detail and good negotiation skills. As the antigun lobbying interests in New York began to target semiautomatic rifles in the 1980's, McVeigh noted the increase in their retail price. He acquired a Colt AR-15 A2 sporter rifle from his hometown gun store in 1987 when the value of these firearms increased almost 30% that year.

McVeigh said he had several interests in his teens: including science fiction, collecting comic books, computers, and outdoor athletics. He played hockey and basketball in the winter and ran track for his school as a senior.

Development of Strong "First Impression" Social Skills

Although not a particularly outgoing social climber as a teenager, McVeigh was definitely not a "loner" in high school. He attended most school functions, worked at Burger King with several of his classmates during his senior year, and admitted that he occasionally snuck across the Canadian border to drink beer with his friends where the age limit for alcohol consumption was lower. Friends and teachers recall his general good humor and sharp intellect.

McVeigh's cleverness with computers stands out. He took every available advanced computer class at Starpoint High. A teacher, who asked to remain anonymous and has not been interviewed by the FBI, recalls McVeigh's proficiency with programming.

When the school first acquired computers for classroom use in 1984, McVeigh was one of the first students to excel he said. "We used very primitive Commodore PET systems at first. Tim designed a software program that sequentially dialed every number in the 433 and 434 calling-area by modem. It was an enormously long program. He did it mainly on his own. That was the age when there was no software to speak of, and it wasn't user friendly. But Tim and some other kids went out and did this. There were so few modems, how would you find someone else with a computer? Maybe one house in a thousand, or a business [had one]. So they were looking to hook up with someone else who had a Commodore PET. In a way, that was fairly advanced. This demonstrates his bright mind and his ability."

During our interview, McVeigh recalled his hobby working with and programming the Commodore 64. McVeigh had a separate Commodore 64 and a 1500 series modem specifically tasked to search through every available phone line to locate other computers, which he and his friends would then attempt to communicate with. He smiled as he described the software program he wrote as a "War Games box," a reference to the movie starring Mathew Broderick. McVeigh further developed his programming skills on the IBM PC systems that were brought to Starpoint High School the following year.

"Tim," "Timmer," "Timbo," and "Chicken McVeigh," were some of the nicknames Timothy James McVeigh had in high school. Friends and teachers remember he hung around the lobby at Starpoint Central School during study hall where he mingled with just about everybody. A photo in his senior yearbook shows Tim on the pay phone in the lobby, standing next to Lynn Miazga. The class of 1986 voted the two "Most Talkative."

Brandon Stickney, a local journalist who has contracted to produce an unauthorized biography about Tim's life for Prometheus Books, stated, "Tim was not the most talkative out of his class of 194 students, but he was by no means introverted. He was certainly an outgoing young man who had many friends and acquaintances."

Stickney also confirmed the general survivalist nature of the community. When interviewed by telephone in early January, he pointed out that a foot of snow had fallen overnight and his wife was at the store stocking up on supplies. "My wife even has a large candle, some water, a blanket, and some candy bars in our Jeep Cherokee in case she ever gets stranded. Just about everyone around here has a four wheel drive vehicle."

Though McVeigh was arguably not the most talkative member of his senior class, he probably talked to the most people, according to classmate Pam Widmer, who has been his friend since junior high school. "We all had study hall together in the lobby of the school. What he would do is go around and sit and talk to other groups. He was actually kind of a popular guy, although I don't recall him having a lot of close friends. He was a friend with just about everybody. [Tim] worked at the Burger King on South Transit Road in Lockport. We would come in late at night and he would be mopping up the floor or working behind the counter. Burger King was like a local hangout the summer of our senior year. Tim would sneak through the side kitchen door and give us free food, french fries and stuff."

"He listened to the basic rock and roll," Widmer said. She recalled McVeigh liked Ozzy Osbourne, the Scorpions, and Van Halen. McVeigh, along with several of his classmates in the summer of his Senior year, grew his straight blond hair long and had it permed. MTV evidently had its influence. McVeigh is quoted in the yearbook as having the following plans for the future, "take it as it comes, buy a Lamborgini, California girls."

In Widmer's yearbook, McVeigh wrote in pencil: "Pam, Geez-uz! You are quiet! Loosen up woman! It's your senior year, I can't read this, how are you going to? 3-D glasses are the best! Best of luck in the future! Tim"

The claim in the December 31, 1995 issue of the *New York Times* that Tim McVeigh was "so withdrawn that his classmates sarcastically voted him most talkative in the yearbook and teachers did not remember him" is patently untrue. McVeigh is featured several times in his high school yearbook, including a photo of him on top of a pyramid of other students. He is quoted making comments about skipping school and falling asleep in class. The record actually indicates he was an ordinary and reasonably popular high school student.

Growing up in a small town tends to create life-long friends. Keith Maurer, who competed with McVeigh at freshman football tryouts in 1982, knew him from their neighborhood hockey games on Myer Road in Pendleton. "He lived a few houses down from me. We played hockey, baseball, and just about every other sport in the neighborhood. He wasn't the best athlete in the bunch, but he showed up to play every day and he always played hard. When we tried out for freshman summer football at Starpoint, he was pretty big for his age and he made the team," said Maurer. "I remember going to a Halloween party Tim had in his basement when he was about fourteen or so. Every kid in our neighborhood went." Maurer also discounted the claim that McVeigh was a gun fanatic in his youth. "I remember starting to hunt at age eleven and Tim never had any interest in this, that I can recall," he said.

McVeigh said one of his most vivid childhood memories when the family lived on Myer Road was the Blizzard of 1977, which took out power and telephones in his hometown for several days when about fifteen feet of snow fell on the community. His father was evidently stranded at the factory for a couple nights. Tim was nine years old. The McVeighs started storing food, water, and other necessities in the basement of their home from then on. Tim remembered well this lesson for survival. His father, however, drew the line and refused to purchase a generator for back-up electricity at his son's request.

McVeigh graduated high school in May 1986 and continued working at Burger King for part of that summer. Again, despite media representations that he was a sullen loner, friends say McVeigh worked hard at his part-time job, clowned around with co-workers, and dated a few girls from Starpoint. "He was just a normal, polite kid," recalled Matt Kiff, whose wife Marcia worked with McVeigh.

Brief, Uneventful, and Ultimately, Unsuccessful College Career

Like almost a third of his senior class, McVeigh started his university education that September. The local computer hacker known as "the Wanderer" on his homemade bulletin board was accepted to study advanced COBOL and FORTRAN programming languages at the eastern campus of Bryant & Stratton Business College in Williamsville, New York.

His college career was cut short within a couple months. In early winter 1986, at age 18, Tim dropped out of computer classes and began looking for a job. McVeigh, who was an honor student through most of his years at junior and senior high school, said he became bored with the simplistic nature of freshman academic subjects and the notion that he needed to obtain a degree to be employable. Also, the Regents Scholarship he was awarded at Starpoint was only for $500. Tim said he did not like the fact that he could not pay his own way through school. His father paid most of his tuition. McVeigh admits he now regrets dropping out of college after only one semester.

Shortly after Christmas, Tim learned about a security guard position at Burke Armored Truck on Main Street in Buffalo, NY. He passed the drug screen and police background check, but before he could take the $6.25-an-hour position, McVeigh was required to obtain a handgun permit in Niagra County. After waiting about three and half months, the permit was issued on April 23, 1987.

McVeigh said he enjoyed the job, and according to former employees, he performed well in the role as an armed guard and messenger, providing security for pick-ups and deliveries of bags of cash at area banks and retail stores. His co-worker and partner, Jeff Camp, of

Cheektowaga, New York recalls with clarity the intensity and diligence of Tim McVeigh on the job. Burke's headquarters office had an indoor weapon firing range upstairs and Tim qualified with his pistol without many problems. He was an excellent shot and had several guns, said Camp.

"He was a very alert guard. He worked a lot of overtime and was polite with our customers," he said. Camp recalled he and McVeigh would also sometimes lose patience in traffic. "If someone was driving badly, cutting us off or interfering with our schedule, he could get pretty mad. His face would turn red and he would yell and scream inside the truck, although he calmed down pretty fast."

Early Indications of Militancy, Intervention, Cumulative Rage

McVeigh never actually got into any altercations with drivers or customers, Camp said. He recalled a minor fender bender accident in the parking lot of a shopping center during one of their delivery runs. A woman backed into the heavy armored car and Camp said McVeigh got out of the passenger side and calmed the lady down. "She was upset about hitting our truck, which wasn't damaged. He told her we would say the accident was our fault, even though it wasn't. He also told her we would not call the police to report the wreck." Camp said McVeigh evidently felt sorry for the woman and did not want to involve law enforcement in the accident. McVeigh recalled the wreck and said there were several minor fender benders involving armored cars during his time at Burke.

Although McVeigh said he did not brandish his weapon or fool around with guns on the job, fellow employees noted his intense interest and knowledge of firearms. "He came to work one day with a Desert Eagle .44 Magnum automatic pistol," said Camp. "Tim had a lot of guns and he knew a lot about them." McVeigh said he bought the Desert Eagle with some of his savings but ultimately concluded that it was an inherently unreliable pistol. Camp pointed out that most certified full-time security guards and law enforcement officers that he has known typically own an assortment of firearms. He said the fact that McVeigh owned several guns was not particularly unusual for an armed guard.

Camp recalled that while on the job, McVeigh did not like to eat at fast food restaurants. "On our lunch breaks he would stop at a convenience store and buy a whole bunch of food. That kid could eat. He was really thin, but he ate a lot of food every day."

During the interview, McVeigh laughed about the often-reported story about him showing up one day at Burke Armored Truck with a bandoleer full of 12 gauge shotgun shells around his chest. He said he and other guards came to work that morning with extra equipment as a joke on the supervisor who was sending them on a high-profile assignment for the day. Camp recalled the incident as well and said their supervisor was not amused by the sarcastic humor of his employees.

For a 19-year old living at home, McVeigh said he was making pretty good money as an armored car guard. He said he bought several guns, got a Visa card and built up his savings account. McVeigh said he enjoyed the outdoors and, with $7,000 of his earnings, he and Dave Darlack, a friend from high school, acquired nine acres of land at a hunting and camping retreat near rural Olean, NY, located about 100 miles south of Lockport.

County tax records show McVeigh purchased the parcel of rugged land on April 12, 1988 from a retired Buffalo police officer. Although he and Darlack and others went to the property a few times to target shoot and hike, less than six weeks after acquiring the campsite, Tim joined the United States Army. The reason for this decision may be explained in a tiny state police blotter entry from the Olean New York State Police barracks log sheet.

First Opportunity for Intervention

In late April 1988, locals in the area near the property began to note loud explosions up the hill from the McVeigh/Darlack parcel. A retired state trooper contacted the local police barracks to have the matter investigated, he said, because several Cranes were nesting in the area and the retired officer knew the sounds were not originating from gunfire. When a trooper arrived along the roadway adjacent to the property, four white males dressed in camouflage fatigues and carrying a variety of military weapons, including an AK47, an AR-15 and a 44 magnum automatic pistol approached and said they were firing the guns and attributed the noise reported to their firearms. The trooper left the area and filed only a "no action taken" report regarding the contact.

Almost exactly seven years later, a team of FBI forensic experts arrived in helicopters and combed through the property and reportedly recovered residue and other evidence of experimentation with pipe bombs and low explosives on the site. Whether this was McVeigh's first exposure to improvised munitions will be forever clouded in controversy, however, it points out the importance of aggressive law enforcement investigation of all reports of explosive function or evidence of bomb testing in the United States. Regardless of the residue, McVeigh almost immediately enlisted into the military within days of this contact.

Virtually every offender interviewed and studied who employed IED's admits he went to a safe private place to conduct testing. This is often the first and only opportunity for law enforcement to identify the offender and the offense prior to an EOD incident involving damage to property, injury, and loss of life.

Perceived Deterioration of Social Safety Net

For McVeigh's family and friends, his decision to join the military was somewhat unexpected. Records show he enlisted with the Buffalo recruiter instead of at the Army office in his hometown of Lockport, about 25 miles away. "He didn't tell anyone he was joining. He just came to work one day and said he was going in the Army. We were all surprised," said Camp. "He was gone in a couple days."

Aside from the apparent IED incident, there were certainly other reasons for Timothy to enlist. According to author Brandon Stickney, the local job prospects for McVeigh were not nearly as assured as they were for his grandfather and father who both spent their careers at the Harrison plant, the biggest employer in the community. Now called Delphi Harrison, the metal work factory employs about 6,000 Lockport and Pendleton area residents and manufactures car radiators for General Motors. McVeigh's father, Bill, has worked the night shift at the plant for almost all of Tim's life.

The predominately white industrial working class area of western New York suffered in the seventies when the American auto industry went sour. The energy crisis reduced car sales and the Harrison factory stopped all hiring and starting laying off workers in the late 1970's according to Stickney. "There haven't been any new hires there in about 20 years," he said.

During the interview, McVeigh said he went into the service because of the career opportunities and the chance to travel. He intended to make the Army his career. Records show McVeigh's General Technical test-score, or GT, was 126, which put him in the highest percentile among new recruits. He said he chose the infantry because it was the core skill a soldier needed to function in the military. He very much wanted to try out for the Army Ranger school. He could have waited a few weeks to get a slot for the option, but instead, wanted to go into the service immediately.

McVeigh said the recruiter misled him about an opportunity to go into the Airborne Ranger battalions once he got to Fort Benning. The chance was actually not open because the basic training unit he ended up in was part of an Army experiment known as "COHORT," an acronym for Cohesion, Operation Readiness, and Training. Unbeknownst to McVeigh, there was no way he could transfer out of the unit into the Ranger program.

Army Regulation 601-210 stipulates the limitations of soldiers transferring out of a COHORT unit into other parts of the infantry. The soldiers had to stay with the program for their entire first enlistment. Because of these restrictions, McVeigh's dream of becoming a Ranger was dashed when he arrived at Fort Benning. During our interview, he smiled and agreed with the observation that if U.S. Army recruiters actually told young men and women what the Army was really about they probably would not get many to enlist.

According to the Department of Defense, the COHORT program attempts to build a bond between enlisted men from basic training all the way to their first duty station by keeping them together. After basic, soldiers are ordinarily sent to different training facilities and duty stations. This tended to eliminate the creation of long-term friendships among new recruits. Pentagon studies from Vietnam suggested that young soldiers are motivated to perform difficult tasks in harsh conditions not simply out of patriotism or a sense of duty as much as out of the bond formed over time between fellow soldiers. Research suggests that heroic acts in combat are more commonly attributable to the bond of trust and honor among soldiers who tend to look out after their "buddies" more than the interests of the mission or of the United States Army. Exploiting this natural function of peer-pressure and friendship was the purpose of the COHORT program, which is still in limited use in the Army today.

Another media misrepresentation, according to McVeigh, is the claim that the pseudonym "Tim Tuttle" originates from the Robert DeNiro character in the cult classic movie "Brazil." Harry Archibald Tuttle is a serial bomber in the film who strikes out at government targets with impunity. Although viewing guide records from the Lockport-based cable company currently called Jones Intercable, show the movie was aired hundreds of times in the 1980's, McVeigh said he never saw the film in his teen years nor did he ever rent the movie. Stephen Jones, his attorney, states that the defense can explain the origins of the alias.

Exposure to Radical Fringe

McVeigh said he also considers unfair and unfounded the notion that the mainstream press has classified him as a racist simply because he had read the *Turner Diaries.* He said he responded to a gun magazine advertisement for the book around 1988 because it was being billed as a novel about what may happen when government comes to confiscate privately owned firearms. McVeigh also pointed out, and his Sergeant confirms, that while in the Army he served alongside black soldiers without incident or problem and when he lived off base he and Michael Fortier routinely gave rides to work to two fellow soldiers who were black.

Although there were no African Americans in McVeigh's graduating class, and few in his hometown, according to the U.S. Army there are no reported incidents of him having any professional problems as a soldier dealing with any other races. Furthermore, McVeigh's platoon sergeant was black and his platoon leader was Hispanic, and both gave him the highest ratings an infantry soldier can attain.

McVeigh admits that he regrets not continuing college, where he attended for a semester on a Regent's scholarship for high academic performance. The university environment was boring and somewhat repetitious in content, he said. McVeigh also found it a waste of his father's money. The Army offered him the GI bill and an exciting change of pace. He was making good money as an armored car guard but the job seemed to have no future, he said. He enlisted on May 24, 1988, a month after he turned 20 years old.

Service in the Army was and probably still is the highlight of McVeigh's life. By all accounts he absolutely excelled as a soldier. What has been claimed about McVeigh's service record is most disappointing to him. He said a number of misrepresentations have been made about his military career, which he wishes would be clarified. Media Bypass has obtained much of McVeigh's military records, which will be outlined in part two of this story.

As confirmed by Sgt. Warnement, McVeigh said he initially enlisted in the Army to participate in the Airborne Ranger enlistment option. McVeigh's GT score of 126 essentially allowed him virtually any military specialty he wanted. Serving in the Army's elite Ranger battalion is what he wanted. McVeigh said he was misled by his recruiter and placed into the Army's experimental COHORT unit at Fort Benning when he arrived. The COHORT program did not allow soldiers to transfer over to the paratrooper battalions. Everyone who arrived for basic training under the program had to stay in their assigned unit all the way through basic and advanced training and to their first permanent duty station, which, for McVeigh, Terry Nichols, Michael Fortier and about 200 others was the newly created 2/16th Infantry Battalion at Fort Riley, Kansas.

The record shows McVeigh was a natural soldier. He scored the maximum possible rating out of training at Fort Benning and was promoted to Private E-2. He made rank faster than just about anyone else in his unit. He said the secret to his success was studying the voluminous training manuals available to every soldier but seldom actually read in their entirety. Instead of spending off duty time drinking at the Enlisted Men's Club, McVeigh carefully read the field manuals, talked to higher-ranking NCO's and took notes about being a professional infantryman. He also took Military Occupational Specialty (MOS) sub-courses, Army correspondence classes available to military personnel to familiarize them with other job specialties. McVeigh took the Psychological Operations (PSYOPS) Course and began taking the Army Special Forces Qualification course by mail.

Special Forces selection was the only way out of the COHORT unit he said. McVeigh passed the initial selection application and received orders to go to the Army's elite school. His orders had him expected to arrive at the Ft. Bragg Selection and Assessment course on November 17, 1990. The Gulf War eliminated this opportunity. McVeigh's unit was activated for service on November 15.

The Road to Becoming "The Ultimate Soldier"

Although McVeigh would not get a chance to become one of the elite in the military, the twenty year-old, 155 pound young man from upstate New York became a soldier at the Second Infantry Training Brigade at Ft. Benning, Georgia. After processing into the Army, getting shots, uniforms, boots, and a haircut he would keep for years afterward, Tim McVeigh arrived at his training unit with several hundred others from across the country. The 112 men of Company E, 4th Battalion were divided into three platoons. McVeigh was part of second platoon, which arrived by open covered cattle car to the Army Infantry School in early June 1988. The first stop was the "sawdust pit."

Military indoctrination is intended to strip away any individuality from a typically teenage American male, and the first few hours of Basic Combat Training are generally remembered by anyone who has experienced it. McVeigh remembers like it was yesterdays.

As fellow soldier and assistant platoon leader Glen "Tex" Edwards recalls, when the cattle cars stopped, the recruits were greeted by a very large, profanity-screaming drill sergeant who ordered them to get off the trucks and into an exercise pit full of sawdust. The soldiers were made to perform push-ups then sit-ups then run in place and then pushups again until each, one by one, fell exhausted onto the sawdust, where they were then screamed at and ordered to get up and exercise more. The recruits are harassed, humiliated, and demoralized in the process. The first few days of infantry training are generally a blur of fatigue, fear, and exhaustion for the civilian recruits.

Edwards recalled Tim McVeigh as somewhat "timid" when he first arrived at Ft. Benning but said he was not the least bit intimidated by the training or the Drill Sergeants. "McVeigh was really motivated to be a good soldier and performed well at everything expected of him, although he pretty much kept to himself during basic," said Edwards.

Edwards, who entered the Army at the age of 22, was made assistant platoon leader among the recruits in the 2nd platoon. The oldest man in the unit, 32 year-old Terry Nichols of Decker, Michigan was appointed on the third day of training to be the senior platoon leader.

"The Drill Sergeant said that because Nichols was older than the rest of us he would hopefully be more mature and able to lead the younger guys in the unit. He also had some college background and came into the Army as a PFC," Edwards said.

Edwards recalls his initial contacts with Nichols. "He said the government had made it impossible for him to make a living as a farmer. He hated the United States government. I thought it strange that a 32 year-old man would be complaining about the government, yet was now employed by the government. Nichols told me he signed up to pull his 20 years and get a retirement pension."

McVeigh and Nichols evidently became acquainted at Fort Benning by necessity. Both soldiers were on the second floor of the barracks and McVeigh would have needed to go through Nichols if he had any question or problem and when he reported for any detail or guard duty according to Edwards. "The platoon leader is the soldier's first chain of command at basic training. If a recruit needs to ask a sergeant anything, he has to first go through the platoon leader," he said.

Edwards also recalled that the E Company First Sergeant, an older South Vietnamese NCO was relieved of his command in their third week of training after forcing the recruits out of bed one night without shoes or uniforms to perform exercises and "combat rolls" after a member of the third platoon went AWOL. This illegal form of group retribution resulted in several injuries. Edwards said the First Sergeant was replaced the following day.

As basic and advanced training progressed, Timothy James McVeigh gained weight and muscle-mass and performed extremely well as an infantryman. "You could load that boy up with 140 pounds of gear and he would carry it all day on the march without complaining. He was thin as a rail but he never fell out of a formation," said Edwards, who recalled the hot Georgia summer of 1988. "It was the worst time of year to go through the course, but it did not seem to bother McVeigh one bit."

Indeed, military records indicate that Private McVeigh scored higher than anyone else in his training battalion when he achieved "the maximum test score on the mid-cycle and end of cycle testing" to be an Army infantryman, according to a certificate awarded by his commanding officer on August 25, 1988. He was also promoted to Private E-2 for his performance in the training. He arrived on Custer Hill at Fort Riley, Kansas in early September to serve with Company C, 2/16th Infantry Battalion, a part of the infamous "Dagger Brigade" of the 1st Infantry Division.

McVeigh embraced the career Army ethic almost immediately out of training, according to Staff Sergeant Albert Warnement, his supervisor at Fort Riley. "He was without question the best soldier I have ever trained with. He was motivated and very interested in learning everything he could about being a professional soldier," Warnement said.

"Hell, that boy was the ultimate soldier," said Edwards. "After we had thrown the thing in the garbage or lost it, McVeigh was still carrying around the basic infantry skill handbook we got issued at [Fort] Benning, months after we got to Fort Riley. He carried it in the leg pocket of his BDU's and referred to it constantly. He knew more about the job and the equipment than most of the officers and NCO's in our unit. He was usually quiet but he had no use for incompetence. I watched McVeigh correct many Sergeants on some aspect of soldiering. The only times I ever saw McVeigh get angry and red in the face was when a Sergeant did something really stupid or did not know how to do his job."

Edwards said that when he occasionally visited McVeigh's quarters, he noticed hundreds of magazines, paperback books, and Army field manuals stacked neatly in his area. "He had *Soldier of Fortune* magazine and *Guns and Ammo* and all sorts of paperbacks on military history." Edwards said he remembered McVeigh reading the biography of Carlos Haithcock, a famous Vietnam sniper. The book *97 Confirmed Kills* is a classic work on the subject. "McVeigh seldom went out drinking with us. He stayed in the barracks and read his military manuals. He saved most of his paycheck, and he would lend the rest of us money when we needed it. To be honest, I still owe Tim McVeigh forty dollars myself," he said.

Warnement also confirmed McVeigh's reading interest, including the *Ranger Handbook, The Special Forces Handbook* and the TM 31-2 1 0 series known as *Improvised Munitions*--the U.S. Army's technical manuals on homemade explosives.

These types of books are widely read on military bases. Warnement, who recently graduated from the Army Ranger course himself, said most of the more serious soldiers in the unit read the available literature on guerrilla warfare, Survival, Evasion, Resistance and Escape (SERE) and improvised munitions. "We all had those kinds of books," he said. "You have to remember, at that time, we were training to fight the Russians in Western Europe and it was expected the Red Amy would probably break through our lines almost immediately. We were encouraged to learn how to improvise. Our survivability on the battlefield would likely depend on our skills in unconventional warfare."

When McVeigh was tested as a gunner on the Bradley fighting vehicle, he scored higher than anyone else in the battalion did. As a soldier, he was promoted faster than anyone in his unit and within a year became the literal poster boy for the United States Army's "Big Red One" 1st Infantry Division.

In 1989, he was selected as the commander's choice to be the gunner on the Division Display Vehicle at Fort Riley. Whenever a senator or visiting dignitary came to the huge installation and wanted to see what the new high-tech M2 Bradley Armored Fighting Vehicle could do, McVeigh and Warnement would report with their "track," designated "Charlie 13" to division headquarters to demonstrate the system.

"We kept that vehicle immaculate," said Warnement. "McVeigh and I spent our own money to buy Armor-All and other cleaning materials to make our Bradley look brand new.

Although records and reports show that McVeigh may have taken his military service much more seriously than the average Infantryman, according to Edwards, "If we ever went to war, every one of us wanted to go to war with McVeigh."

Tim became a close friend with Terry Nichols and Michael Fortier in his first year at Fort Riley. They would go shooting together at the range and also at a private farm along the Republican River and Tuttle Creek Lake near Manhattan, Kansas. Nichols had a small house off base and McVeigh would sometimes visit.

McVeigh had a number of personal weapons he kept off base in a gun safe he bought and kept at Warnement's house. "He had an H&K 91 with a heavy barrel and a bipod, an AR- 15 A2 Sporter, a Desert Eagle pistol, a Mossburg shotgun and a Taurus 9mm," said Warnement. "I bought his Taurus from him before I shipped out to Germany in 1990. I still have his gun safe," Warnement said in a telephone interview.

McVeigh recalled going shooting with Warnement and others. Most infantry soldiers have their own personally owned weapons, called "POWs" in the military jargon, he said. McVeigh bought the H&K 91 at his hometown gun store. He said he went in one day and the classic German rifle was on display and for sale at a good price.

Starting a "Private Army"

Terry Nichols drove the commander's Humvee vehicle in the unit. His military career was cut short because of problems at home with his son Josh, according to Army records. According to Edwards, shortly before he left the Army on a Hardship Discharge, Nichols invited him to be a part of a "private army" Nichols said he was creating. "He told me he would be coming back to Fort Riley to start his own military organization. He said he could get any kind of weapon and any equipment he wanted," said Edwards, who recalled Nichols told him he intended to recruit McVeigh, Fortier, and others for the same purpose. "I can't remember the name of his organization, but he seemed pretty serious about it." Edwards said that he reported Nichols' offer to the FBI shortly after the Oklahoma City bombing.

According to Army records, the 2/16 had a number of problems with morale and individual misconduct. Edwards himself was put out of the Army for alcohol abuse while in the unit. One of McVeigh's platoon sergeants was kicked out of the Army for drugs within the first few months of duty at Fort Riley, according to Edwards, who also recalled that a number of soldiers in the unit listened to heavy metal rock music and engaged in satanic cult-like behavior. "There were guys who hung a crucifix upside down on the wall in their rooms. The whole unit had a lot of weirdness to it," he said.

A Company Commander in the First Brigade, Major Jeff Coverdale, who incidentally lost two nephews in the Oklahoma City bombing, has a discrimination complaint against the Army over his experience at Fort Riley. In a telephone interview he recalled the problems with McVeigh's unit, including an officer in the 2/16 who was caught twice by Army criminal investigators attempting to set fire to a barracks. "CID caught Major Hunsinger in the act two times, yet he was simply put out of the Army with no criminal charges filed. They turned a serial arsonist back on the streets without a word of warning," he said.

Despite this environment, McVeigh took soldiering seriously. Any free time he had away from the Army was generally spent at home in New York. Service in the field was something Edwards said almost all soldiers in the unit looked forward to.

McVeigh and Warnement would sleep inside the cramped quarters of the Bradley when they were in the field. "One of the perks of being a gunner or a driver is that while the rest of the troops, or dismounts had to dig in their defensive positions outside, we got to stay in the track and monitor the tactical radios," Warnement said. "I would plug my walkman into the intercom so we could listen to tapes and Tim and I would talk for hours. He talked about home a lot. He told me he held his mother responsible for the break-up of his family."

Much has been made about the reported resentment McVeigh had over his mother. Tim dismisses these stories. His parents separated and then divorced when he was in his early teens. During the interview he said that when he was younger it might have bothered him that his parents had problems, but he understood when he became an adult that things are not always perfect in relationships and families. McVeigh said as an adult he has not been affected by what happened between his mom and dad over fifteen years ago.

As an adult soldier, McVeigh's record was exemplary. Colleagues say he had little patience with incompetence or laziness from fellow soldiers or, for that matter, from leaders. Sgt. Chris Barner, who served with McVeigh, said Tim was a natural born leader. "He had a lot of leadership ability inside himself. He could command soldiers of his own rank and they respected him. When it came to soldiering, McVeigh knew what he was doing. He had a lot of self confidence," said Barner.

The unit traveled to West Germany in April 1989 for a one-week orientation with the German Army. Charlie Company landed in Heidelberg over the Easter Sunday weekend, according to Edwards. The soldiers of the German Army, or Bundeswehr, are two-year conscripts, well educated and very motivated. "We went to a German war museum and we went down on a border patrol mission with the Germans," said Edwards.

"A Way Out"

In the summer of 1989, after returning from Germany, McVeigh said he heard through a friend that the way out of the COHORT unit was through the United States Army Special Forces program. He learned of the rigorous training requirements of the elite "Green Beret" or SF units and began to study the sub-courses on his own time, and got himself into a high state of fitness.

McVeigh admitted the often-reported stories that even when off-duty he would constantly do push-ups and sit-ups and go on ten mile marches while carrying over a hundred pounds of sand in his rucksack are true. He said he wanted to make it through the Assessment and Selection Course at Fort Bragg and he knew the physical training there was some of the most grueling in the United States Army. He said he trained hard for his chance to make the cut.

According to Army Regulation AR-601-25, the physical requirements to even qualify for the Special Forces Assessment and Selection (SFAS) Course are generally beyond the capabilities of all but the most physically tough U.S. Army infantrymen. Other than being required to swim a minimum of 50 meters with full uniform and gear on, the soldier also has to be able to perform a minimum of 42 pushups in 2 minutes, 52 sit-ups in 2 minutes and then run two miles in less than 15 minutes and 54 seconds in order to qualify to take the course, which is recognized as the most physically and psychologically stressful training the Army offers.

McVeigh said he passed the SF physical fitness test in the late summer of 1990 and was issued orders to report to Fort Bragg, North Carolina to start the assessment course on November 17, 1990. He re-enlisted in the Army for four more years on September 20th, shortly after learning about his appointment to the Special Forces School. The brewing conflict in the Persian Gulf changed everything.

A Soldier Goes To War

On November 8, 1990 all leaves and training assignments were canceled by the Pentagon when McVeigh's unit was activated for deployment to Saudi Arabia, just days before he was to travel to Fort Bragg. McVeigh, who had privately trained hard for months to attend the school, missed his chance.

"He was against the National Command Authority's decision to go to war," said Warnement. "McVeigh did not think the United States had any business or interest in Kuwait, but he was a good soldier. He knew it was his duty to go where he was told and he went."

When McVeigh's unit arrived in Saudi Arabia just a few weeks before Christmas, 1990, they were issued brand new Bradley Fighting Vehicles. He immediately disassembled his new Bushmaster 25mm gun, carefully cleaned it, and zeroed the weapon at 1,000 yards. The vehicles were also modified to reach a top speed of about 70 miles per hour. The men of Charlie Company 2/16 spent Christmas and all of January living in tents in the desert and waiting for orders to advance into Iraq. On February 1, 1991, Tim McVeigh was promoted to the rank of Sergeant.

When the air war began, U.S. troops were on a high state of alert because of incoming Scud missiles and the constant threat of chemical and biological weapons. Many soldiers listened to news updates on portable radios. McVeigh said he recalled the sick feeling he and his troops had when they heard about the accidental allied bombing of an air raid shelter in Baghdad about two weeks after he was promoted.

According to Al Kaissy, an information officer at the Iraqi Interests section of the Algerian Embassy in Washington, on February 13, 1991, a U.S. Air Force "Stealth Bomber" dropped a 1,000-pound laser guided bomb on the roof of the Al-Amira air raid shelter in Baghdad. "Then another 1,000 pound bomb followed. We lost 294 women and children," he said. "We thought it was the best built bomb shelter in the Middle East," said Kaissy. "We were wrong." Kaissy said all of Baghdad has been rebuilt since the war five years ago. Except Al-Amira. "Our citizens have turned the rubble into a shrine. There are pictures of the children who died in the bombing and family members go there almost every day to pray," he said. "The U.S. military considers the murdering of our children nothing more than 'collateral damage.' They have never apologized or even admitted their mistake."

As the date for the ground war approached, the infantry units expected to punch through the Iraqi lines were more than a little nervous, McVeigh recalled. Between training accidents and friendly fire casualties, McVeigh told fellow NCO's that he was worried less about the much touted and battle-hardened Iraqi Republican Guard soldiers than he was about U.S. aircraft and tanks accidentally attacking members of his squad.

Loss of Patriotism-"This Buds For You"

U.S. Army helicopters destroyed over 600 enemy tanks during the action in the Gulf. The first ground war casualties caused by Army aviators, however, were Americans. Around midnight on February 17, 1991, members of McVeigh's division were approximately three miles into Iraqi territory when a squadron of AH-64 Apache helicopters arrived behind the Bradleys and Ml tanks to provide Close Air Support (CAS) for the unit, now designated "Task Force Iron". Because of 25 mph winds and a glitch in the guidance systems, the Apache Squadron

Commander, 42 year-old Colonel Ralph Hayles, Jr. mistook a Bradley and an M-113A1 APC for enemy and fired on both vehicles.

Transcripts of the tactical radio traffic obtained by *Media Bypass* indicate that as the helicopter "lit up" the Bradley with a laser-target designator, Hayles' co-pilot, Captain Garvey, said, "There you go, now do the mother f---er." To which Colonel Hayles responded as he fired a missile at the track, "This bud's for you."

Twenty-three year-old Specialist Jeff Middleton and 18-year-old PFC Bob Talley died when Hayle's rocket hit and instantly incinerated their Bradley. He then fired another rocket and hit the APC. As Hayle brought his 7.62-mm "mini-gun" sites on the soldiers who were fleeing the wreckage, he was advised by a ground commander to stop, telling him on an open frequency that he had just killed U.S. ground forces. Hayles was relieved of his command for the incident and retired from Army shortly afterward.

Infantrymen in their aluminum Bradleys were horrified as they monitored the entire friendly fire attack on their tactical radios. As the ground war progressed McVeigh said he attempted to reassure his younger soldiers that the incident was accidental, but he never forgot it. When he got back home from the Gulf War, he recorded a CBS News *60 Minutes* documentary on the incident and other "friendly fire" accidents. He said the FBI has since confiscated the videotape from his family.

The 2/16 was ordered across the southern Iraqi desert along the same path their fellow soldiers took at 3:00 p.m. on February 24, 1990. McVeigh, a 22 year-old Army Sergeant, along with driver Jason Smith and the vehicle commander, Lt. Jesus Rodrigues, were the lead tracks in the platoon. As the "top gun" in the unit, McVeigh was volunteered to be on point. He fired the first shot when he took out an enemy armored vehicle with a TOW missile, killing four Iraqis.

On the following day, Sgt. McVeigh became somewhat of a legend in his unit when the battalion encountered a dug-in enemy machine gun emplacement. The unit came under small arms fire from a platoon of Iraqi soldiers. At a kilometer away, the enemy weapons were relatively ineffective. The U.S. troops would have to advance closer to engage them. McVeigh brought his 25mm gun site onto the chest of one of the enemy soldiers and fired. He took the man's head off at 1,000 meters. McVeigh said during the interview that reports of him shooting the soldier in the head are not accurate. He said his round hit the Iraqi in the neck. McVeigh killed another soldier the same way as the rest of the platoon sat there in stunned amazement. "Jesus, did you see that?" said another gunner over the radio. "Great f---ing shot!" The record shows that the next thing the platoon witnessed was the waving of a white flag and the raising of over 60 hands up into the air around the machine gun emplacement. All were taken prisoner without another shot being fired.

McVeigh's unit commander, Colonel Anthony A. Moreno requested that he be awarded an Army Commendation Medal which reads in part "*...he inspired other members of his squad and platoon by destroying an enemy machine-gun emplacement, killing two Iraqi soldiers and forcing the surrender of 30 others from dug-in positions."* The Commendation medal was issued for "Meritorious Achievement with Valor," four months later in Washington D.C., and signed by The Secretary of The Army.

Colonel Moreno said McVeigh's unit killed over 650 Iraqi soldiers in the first two days of the ground war. McVeigh also earned the Bronze Star Medal "for Flawless Devotion to Duty," during Operation Desert Storm. There were no deaths in the 2/16, although another "friendly fire" incident in the 5/16 unit took the lives of three of McVeigh's fellow infantrymen within days of the cease fire when they stepped on a U.S. mine fired from an artillery shell cluster bomb.

Because of their exemplary combat performance, the 2/16 was invited by General Norman Schwarzkopf to provide security on the inner perimeter at a captured Iraqi airstrip known as Safwan Airfield in Southern Iraq when the armistice was signed. ABC News has obtained a file photo of Timothy James McVeigh smiling as he points a camera at General Schwarzkopf from about an arms-length away.

Pursuit of a Dream "Hurt more than it should"

McVeigh recalled he met a few Army Special Forces soldiers at Safwan Airfield from the 5th SF Group. He said it was an unexpected surprised when he was issued orders on March 28, 1991 to again report to the Selection and Assessment Course at Fort Bragg, North Carolina. He knew he wasn't ready. McVeigh said after living in the desert for four months he was not in the best physical condition. His military issue field gear was worn out and he had just replaced both sets of combat boots. They were not even broken in, he said. He packed up his gear and left the desert the same day. McVeigh said he went home for a few days and then flew to Pope Air Force Base, outside of Fort Bragg, North Carolina, where he arrived on April 5, 1991.

McVeigh actually spent less than two days at the SF school. He and another member of his unit, Mitch Whitmyers, both knew they were not in the requisite physical condition for the course, he said. When they got to Camp McCall at the Special Forces training facility west of Fort Bragg, he and Whitmyers and a couple other Gulf War veterans were pulled from the formation of volunteers and asked if they wanted to consider returning to their unit for a few months and get back into shape. McVeigh said one of the veterans yelled out that they were ready, and, perhaps out of a sense of gung-ho pride, no one decided to leave the course.

Media reports claiming McVeigh was rejected because he failed the psychological test are not true, according to Col. Ken McGraw, information officer at the Special Operations Command at Fort Bragg. "McVeigh dropped out of the course on the second day. His psychological test work would not have even been graded yet," McGraw said.

Despite these facts, FBI agent John R. Hersley told grand jurors in the Oklahoma City bombing case that McVeigh was rejected by the Special Forces for psychological reasons. Hersley, incidentally, is one of the two FBI agents who visited and intimidated grand juror Hoppy Heidelberg at his ranch in May 1995 after he accidentally took his grand jury notebook home with him. McVeigh's attorney Stephen Jones told *Media Bypass* that Army records indicate his clients' SFAS psychological tests were not actually graded until after McVeigh was arrested in April 1995.

The first day of the SFAS course begins with a physical and a PT test and then a 4-5 hour psychological screening examination, according to McGraw. Army psychologists give candidates three tests; the Adult Personality Inventory, the Minnesota Multiple Phase Personality Test and a sentence completion exam, he said.

McVeigh said he had no problem with any of the questions in the psychological screening, many of the same questions were asked several times. He said the second day of the course began with physical training and an obstacle course, which tested the soldiers' confidence. He passed the course without difficulty. After lunch, McVeigh said the soldiers were ordered to report to a formation where they were told they were going on a high-speed forced march. They were not told where they were going, how long they would be gone, or what distance they would cover. McVeigh said he was ordered to pack his rucksack with whatever he thought he would need for such an activity, and that the total weight of his LC-Medium pack must exceed 45 pounds when the march was over. McVeigh said he packed his usual infantry gear and two extra pairs of socks. He said he then filled several zip-lock bags with sand to get the weight over 45 pounds.

McVeigh said his new-issue boots tore into his feet on the march, which he estimated was about five miles. Out of condition and physically drained from the war, he said he met with Whitmyers out by a water billet where they were filling up their canteens. Both soldiers knew the worst was yet to come and decided to drop out of the course and try again in a few months. McVeigh said he filled out a Statement of Voluntary/Involuntary Withdrawal from the SFAS school that was a single sentence in length. It read, "I am not physically ready, and the rucksack march hurt more than it should." McVeigh said he was invited by the commander of the school to return to try the course again whenever he felt he was ready.

The claim that McVeigh was completely "burned out" about U.S. military service after the SFAS course is not true, he said. Furthermore, his records reflect that he was given the highest rating a NCO can obtain by his commander two months after reporting back to Fort Riley. McVeigh also earned another Army Commendation Medal six months later when he fired his 25mm gun at a competition at Fort Riley and "Scored a perfect score of 1,000 points," earning the title "top gun" of the division on September 27, 1991.

As the military force reductions came on-line in late 1991, McVeigh transferred to the Army National Guard in Buffalo on January 1, 1992. He got a job as guard with Bums International Security and worked night shift at Calspan Research. He did well at Burns and was promoted to the rank of Lieutenant in May 1992.

Final Stage- Waco, Short-wave Radio, and Mobilization

As a civilian, Timothy McVeigh registered to vote as a Republican in Niagra County, joined the NRA, and served in the National Guard until June 1992. The 23 year-old war hero led a relatively ordinary life back in his hometown. He sold his property in September and moved out of his apartment early in 1993. He traveled to Kingman, Arizona and to Decker, Michigan to visit his Army buddies Terry Nichols and Michael Fortier. He admits that he, like thousands of other former soldiers, was concerned and troubled when he saw tanks and an M2 Bradley Fighting Vehicle pull up into the front yard of a church in Waco, Texas in March 1993. Tim drove from Kingman to the scene and acknowledges that he was among a group of citizens protesting the raid on the roadway in front of the Branch Davidian church.

McVeigh said he was at Waco for about a day and half and then traveled up to Decker, Michigan to again visit James and Terry Nichols. He was at the farmhouse in Decker when they watched Waco burn to the ground on April 19, 1993. "Tim did not say a word," said James Nichols, who was in the room while he and his brother Terry and McVeigh looked at the television screen in a stunned silence. "We just stood there and watched the live television footage as the church burned and crumbled. We couldn't believe it."

McVeigh had a short-wave radio he listened to regularly in 1993. He said he bought a Realistic Model DX-390 and tuned in to the news on the BBC and Voice of America. He said he also listened to Chuck Harder on WWCR and also monitored radio programs broadcast by Jack McLamb, Bo Gritz, and Kevin Strom on short wave. He said he listened to the religious and patriot programming on 7435 kHz until April 1993, when the WWCR transmitter burned down just outside of Nashville. McVeigh said he is curious about the coincidence of the fire, which occurred during the Branch Davidian Siege. The station said the fire was the result of an electrical problem.

As the interview drew to a close, McVeigh dispelled a number of other media and government misrepresentations. He did occasionally read Bo Gritz's *Center for Action* newsletter but never met him. He also said he never saw the movie *Brazil*. He was familiar with the Linda Thomson videos about Waco, copies of which he sent to Sgt. Warnement.

Final Opportunities for Intervention

Three more contacts with law enforcement did not send up any evident flags over Mr. McVeigh's escalation, nor would they be likely to in the future. By winter of 1993-94, Timothy was experimenting with explosive devices routinely with friends on the Nichols Farm, though no police responded, despite neighbors calling the Sheriff and complaining.

At a gun show in summer 1994, McVeigh explained to retired ATF agent Rick Sheffow how to modify the PVC tubes and flare guns he was selling to "take out helicopters." At another gun show in Phoenix in September 1994, a criminal intelligence agent with the Sheriffs Department filed a brief report regarding similar representations McVeigh made to him.

In February 1995, a huge ANFO explosion that rocked the community of Kingman, Arizona may have involved Mr. McVeigh, who was identified by the victim, Rocky McPeak, as a likely suspect, according to the investigative file obtained under the Freedom of

Information Act. McPeak also made this representation to the Grand Jury in the Oklahoma Bombing investigation.

And finally, at the time of his arrest on April 19, 1995, McVeigh actually had an outstanding warrant for his arrest in Arkansas for failure to appear on a traffic citation. He was also named and wanted for questioning in the home invasion robbery of gun collector Roger Moore of Royal, Arkansas. Any one of these law enforcement contacts could have hampered or perhaps incapacitated Timothy James McVeigh from what he now stands accused of. We find, over a period of seven years, at least three known instances of constructive possession or development of improvised explosives in this subject's biography, yet, none of these events in and of themselves are currently regarded as incidents indicating a predisposition to violence or terrorism.

Psychosis Attributable to Drug Use?

Contrary to claims he was a chronic user of speed, McVeigh does not deny casual experimental use of methamphetamine a couple times while visiting Michael Fortier in Arizona. But he said he was never a serious user of the drug, and, unlike codefendant Terry Lynn Nichols, McVeigh said he never renounced his U.S. citizenship or refused to pay income taxes. Though McVeigh dismisses his claimed rare indulgence in narcotics, the paranoid delusions associated with even experimental use of methamphetamine should not be overlooked in this case.

Conclusion

The need to collect intelligence in an open society should be considered carefully as the rights of citizens and issues of public safety often afford little commonality of purpose. However, once again, we find an accused offender engaging in paramilitary training at an early age who was also evidently experimenting with and testing improvised explosive devices under the eye of his neighbors and the suspicion of law enforcement. We find an escalating pattern of cumulative rage in an otherwise ordinary, frighteningly normal human being that was and still is being exposed to the influential radical right alternative media that foments paranoia as a matter of purpose and intent. And finally, we find a society forever altered by the notion that this deadly brand of terrorism can indeed, happen here.

Historically, the Oklahoma City bombing and the case of Timothy James McVeigh will likely alter the path of this country for decades to come. For the sake of history, an accurate biography of this young man needs to be compiled, documented and carefully crosschecked.

Based on recent defense motions, the Oklahoma City bombing trial is expected to uncover a number of disturbing details about America and its current government. McVeigh's attorney, Stephen Jones, said in a speech in January at the fifteenth annual Advanced Criminal Law Seminar in Aspen, Colorado, "If you believe the Oklahoma City Bombing was the result of two rogues mixing fertilizer, then you can believe that if you put your tooth under the pillow, you'll find five dollars under it the next morning."

What the trial may reveal is unknown. Its impact undetermined. The only clue comes from Mr. Jones' rather grim prediction in his closing remarks at a speech in Oklahoma City in November 1995. "Some day, when you know what I know and what I have learned, and that day will come, you will never again think of the United States of America in the same way."

In a solitary cell, inside an ancient federal prison in the middle of Oklahoma, 27 year-old Timothy James McVeigh, along with the rest of America, is waiting anxiously for that day to come.

On June 2, 1997 Timothy James McVeigh was convicted of conspiracy to use a weapon of mass destruction, use of a weapon of mass destruction, destruction by explosive, and eight counts of first degree murder and sentenced to death by lethal injection.

On January 2, 1998 Terry Lynn Nichols was convicted of conspiracy to use a weapon of mass destruction and eight counts of involuntary manslaughter and sentenced to life in prison.

Lawrence W. Myers, *a U.S. Army-trained Explosive Ordinance Disposal technician, has five published books on bombings and terrorism and is currently under contract to produce a book on serial bombers. Since 1987, he has been on the Editorial Advisory Board for Security Intelligence Report in suburban Washington, DC. Also on staff at Media Bypass Magazine as Chief Investigative Reporter, Myers has served as a consultant to ABC News and has published widely in newspapers and magazines on federal law enforcement and violent crime.*

AVIATION SECURITY AND THE CURRENT TERRORIST THREAT

Frank J. Donahue

While the focus of this chapter will be directed at aviation security, please keep in mind that aviation is not the only targeted mode of transportation for terrorist threats. Other examples of targets in recent history have been the Arizona Amtrak derailment, the chemical terrorist incident in Japan on board a commuter train, the Achille Lauro, a terrorist maritime incident, and the recent terminal bombing outside of Madrid.

The exposure and emotion directed at the security and safety of air travel, domestically or internationally, today has not been seen or felt since the bombing of Pan Am 103, prior to that the hijacking of TWA 847 in 1985 and the Rome and Vienna airport massacres. The nation and the world was shaken by terror and to those who needlessly died and the relatives that were left behind were victimized by terrorists' who base their actions on various foundations that have no more concrete than a gravel road. However, do not misunderstand, terrorist groups are well funded, well organized and well educated. They can be civil engineers at an airport, airline employees, or administrative types.

Terrorism has no boundaries. During World Wars I and II there were many theaters of operation. The Axis powers kept trying to expand their control and intimidate, while the Allied powers kept trying to reduce their sphere of influence. In today's world we have basically the same situation. The difference is that during those two wars, Congress pulled out all their resources, financial and personal, until they were defeated. Today we only see the money, the people, and the passionate speeches after the fact.

There was a move within Congress to divert monies from the Airport and Airways Improvement Act to some other programs. On August 2, 1996 the House passed HR 3953 Aviation Security and Antiterrorism Act of 1996 that directed the FAA to deploy commercially available explosives detection devices on an interim basis pending a fully certified system.

The FAA will also be required to increase security standards for aircrafts with fewer than 61 seats. The Bill also requires a more rigorous background check on the screening of personnel and establishing performance standards for them. Three key issues are important to airline security: money, focus, and attitudes.

In the late 1960's and early 1970's, the homesick Cuban or the general criminal element thinking they could avoid prosecution with their Cuban riches were the main threat to aviation security. Based on a rash of hijackings, Congress immediately reacted by placing federal agents and military on airplanes. Eventually laws and regulations directed toward airports and airlines to institute security measures that protected the traveling public were established, such as the creation of the FAA's Office of Civil Aviation Security.

The basic differences between airport security and airline security, and standards for screening personnel are as follows: Airports are primarily responsible for external physical security, law enforcement, airport access control, personnel security, air operations areas, signage, lighting, fencing, five-year backgrounds and normally act as the host of the airport and tenant security committee; airlines have the responsibility for the screening of all individuals who pass through into designated sterile areas of the terminal, access control of assigned areas, airplane security, employee identification, and five-year background investigations of their personnel.

The airlines in the majority of cases contract with private security firms. These firms must comply with the standards set upon the carriers. However, they are not legally responsible for enforcement sanctions, the carrier is. In some cases now, the carrier stipulates in the contract a return of sanctions if they are in violation of FAA rules.

Checkpoint security screeners prior to working the checkpoints are required to undergo initial training that in part involves the total screening process; identifying the threat, screening the passenger and hand-carried items, special situations, alarm procedures, equipment operation, and air carrier procedures. It is important to remember that these are minimum wage employees. FAA Special Agents and the airline do in fact conduct periodic testing of all checkpoints with mock test objects under realistic conditions.

Having covered many of the first three issues, let me turn to focus. In essence we have a number of elements in aviation that are trying to forge ahead into the 1990's and beyond with respect to aviation security. However, we also have those with a mindset that aviation security is still the same and should be the same as in the early 1970's. We need to move forward collectively amongst worldwide governments and industry, for those who swim out to sea by themselves will drown and those who swim together will continue.

After Pan Am 103, Congress had public hearings and asserted blame. Our president created a commission on aviation security to make recommendations and the 1990 Aviation Act was passed, directing the FAA to carry out a number of recommendations with respect to newer technology and placing more agents overseas. Today, for whatever reason, a number of them have not been enacted.

President Clinton directed the Vice-President to create yet another commission on aviation security and safety. The focus problem does not lie just within the government. It lies with the industry, as well. The focus is not just for the commercial aviation industry but also for corporations who have their own aircrafts flying domestically and internationally.

A third factor on the same plane (no pun intended) as the money and focus problems, is attitude. The attitudes of government, the industry, the flying public, and yes, the media all have a major impact. Some considerations to contemplate.

- When the media has an exclusive, it's a reporter's job to beat the competition providing all the facts are there. This certainly increases the ratings! It is also the right of the traveling public to know the truth. But one has to ask whether the "exclusive" or "expose" can cause public panic or, even worse, give the bad guys information that they can use to cause more terror.
- The traveling American public, unlike people in other countries, has not and will not accept showing up at an airport three hours in advance for security purposes. They will not accept having their personal vehicles searched when they arrive at the airport. And they will not accept seeing heavily armed SWAT or military personnel on the rooftops. The irony is that when U.S. citizens fly overseas, they are cognizant of security and they do arrive three hours early.

The technical aspects of aviation security and the technologies, while not always foolproof are out there, like the EGES, the CTX Scanner, and the Altitude Cargo Chamber. So what has been the hold-up in getting such systems included as standard equipment in most airports? In a number of instances, they are still in the experimental stages and not certified. Other issues or imperfections to still be worked-out include their size, where is the best place to put them and the money issue. For example the Thermal Neutron Explosive detectors (TNA devices) that are now in San Francisco and Atlanta cost anywhere from $1.2 million and up.

However, there are a number of things that could be accomplished within a reasonably short time period. Seven points I would like to make related to this:

1. Previously as a result of Pan Am 103, there had been a commission on aviation security to make recommendations to the FAA for implementation. We now find ourselves with a different administration directing the Vice President to establish a second commission on aviation security. How many commissions on aviation will be convened before we can get it right?
2. At category X airports, major airports such as O'Hare, Detroit, San Francisco, Atlanta, Boston, JFK, and Miami, there is a daily presence of FAA security, and all screening personnel undergo specialized retraining on all aspects of their jobs. The difference would be that FAA Special Agents do the training and the certifying. This is a little stronger than the house bill that was just passed, but still workable. If we have higher standards and certifications, then higher pay would logically follow. This would eventually lead to a higher degree of applicants.
3. At those airports where FAA Special Agents do not have a presence, assigned law enforcement for the airport should assist in local initial and recurrent training. This could be done with the local FAA manager.
4. The Department of Transportation publishes on-time records of airlines and other criteria in the media. Add another category - the overall nationwide pass/fail rate of security tests of the carrier - not by airport. We do not want to give our literate terrorists the opportunity to focus in on one particular airport.

5. The basic standards for the employment of contract security personnel at airports are minimal. As mentioned, a higher degree of standards, training and certifications need to be addressed and implemented.
6. Currently every regulated airport and airline have separate and distinct FAA approved security programs that are not necessarily uniform. While there are basic standards that are called for in each, it would be easier to run an airport if everyone was singing from the same hymnal. At a particular location, there should be one security program for each airport that applies across the board between airlines and airports.
7. Institute a positive bag match-up, either electronically or administratively, for domestic flights. But when doing so, insure that the bag match is tied into both inter and intra line baggage.

Outlined above are just a few possibilities that do not cost a lot of money. While there are things that can be done better, air travel is still the safest mode of transportation available. The high cost of technology is worth it. When we send millions of dollars in aid to other countries and then say that we cannot afford devices that can save U.S. citizens here, something is drastically wrong.

Frank J. Donahue *is a security, safety and crisis management consultant to a number of corporate clients and airlines. His prior U.S. government work was in the Department of Transportation. His extensive experience in the Federal Aviation Administration included National Crisis Management Coordinator and service in the Chicago field office. Donahue's earliest security training and efforts were with the U.S. Air Force and the Department of Defense.*

THE CONVERGENCE OF TERRORISM AND DRUG CRIMES

Marc Steven Colen

Terrorism[1] and drug-related crime are two of the most pressing and difficult problems facing governments, law enforcement and the criminal justice system on an international basis. [2] The connection between terrorism and drug related crimes has evolved on several fronts, from terrorists who use drug trafficking as a means of generating income to drug cartels who use terrorism as a means to maintain power. This connection became evident in the late 1970's and early 1980's when the drug cartels and terrorists began their alliance, each wanting what the other had. The drug cartels and traffickers had virtually unlimited resources and the terrorists were skilled in weaponry, intimidation, provocation of fear in law enforcement and governments, and killing those who opposed them. Narco-terrorism was born, particularly evolving in Latin America, the Middle East and Asia.

Several recent changes have occurred which have had significant effects on efforts to understand the relationship and to effectively counter it. First, there is a general decrease in the availability of funds to sponsor and support terrorism. The Soviet bloc no longer exists and Russia has enough problems with its own organized crime to be concerned with exporting terrorism. East Germany no longer exists. The communist dogma of Eastern Europe is largely gone. The decreased volatility in the Middle East and the financial distress of certain countries historically acting as sponsors of terrorist activities have decreased the funds emanating from that area into terrorist hands.

Second, the drug cartels and traffickers are under tightening scrutiny, no longer able to operate as freely as they did in the past. International cooperation, law enforcement techniques and technology and the judicious application of the military have increased intelligence gathering and communications. Computer technology has been applied to monitor the cash transactions necessary to launder the money generated by the sale of narcotics.

Third, new players, including ones in the Middle East and in Russia, are becoming involved in the increasingly global activity of drug production and trafficking. Some of these players are non-ideological in their philosophies and driven by economics. Some may be characterized as organized crime. Some have a long and intense history of violence and the use of terrorist techniques to achieve their goals.

Perpetrators come from either of three backgrounds. First are the "classical" terrorists, with which we have already had more experience than anyone ever wanted. For simplification, we will refer to classical terrorists as those motivated by ideological, nationalistic, ethnic, religious and/or separatist causes. For the most part, the nature and extent of their violence is constrained by their supporters and sponsors, although that constraint may be limited in its application and consequences. Several well-known terrorist groups, including the PLO and Hizballah, are known to be engaging in drug trafficking and sales. Lebanon is a known processing and distribution center for heroin and marijuana; the Bekaa Valley is the site of hashish plantations.

Second are the drug cartels, comprised of drug manufacturers and traffickers, whose motivation is simply money and power. Violence is simply a means to a financially beneficial end. There are no limits to the level of violence that may be used by drug cartels: they do not have anyone to whom they must report.

An example of this type of violence occurred in November of 1985. The leftist M-19 insurgent guerrillas, working on behalf of a Colombian drug cartel, invaded and seized the Palace of Justice in Bogota. Their intent was to intimidate the Colombian government, particularly the judiciary, to preclude the further extradition of drug criminals to the United States. Almost 500 hostages were taken, including numerous Supreme Court judges and members of the Council of State. Security forces attacked and a battle ensued. Eventually, all of the terrorists were killed, as were all of the Supreme Court judges and about fifty other hostages.

It is estimated that in the 1980's over one thousand public officials were killed at the behest of the drug cartels. The effect of these killings has been profound and continues to this day.

Third are the organized crime groups, particularly those evolving in Eastern Europe, who are motivated by money and a desire for power. More likely to be involved in distribution and sales rather than manufacturing, these same groups will sell illegal weapons, nuclear materials, agents of biological warfare, or any other items that may be sold on the international market at a high profit margin. History has shown that organized crime will stop at nothing to achieve their goals.

The potential targets differ for the different types of perpetrators. Terrorists may be expected to continue to attack targets that in some way represent the enemy, be that the United States, England, Israel, et cetera. Bombing will doubtlessly continue to be a preferred method of terrorist actions, rendering buildings and airplanes as most likely targets.

Narco-terrorists seeking to strengthen their crime empire may be expected to attack those targets most likely to advance their economic purposes. The law enforcement and criminal justice systems may bear the brunt of these attacks. In order to increase the likelihood of advancing their invulnerability to challenge, narco-terrorists may find it preferable to strike at larger infrastructure systems, such as the government and the country's financial institutions. Cyber-terrorism[3-4] will be the growth area of the coming decades.

Bombing has historically placed high in the choices of terrorists.[5] Assassination and kidnapping are effective alternates. Traditionally, terrorists have avoided what may be termed "white collar terrorism." Narco-terrorists may be expected to attempt to use cyber-terrorism and cyber-crime to directly affect their profits by attacking computers which aid law enforcement in database processing and analysis of crimes, criminals, and fund transfers. Sabotaging a computer system controlling financial markets or even utilities is not as dramatic as a bombing, nor is it so technically trivial. Nonetheless, certain terrorists will be moving on beyond bombings and kidnappings into the virtual world of cyber-terrorism. Their motivation will continue to be the same. But their techniques, however, will have advanced given that it has been shown that a mere building or airline bombing will simply not alter government policy. As new weaknesses in the "system" arise, e.g., computer access and the Internet, where the consequences are actually far more intense than the loss of even a few hundred people, there will be terrorist activity.

As to the present, the United States has joined much of the rest of the world in directly suffering the consequences of a terrorist attack on our own soil. The World Trade Center and the Murrah Federal Building bombings are excelling examples of the terrorists' art. On a more local scale, we have the burning of numerous Afro-American churches in the southern United States. White supremacist terrorists are involved in most, although not all, of these incidents.

Most relevant to this discussion, however, is the terrorism presently seen in the border areas of Texas, where drug traffickers have undertaken major actions to ensure free access to the land on the United States side of the border. Ranchers are being given the proverbial offer too good to refuse and are selling out to drug traffickers or their fronts.

At present, the drug trade continues virtually unabated. While it is unnecessary to delineate the numbers defining the magnitude of the problem, as an example consider that it is estimated that the volume of cocaine trafficking by the Colombian drug Mafia in 1994 was approximately 850 metric tons with a street value of between $10,500 and $40,000 per kilogram.

The future is problematic. Drug trafficking is an expanding enterprise. It is able to generate incredible amounts of money. As the established drug cartels lose their hold due to the work of law enforcement and the criminal justice system, new players arise. Middle Eastern countries are becoming the harbors for drug manufacturing and distribution. Many of the people involved are the same ones who have been involved with international terrorism for many years. Drug trafficking is a means to their ends. As the Russian organized crime syndicates expand, drug trafficking may be expected to be a favored source of revenue. The profit margin far exceeds that of other criminal ventures.

Of primary concern is the termination, or at least the significant reduction, of the supply of illicit drugs prior to their importation into the United States. History has indicated that it is impossible for the grower and producer countries to handle these matters alone, resulting in the necessity for the involvement of United States agents and intelligence assets to operate outside of the continental U.S. In some instances, but certainly not all, the presence of Americans is the result of "negotiated" agreements. In general, financial aid to a foreign country accompanies these agreements. However, there have been controversial court decisions supporting the right of United States law enforcement agents to arrest drug suspects in foreign countries.

Although national sovereignty is a critical concern for most countries, for those "outlaw" countries that support terrorism and drug trafficking, the international security issues of those countries, such as the United States, that are the target of terrorism and drug trafficking may be of overriding concern. Intentional discord may result from unrequested intrusion, but may be inevitable if target countries are to protect themselves.

As an example of the political consequences, consider the very unusual action of the United States wherein the U.S. visa of Colombian President Ernesto Samper was revoked on July 11, 1996. This is not a direct result of Colombia's refusal to extradite criminals, but rather from the allegations that Samper knowingly aided and cooperated with the drug traffickers operating in Colombia in exchange for monetary rewards.

The basis of counter-narco-terrorism as differentiated from terrorism in general, is the requirement for the functions of drug enforcement, which can be conveniently broken down into several areas, as follows:

1. **Investigation and prosecution**. Law enforcement and the criminal justice system must be brought to bear with their most intense application.
2. **International drug control**. No single country can deal with this international problem. No single country is immune from the dangers and consequences of the problem.
3. **Intelligence.** The gathering and sharing of intelligence is critical. In some cases, certain countries such as the United States, have vast advantages in COMINT (communications intelligence) or ELINT (electronic intelligence), while other countries may have better sources for HUMINT (human intelligence, that is information derived from working field assets).
4. **Diversion regulation**. The diversion of controlled substances from lawful purposes to criminal purposes must be precluded. Countries where organized crime flourishes, such as Russia, need take particular heed of this area.
5. **Analogue regulation**. Substance analogues are chemical variants of controlled drugs and need to be carefully controlled. Countries where sophisticated laboratories exist need to be concerned.
6. **Detection and monitoring**. Related to and overlapping with intelligence gathering, it is requisite that the existence of and trafficking in drugs and source materials be detected and monitored. Detection and

monitoring has been shown to be a very difficult, although critical, part of the counter-narco-terrorism program.

7. **Interdiction**. To the extent that controlled substances can be interdicted, the "owners" are penalized financially. This may be minimal in actual effect since the cost to procure and manufacture the narcotics is insignificant compared to the street value. Further, those apprehended are rarely of such stature and significance that they will have a major impact on the general flow of narcotics. Nonetheless, every kilogram of material that is removed from circulation is one less kilogram that will fund cartels and terrorists and one less kilogram to kill its users and devastate society.

8. **Border control**. All countries must consider border control as critical, both with regard to materials being imported and those being exported. Control within a country reduces the necessity for operations by other countries within their borders. It is easier to monitor one's own citizens than it is to try to watch the entire global community. Control of persons, narcotics, and weapons to preclude their importation into a country is clearly critical, but most difficult.

Extraordinary dangers exist when operating either in the "hot zone," that is, the inside of the laboratory, or in the "warm zone," the size of which is dependent on, *inter alia*, environmental factors such as wind. It may be expected that the people involved in the actual drug production, known as "cookers" have been effected psychologically by the extended exposure to the hazardous chemicals, typically leading to extreme paranoia. Such individuals frequently have access to very effective weaponry, including automatic weapons, explosives, booby-traps, as well as countermeasures such as detection equipment and monitors.

Unfortunately, these weapons are also those preferred by terrorists and the techniques applicable to the manufacture and production of drugs is not dissimilar to the techniques required for the production of terrorist devices from simple explosives to weapons incorporating chemical agents and agents of biological warfare. Within the United States, the majority of clandestine laboratories have been discovered in California, Texas, Oregon, and Washington.

The military may play a critical role in counter-drug terrorism, providing the requisite manpower and equipment to effect border control and the international intelligence required. The military has a well-developed methodology for C^3I–that is command, control, communications and intelligence–which may be applicable to counter-narco-terrorism activities.

Use of the military in the U.S. is limited by Title 18 of the United States Code (particularly Section 1385, the Posse Comitatus Act of 1878) and Title 10 of the United States Code. While the former generally prohibits the use of military personnel to enforce civil law and the latter prohibits Department of Defense organizations from arresting or conducting intelligence gathering against American citizens, there are relevant exceptions. Further the Defense Appropriations Act of 1989 and the 1989 Defense Authorization Act further authorizes military assistance. Examples of conditions where the application of military force is permitted include the following:

1. To prevent the loss of life or wanton destruction of property in an emergency if it is determined that local authorities are unable to control the situation;
2. To protect federal property and federal government functions if it is determined that
3. Local authorities are unable to control the situation;
4. To suppress an insurrection if requested by the governor or legislature of a state;
5. To suppress unlawful conspiracies or rebellion against the federal law;
6. To enforce the civil law of a state or the United States if it is determined that the law enforcement authorities of that state are unable or unwilling to protect the constitutional rights of citizens.

Two things are certain: the convergence of terrorism and drug crimes will continue to develop and expand, intruding into all countries, and 0this convergence will result in the escalation of terrorist activities, including the increasing use of high technology weaponry, like cyber-terrorism. Cooperative international efforts must be continued and expanded to conquer this enemy. Interagency cooperation must similarly be expanded. New techniques must develop and brought to bear in combating the new challenges of high technology terrorism. Both pro-active and responsive methods are critical. It is obvious that the countermeasures in place today are woefully inadequate to address the requirements of not only the future, but also even today.

Marc Steven Colen *is a Senior Research Fellow at the Institute for Security and Intelligence (ISI), in Stanford, California. He is ISI's Geopolitical Terrorism issues expert as well as a member of the Institute's Board of Advisors. Mr. Colen was a consultant on terrorism and legal issues to Rand Corporation and member at ISI, and is the author of more than 20 classified and open source papers on topics including potential terrorist use of biological and chemical weapons, criminal prosecution of terrorists, and explosives. Colen also has been a prosecutor and has taught weapons issues to the Los Angeles Police Department.*

NOTES AND REFERENCES

[1] The conventional definitions of terrorism may fail or at least appear to fail, to properly address the issue of narco-terrorism. For example, the Department of Defense (DOD) definition of terrorism, specified in DOD directive 2000.12, is "the calculated use of violence or the threat of violence to inculcate fear; intended to coerce or to intimidate governments or societies in the pursuit of the goals that are generally political, religious, or ideological." This definition, at least on the surface, specifically seeks to discriminate from violent actions intended to further personal gain. Nonetheless, it is necessary to include violence by criminal organizations, including drug cartels and international organized crime, when the purpose of the violence (or threat of violence) is intended to influence government function, even though the terminal goal is strictly economic. It is possible to read the DOD definition in that light. To the degree that a definition precludes narco-terrorism, that definition is obsolete.

[2] For the purpose of this discussion, we will differentiate law enforcement from the criminal justice system as the latter is largely concerned with reactive measures, that is, subsequent to the incident, whereas law enforcement is additionally tasked with proactive measures.

[3] Collins, Barry C., *CyberTerrorism: A New Era in Law Enforcement and Intelligence Agency Cooperation*, Institute for Security and Intelligence, submitted
upon request to the Senate Subcommittee on Investigations on June 18, 1996.

[4] Colen, Marc Steven, *Cyber-terrorism-The Terrorism of the Twenty First Century*, Institute for Security and Intelligence, submitted upon request to the Senate Subcommittee on Investigations on June 18, 1996.

[5] Colen, Marc Steven and Edward Ellistadt, *Bomb - Non-Military Anti-Societal Use*, Institute for Security and Intelligence, 1994.

HIGH NOON IN NORTHERN IRELAND

Paul Clare

I believe in fighting against the republican movement and not against the Catholic community. Killing one IRA member is better than shooting ten people in a pub. But I think after Teebane and the bookies on Ormeau Road were hit, it was massacre for massacre. When the Protestants seen the reaction that a massacre got, it encouraged them, because they had been killing nationalists and IRA men for years but at an accepted rate of violence. They kept it down to maybe ten or twelve a year or whatever. That was O.K. as far as the British government was concerned. They went on to Greysteel, and they went on to Lockinisland (locations where loyalist terrorists committed multiple murders). You see the Protestants got more feedback from the government. They were more accepted as a real threat killing innocent people than they were for killing the right people, as I would call them. When we were killing so many, ten a year or whatever, we were just seen as bit actors in a play. The IRA was the main star. The IRA and the British Army, the "British war machine" as they would call it, were the main players, and the loyalists were just bit-part players. Now however, they (the loyalists) have proved that they can kill six or seven people at a time and have the determination to do it. The British government realized how much of a threat they were. So, all of a sudden, we're invited to talks. We're asked to come to the table with Sinn Fein, and we're told--promised--that "if we, the British government, talk to them we'll talk to you." So it proves, although it (killing innocent people) is harder to do, that the end justifies the means. It always justifies the means.

The man who expressed these views to me, in a pub on the outskirts of Belfast in August 1994, was, and still is, a key member of the loyalist paramilitary (terrorist) organization known as the Ulster Freedom Fighters. Originally a nom de guerre for the Ulster Defense Association before the UDA was outlawed; the UFF is perhaps best described as the UDA's killer squads. Since the UDA was proscribed in 1992, there is little need for the organization to use a cover name when taking credit for its acts of violence. Nevertheless, UFF is a name that stuck, and the Protestant killers who proudly label themselves as Ulster Freedom Fighters will, in my opinion (every bit as much as will the Provisional IRA), determine the future of Northern Ireland.

I will refer to the Ulster Freedom Fighter, who was my companion on that August day, as the Big Man, a name used within some Northern Irish social circles for a person deemed to be of considerable importance. Admired by many in the working-class Protestant neighborhoods and feared by his republican adversaries, the Big Man is a 22-year veteran of Northern Ireland's terrorist wars. Yet he remains something of an anomaly, being from a different generation than the young men who now dominate the UDA/UFF.

Many of his contemporaries ended up in prison, while others were forced to step down from positions of power within the organization when, starting in 1989, younger and more aggressive members took control of the UDA/TJFF.[1] Some within the old guard met violent deaths at the hands of their younger rivals. When they shot dead a UDA supremo by the name of Jim Craig, who virtually everybody considered to be the biggest racketeer in Northern Ireland, the young bucks were sending a message to the old timers. Craig was not only more of a gangster than he was a paramilitary leader, he was accused of engaging in sinister 'behind-the-scenes' negotiations with the two major republican paramilitary organizations (the Provisional IRA and the Irish National Liberation Army).

The UDA's top man, John McMichael, who was said to be cracking down on Craig's racketeering activities, was assassinated by the Provos. The hit was allegedly to have been set up by Craig. So the word was out; no more cozy deals with republicans such as those in the past that involved dividing up territory for racketeering purposes. Make no mistake about it; the UDA is still involved in organized crime, but extortion monies and other funds gained from the rackets are now more likely to go to "the cause" than into the pockets of loyalist gangsters. Forget about any "understanding" between republicans and loyalists that neither side would, as a rule, go after the top people in the other camp. From now on it was going to be a real war.

If the Big Man had not possessed the same dedication and mind set as the younger leaders, he would have been pushed aside. The fact that he remains an important figure within the UFF command structure is a testament to the respect that his juniors have for him. His importance, as one of the major players in the war, was attested to by the fact that he was being relentlessly hunted by PIRA assassins who were intent on killing him before their leaders called a cease-fire. The fact that he was on the run from the Provos on that August day necessitated our out-of-the-way meeting place. Three of his best friends had been recently shot dead by the PIRA.

About two weeks prior to our meeting, the Big Man had spent the day socializing with Ray Smallwoods, spokesman for the UDA-linked Ulster Democratic Party but perhaps better known for serving a prison sentence for shooting the famous, or to some infamous, republican activist Bernadette Devlin.[2] The next day Smallwoods was murdered by the Provos. A few days after Smallwoods' demise, two other close friends of the Big Man, Joe Bratty and Ray Elder--said to be the UFF's most ruthless killers--were ambushed and killed by another PIRA hit team. As the anticipated cease-fire approached, the INLA also killed two other prominent loyalist paramilitary leaders. Colin "Crazy" Craig and David Hamelton were important figures within the other major loyalist terrorist organization, the outlawed Ulster Volunteer Force.

The republican paramilitaries were obviously attempting to eliminate as many as they could of their most hated enemies, such as the Big Man and some of the more articulate spokesmen for hard-line loyalism, like Smallwoods, before ending their hostilities--at least temporarily. Ray Smallwoods might have also been targeted because of his direct involvement in loyalist terrorist activities in the past. However, others, such as the outspoken Reverend William McCrea of the Democratic Unionist Party, who survived an assassination attempt by the Provos, may have been on their hit list because he was viewed as a potential formidable foe across any future negotiating table. Gary McMichael, the leader of the UDP, would also fit into the same category as McCrea. While he is the son of the late John McMichael, the purported creator of the UFF, he does not appear to have any history of direct paramilitary involvement.

A few days before I met with the Big Man, I spent some time with Gary McMichael. At that time he also knew that he was a prime target of the republicans. During a conversation that I had with him after the cease-fire was in place, he mentioned that shortly after he last talked to me he received intelligence information that a PIRA active service unit (hit team) was specifically assigned to kill him and given instructions "not to return until they did." McMichael told me that he left the country and did not return until the cease-fire was called.

In a kind of blood frenzy before the cease-fire, the Provos also eliminated a few soft targets as well; a Protestant grocer here, a couple of village constables there, and placed bombs in several loyalist pubs, seemingly just to prove that they could do it. However, the easy hits were just icing on the cake for them. More importantly, they had answered those, and there were many, who regarded the PIRA to be a tired, demoralized, and nearly defeated army. In fact if one can view the situation in purely military terms, it must be admitted that the Provos' last minute killing spree was indeed impressive. They managed to take out some very important loyalists and send others scurrying for cover. However, while the PIRA ended the hostilities with quite a final flurry, it was, in reality, only the last skirmish in a terrorist war that had intensified greatly over the previous three years and had taken a greater toll on the Republicans and, most tragically, on a number of Catholic families who had no connections to the republican movement than it had on the loyalists.

The UFF, and to a lesser degree, the UVF had been giving Sinn Fein/PIRA a pounding. Picture a pint-sized replica of American boxer Tommy Morrison with an Irish accent, clad in a baseball cap and the latest jogging gear and you have Johnny Adair, Commander of the UFF's C-Company. This former lead singer of the punk rock group Offensive Weapon and his similarly-dressed killer elite sidekicks (one of Adair's top two lieutenants could usually be seen sporting a San Francisco 49ers warm-up jacket) for a period of time were moving in and out of Provo territory seemingly assassinating republicans at will. A recruitment magnet and always a joker, Adair urged Protestant youth to join up with him and not with the UVF, which he referred to as "the peace people."[3] This was Adair's way of reminding his fellow loyalist of how far the UVF had fallen behind the UFF in the killing game since he had become a dominant force in the organization. He became the toast of drinking clubs and pubs in the staunchly loyalist Shankill Road neighborhood of Belfast and achieved folk hero status, especially among the impressionable working-class youth of the area, while increasingly striking fear into the hearts of many of the residents of Catholic West Belfast.

What did the Big Man have to say about the then 31-year old flamboyant Adair? The Big Man is intelligent, articulate, and does not appear to act on impulse. Would he place his friend in the same category?

> *No, I would say no, but sometimes my sort of person is not the person for the situation. Johnny came at the right time and the right situation. Some people, after the Shankill* bomb *(a PIRA bomb that killed eight people on the Shankill Road) would have said, "Hold on ... we'll have to see what we're going to do." The likes of Johnny, and his friends would have said, "There is only one answer to this and that's it." No second thoughts about it. Just "they done this. We do that." Regardless of what anybody wants to say about him--I wouldn't say anything bad about anybody in the UDA, but regardless of what anybody says about it, he's the right man in the situation. Sometimes everything just comes together like that. Johnny might not fit in ten years from now. He mightn't fit in two years time, but at that particular time he was the right man to be there because after Teebane and the Shankill bombing--the shootings on the Shankill Road--he's the sort of man that just says "Right, listen, we do this and we do that."*

This was the time when the loyalists' terrorists were at the peak of efficiency. While a PIRA bombing campaign was also in full force, the loyalists were exploding incendiaries in the Irish Republic, attacking Sinn Fein advisement centers, and hitting mostly what the Big Man termed "the right people." Thirteen members of Sinn Fein were murdered; many killed in neighborhoods that were supposedly under the control of the Provos.[4]

The street scenes on the Falls Road, the heart of PIRA territory, began to change. Known republicans were no longer as visible; they started to bunker down. One used to be able to drive around the area and see some of Ireland's most notorious characters interacting with the local population. Isn't that angry looking man with the buzz cut and the red face, the one threatening the election observer, Sinn Councilor Alex Maskey? Look: there's Sinn Fein publicity director Danny Morrison holding court on that corner. However, as the loyalists' offensive became more intense, sightings of recognizable republicans on Belfast streets became few and far between. They were now confining most of their activities to their fortress homes and only the safest clubs and pubs. The UFF was on a roll. After one killing spree a UFF spokesman was quoted as saying, "Yes, this week has been a success, and it is still only Thursday."[5]

While it is admittedly a crude measure of success, the number of murders committed by each side, in recent years, is indicative of the increasing tenacity of the loyalist paramilitaries. In 1990 the republicans were still out-murdering the loyalists (41 to 19), but 1991 saw "the bit players" starting to nearly pull even, trailing only by a 47 to 42 score. In 1992 for only the second time in the history of "the troubles," the loyalist outscored the republicans in the killing game, 39 to 36 (the first being in 1975 when loyalists recorded 114 kills to the republicans 100). In 1993, the number of loyalists' victims numbered 47, while the republicans killed only 35.

The overall murder rate has decreased significantly in recent years. The highest number of recorded deaths was in 1972 when the republicans killed 257 and the loyalists' victims numbered 103. However, the more recent increase in loyalist violent activity has been dramatic when one considers they were responsible for only a fraction of the murder and mayhem that took place through out the duration of the conflict which began in 1969.[6] Again, it must be remembered that the large number of recent victims of loyalists assassins included many hard-line republicans, the type of people that loyalist terrorists in past years were either unable to hit or did not attempt to do so out of fear of retaliation.

There is no doubt in my mind that the success of the loyalist paramilitaries and the consequent serious threat to the lives of top republicans played a major role in Sinn Fein President Gerry Adams and Sinn Fein/PIRA deciding to call a cease-fire. However, what is obviously more important than what any other observer or I believe to be true is how the loyalist paramilitaries gauge the success of their efforts. If they, in their minds, had developed a strategy that was effective prior to the cease-fire, they undoubtedly will employ it again if the hostilities resume. One would be hard-pressed to find a loyalist terrorist who did not feel that by bringing the war directly and fiercely to the enemy, they drove Adams and the PIRA to attempt to accomplish their goals by other than violent means. Again, it stands to reason that, if the conflict reignites, the loyalists will pick up where they left off.

Some loyalist paramilitary leaders (such as Billy "King Rat" Wright, the notorious UVF kingpin in mid-Ulster) have been quite willing to state publicly that their hellacious attacks on ordinary Catholics as well as republicans, which they contend were in retaliation for atrocities committed by the PIRA in places such as the Shankill Road (where nine people were killed by a PIRA bomb) and a town called Teebane (where the Provos murdered seven Protestant construction workers), resulted in the Provisional IRA calling a cease-fire in August 1994. As other loyalist terrorists have, "King Rat" has warned the Southern Irish government that, when and if they return to violence, in response to what the loyalists believe has been that government's interference in the internal affairs of Northern Ireland, Dublin will be a prime target for loyalist bombs and bullets.[7]

It hardly seems to be a coincidence that as far back as the summer of 1992, when the loyalists first jumped ahead of the republicans in the killing game, that Sinn Fein started to develop a downright conciliatory attitude in comparison to the hard-line stance that they had consistently adhered to over most of the prior twenty-odd years. Sinn Fein spokesman Jim Gibney announced that they would go to "any lengths" for peace, and Adams and Martin McGuinness, Sinn Fein vice-president and former PIRA leader in Derry, talked about "taking risks" to obtain peace.

In the meantime, at least a few top republicans exited the North, including Jim Gibney's brother Sinn Fein Councilor Damien Gibney, evidently developing a new appreciation for the safer confines of Dublin and its environs. For those republicans who feared for their lives during quieter times, the upsurge in loyalist violence was, indeed, traumatic. I noticed changes in the attitudes and behavior of several republican acquaintances during that time period. For example, a high-ranking Sinn Fein/PIRA man, whom I know well, mentioned to me on several occasions that the loyalist would consider it to be a major accomplishment if they were able to "stiff" him.

He always seemed to me to have an inflated view of his own importance. At least somewhat fearful of being assassinated by loyalists, he frequently wore a bulletproof vest and concerned himself about such things as what was going on in the parking lot when we drank in a pub. When I visited him in a new apartment that he was in the process of moving into, he would, as the sun started to go down, stretch dark blankets over the windows so that some unknown sniper would not be able to see our silhouettes. When I sought him out during the period of time when the loyalists were on a rampage, he was nowhere to be found. A friend of his told me that he had "fucked off" to Dublin with the UVF hot on his trail.

Here was a man whose whole life, his sense of self-worth, it seemed to me, revolved around being a big shot in West Belfast. He certainly would not be considered to be worth much elsewhere. If loyalists could intimidate him to the point of driving him out of perhaps the only environment that could stimulate his rather large ego, I imagine they were striking absolute terror into quite a few fainter republican hearts.[8]

Perhaps there is no such thing as a clean war, but the Irish one was beginning to get downright dirty when the "right people" became more difficult to locate. The struggle entered a new stage in which innocents became the main targets. Remember what the Big Man was saying:

> *"I think after Teebane and the bookies on Ormeau Road (where the UFF shot dead five Catholics and wounded seven others) it was massacre for massacre. When the Protestants seen the reaction a massacre got, it encouraged them...."*

On October 23, 1993, a PIRA bomb exploded in Fizzell's Fish Shop in the heart of the Protestant working-class Shankill Road area, killing nine shoppers and one of the two bombers. The bomb, according to the PIRA, was intended to kill Johnny Adair and the other UDA/TJFF Leaders (the Inner Council) who, the Provos believed were holding a meeting on the upper floor of the fish shop. As if the murder of ordinary people, including children, were not enough, a few days later Protestants and, for that matter, most Catholics had to endure over their morning coffee, newspaper pictures of Gerry Adams serving as a pall bearer for Thomas Begley, the dead PIRA bomber.

Retaliation was swift. The UFF shot two Catholics to death in a cleaning depot and followed that up by carrying out the most outrageous mass-slaughter of innocent people in Northern Ireland since a 1987 PIRA bomb killed eleven and maimed nineteen Protestants who were attending a memorial service in Enniskillen. A week after the Shankill exploded, two UFF killers entered the crowded Rising Sun Bar in Greysteel, County Derry, interrupted the Halloween festivities with a shout of "trick or treat," and then opened up with automatic weapon fire, killing seven and wounding eleven. During one week, loyalists and republicans had killed twenty-three people; all of which, with the exception of Thomas Begley, were innocent victims. O'Toole's Bar in Lockinisland was the setting for the next massacre, where the UFF shot dead six patrons.

The Greysteel massacre and related murders marked a turning point in the war. It represented a change in strategy on the part of the loyalist leaders. Unlike the UDA/UFF bosses who preceded them, the new breed of loyalists had gone after top republicans as well as moderate nationalist politicians, such as the Social Democratic Labour Party's Joe Hendron, who unseated Gerry Adams as MP from west Belfast, and Brian Feeney, another well-known and respected SDLP politician. Both of the SDLP men's homes were bombed.

Now the killing of innocents had become part of the overall strategy that was masterminded by the leaders of the loyalist terrorist organizations. All evidence indicated that the massacres were authorized and coordinated from the top, at least at the upper echelon of the UDA/UFF if not by the Combined Loyalist Military Command which was made up of the leaders of the UDA/UFF, UVF, and Red Hand Commando. Yes, loyalists had certainly killed ordinary Catholics before, but such murders in the past were usually committed by, more or less, renegade killers within the organizations. Those who were responsible for Greysteel, as evil as they may be, were not in the mold of Lenny Murphy who led a dissident band of UVF thugs (the Shankill Butchers) in committing 19 tortured murders of innocent people. Nor were the killers at Greysteel like the undisciplined group of gunman who a few years ago turned their automatic weapons on drinkers in a City Centre pub and took credit for the massacre under the name of the Protestant Action Force. No, the ones who planned out the latest round of killings knew exactly what they were doing and anticipated what the reactions would be. As the Big Man said, "The end justifies the means. It always justifies the means."

Shortly after the Greysteel massacre, I spent a considerable amount of time associating with some members of the Royal Ulster Constabulary (Northern Ireland's police force) in Belfast and Derry. I had known some of these officers for as long as twelve years and, therefore, can say with certainty that despite all of the tragedy and political and social chaos these men had witnessed, Greysteel and its potential political aftermath had more of a profound effect on some of them than had anything else that had taken place over the last decade. It was not as horrific in terms of the body count as some mass killings had been, but if it was a portent of things to come, the political and social structure of the country was in danger of being destroyed. As soon as the dust from the Shankill bomb cleared, the RUC knew that the loyalist paramilitaries would strike hard and fast, not only at those who were responsible for the outrage, but also against vulnerable Catholics. If the RUC could not stop an anticipated murderous loyalist rampage, the country would be thrown into chaos.

Knowing that Adair's C-Company would be the most likely to swing into action immediately, the RUC proceeded to round up its top killers and interrogate them. The frustrations associated with knowing that something was going to happen, but being unable to pry any useful information out of the UFF killers, was described to me by the police. Unlike many of the UDA/UFF volunteers of old, the new breed would not crack. Far from being intimidated by RUC detectives, one of Adair's top lieutenants reportedly masturbated while being interrogated.

Cocky and self assured, the young UFF supremos let the officers know that something was going to happen but offered few clues as to what. I only possess second-hand knowledge about what transpired during the interrogations. Therefore, any additional commentary on the subject is probably not in order. I was, however, told that one UFF man asked with a smirk on his face, if "anything had happened up north yet," or words to that effect. Calls were made to RUC installations north of Belfast, including Derry, and security was intensified, but to no avail. The outrage took place in the small neighboring village of Greysteel.

Ever since the 1985 Anglo-Irish Agreement, many Ulster Protestants have felt that the British government, aided and abetted by the Southern Irish government, has been selling them out. The 1985 Agreement had given the Irish Republic a role to play in the affairs of Northern Ireland and did so without consulting with any of the Unionist parties beforehand. Things, from the Unionists/loyalist perspective, went downhill from there. Too many concessions were made to the nationalists. Dublin politicians keep interfering in the internal affairs of Northern Ireland and are even dictating policy for the Royal Ulster Constabulary. Alienated, defiant, and feeling that they have no one else to turn to, a growing number of Protestants have offered both their moral and financial support to the paramilitaries. In the early 1990's, for the first time in the history of "the troubles," a significant number of middle-class citizens were contributing to "the cause."

Financial contributions, both voluntary ones and those contributed under duress, bought weapons and the knowledge that the loyalist paramilitaries now possessed weaponry and technical know-how that was far superior to anything that they had had in the past was a major concern of the police. A large cache of weapons, including 200 assault rifles and two tons of explosives destined for the loyalist paramilitaries, was seized from a cargo ship off Teeside, England in November, 1993. Loyalists openly bragged, however, that other shipments had reached them and proudly distributed photographs of masked UFF "volunteers" posing with samples of their new acquisitions.[9]

In the recent past, the UFF had demonstrated their ability to bomb significant targets such as a Sinn Fein advisement center in the heart of Provo territory. The UVF had shown a degree of military sophistication by scoring a direct hit on another Sinn Fein advisement center with RPG-7 rockets. However, in comparison with what seemed to be in store for the future, such assaults were small potatoes. In the past, most UFF bombs lacked the booster mechanisms necessary to create massive damage. The RUC believed, however, that by 1993 the loyalists possessed the materials that would eliminate that problem.

If the RUC could not halt the loyalist onslaught, if it could not prevent the slaughter of Catholics, if Dublin and the border towns in the South received massive bomb damage, if even moderate nationalist politicians were assassinated on a large scale; then it was at least conceivable that the loyalist paramilitaries would unwittingly accomplish something that the 25-year-old terror campaign of the PIRA failed to do: create the international climate in which a united Ireland could be established. If a united Ireland became a reality under those circumstances, I am convinced that a civil war would soon follow.

With a little luck and excellent detective work, the crisis was averted. The Greysteel killers were captured, Johnny Adair (under questionable new legislation that critics claim was specifically designed for him) was taken off the street and at least temporarily incarcerated. About a year ago I asked a senior RUC man, who had shared his concerns with me at the time, about that period when the loyalist terrorists appeared to be changing the course of Irish history.

> *It was a combination of a horrendous month when 27 people were killed in the aftermath of the Shankill bombing. Things had never been as*

dangerous as it was during that month. It seemed to me that the UFF murder squads were running rings around the police, and we weren't getting any closer to them. Then we got a couple breaks. Got a guy and a girl for killing two workmen at Kennedy Way and [He names the lead RUC detective in charge of the Greysteel investigation] did the Greysteel. There was some speculations at that point that internment were being considered. Certainly the RUC was under very severe pressure. I was never as concerned during my police service as I was during that period of time. Certainly the whole society was in the grip of fear, terror, and depression. The police were going to have to catch one or more of the killer gangs and then [the same RUC detective] produced the goods--settled everyone's mind down. Because all of the indications were that the UFF were getting fed-up with individual kills. They were looking for mass killings. You had Greysteel where eight people died. You had Lockinisland where six people died. They were probably disappointed in the number of people killed. They were trying to kill more. If they had not been caught, there would have been another mass slaughter--within two weeks or even the next week. Obviously the IRA, at some stage, were going to respond, as they did with the Shankill bomb.

If the troubles start up again I don't think that there will be any holding the loyalists back. I think that they will go for victory. They have never gone for victory. They have always, in a sense, been defensive. They have reacted to IRA violence, but I think, should there be a return to violence, for the first time the loyalists will decide that they are going to teach the IRA such a lesson. If the IRA breaks the cease-fire, I think that there will be more support for UFF killer gangs than ever before. I think that it will be exceedingly difficult for the police to actually deal with them because they are all experienced guys. They all have been arrested and interviewed. They understand the significance of forensic examinations. I think that they are even moving toward the Arab stage where they are prepared to die for the cause. That has never been seen before, but I think that there is a strong possibility that their gangs will start producing kamikaze people. I think they will be able to do it more easily than the Provisionals. Prior to the cease-fire all of their top people had actual experience in killing people. The UFF is a young army. They are becoming more professional all the time. I would think, if the cease-fire breaks down, you would see killings on a level that you've never seen before. I would think you are moving into the first stage of a civil war-type situation. I would have deep concerns about the breakdown of the cease-fire. The level of violence will dramatically escalate.

Things were changing dramatically on the political front. In April 1993 John Hume, leader of the moderately nationalist SDLP, began secret talks with Gerry Adams, the President of Sinn Fein. When knowledge of the Hume-Adams meetings became public, it was greeted with much skepticism, particularly on the part of Protestants who despised Adams and generally did not trust Hume. In November it was revealed in the press that, despite past denials by the British government, negotiations between Sinn Fein and representatives of the government had been taking place. To say that this revelation deeply upset the Protestant population is an understatement. In the minds of many (if not most) Protestants, Britain had sold them out again, a particularly disheartening turn of events for those who saw the PIRA as a tired army that was on the verge of defeat. To those with a paramilitary mindset, it was the straw that broke the camel's back. The Big Man was livid.

The British government said that they weren't talking to Sinn Fein. Gerry Adams said they were. I hate to say so but you can believe what Gerry Adams said at that time, but you couldn't believe what John Major said. You know the way the government has been manipulated by trying to stop the bombing campaign in England. They blew up the exchange and cost millions of pounds worth of damage. Again, they say that violence achieves nothing. That explosion achieved secret talks for the IRA. John Major was

> *telling lies. Gerry Adams was telling the truth. What's the loyalist person supposed to think? No matter what they would ever say to us again, we would have to believe that we're being sold down the river, and it's only a matter of time.*

When the revelations about the secret talks occurred, John Major and the then Irish Taoiseach (Prime Minister) Albert Reynolds were engaged in negotiations that culminated in a "peace declaration" that was made public on December 15th. The two governments agreed that a united Ireland would only become a reality when the majority of the people of Northern Ireland agreed to such unification; the Southern Irish government would "encourage" its citizens to reconsider the territorial claims to the North that are included in the Irish Constitution, and Sinn Fein would be allowed to participate in peace negotiations if the PIRA called a cease-fire and maintained it for three months. While the "declaration" did not come close to satisfying the demands of Sinn Fein, the anticipated cease-fire was announced by the PIRA in August 1994 and followed, in October by a similar declaration by the Combined Loyalist Military Command.

The British, Irish, and Americans were, for the most part, pleased as punch with the cessation of violence. That was to be expected. However, all those who are ecstatic over peace finally coming to the violent North should pay heed to what *Irish Times* journalists Kevin Meyers has to say. "Understand this clearly: the IRA and its political wing, Sinn Fein, are fighting a total war. Everything within a society is to be bent towards achieving their goals: Brits out of Northern Ireland and a single Irish state, regardless of the wishes of the Irish people."[10]

I agree; Sinn Fein/PIRA will not be satisfied until they accomplish their ultimate goal, a united Ireland, regardless of whether the rest of the Irish population wants it or not. The declaring of a cease-fire did not, in any way, mean that they have abandoned this goal.

Meyers goes on to argue that the governments of Britain, Ireland, and America were duped, with the help of "a credulous, absurdly optimistic media." "The peace process" he writes "was merely a ploy, an interim tactic by the IRA." While Adams was shaking hands with President Clinton in the White House, he claims the deadly bomb that destroyed Canary Wharf in London was being assembled.

I take a little more optimistic view. Granted, it is possible that the Army Council of the PIRA may have called the cease-fire because they needed time to re-group and better prepare their organization for continuing the war. But it is also entirely possible that Adams and Sinn Fein/PIRA felt that, while the "armed struggle" was not going that well, they just might be able to achieve their goals through peaceful means. Adams certainly had to be encouraged, if not overwhelmed, by how he was received on his first two American visits. President Clinton's obvious animosity toward Prime Minister Major was also a point in his favor. During his time in the United States, the world and American press was sometimes critical of him, but he was playing Larry King and Larry King-types on the talk show circuit like a fiddle and the media, or for that matter, the Clinton Administration, did not seem to give a hoot about what the Prods thought. Adams' army might have been knocked around a bit before the cease-fire and he might have been rejected by West Belfast voters, but he was riding high in Irish America. Would he be considered to be another Mandela? Perhaps he would share a Nobel Prize with Hume.

In Ireland, Adams' success in America predictably delighted his supporters and incensed his Catholic and Protestant detractors. It also helped to persuade some Catholics, who had no use for him in the past, that he was becoming a legitimate politician and no longer simply a spokesman for terrorists. Others, however, fearing that Adams and Sinn Fein could possibly achieve their goals through political maneuvering, were becoming radicalized.

The new radicals were largely, but not exclusively, Protestant. They were people who had never taken the law into their own hands before and had never supported loyalist terrorists in any way. Now, they were privately expressing a willingness to go to any lengths to prevent Adams and his kind or, for that matter, the British or the Americans from taking their country away from them. They will have a major say in what the future in Northern Ireland will be like, and from their perspective, the closer Adams and his kind come to achieving their goals, the closer the country comes to being engulfed in civil war. Most of the new radicals were educated professionals, and many had military and/or security force backgrounds. After Adams' second trip to America, I visited with an old and close friend, a Catholic with extensive security force experience. My friend's life story would read like that of the hero in the wildest of spy novels. He was not in a good mood.

> *They are going to have to deal with the likes of me. They are not going to produce propaganda to me. I'm only interested in truth, justice, decency, and I-*

71 die for that before I-71 ever let propagandists, murders--evil people like Adams--win. There'll be a day of reckoning at some stage. So I'm not interested when propagandists try to pervert the truth. I'm a much more honest and honorable man than Adams ever will be. At the end of the day, if he wants to win the prize, he is going to have to beat the likes of me and the likes of [a friend]. We'll just see how good he is at that stage. Conor Cruise O'Brien was saying the other day that no that matter how moderate southern Irish politicians want to try to appear, at the end of the day, they are still speaking on the basis of Northern Ireland being a part of the whole of Ireland. I get fed up with people talking about the future, not mine so much, but the future of good honorable people in this country, Protestants and Catholic people, but particularly Protestant people who don't appear to have an international voice at this point. But I'm giving them my support. In the main, they are honorable. They've done very little that is wrong. They believe in the democratic process. They believe in politics and sharing with Catholics. Perhaps they didn't in the past, but they do now. A substantial number of Catholics feel the same way.

In light of the above comments, it is probably wise to point out again that many Catholics have a much more favorable view of Adams than they did in the past. While Protestants still despise him, Catholics are more likely to give him the benefit of the doubt. He owes his newfound credibility among a growing number of Catholics primarily to John Hume. As a result of his participation with Hume in the secret talks that marked the start of the peace process, many Catholics, who still would not vote for him, now regard him as a legitimate politician, if not a statesman.

The fact that Gerry Adams does not speak for the majority of Catholics in Ireland should not even have to be mentioned. However, there are always some in the American press and a few politicians who treat him as if he is the voice of Catholic Ireland misled the chance that some readers might have. Sinn Fein gained about five to seven per cent of the island-wide vote prior to the cease-fire, while its post-cease-fire vote will probably run at about ten percent. The May 1996 elections in Northern Ireland garnered Sinn Fein 15.5 percent of the vote, indicating a significant increase in the party 's popularity since the cease-fire. The most popular Catholic political party in Northern Ireland is the SDLP.

Adam's reputation in America and in Ireland is largely dependent on his relationship with the Clinton administration or, perhaps, to Clinton himself and a few close associates. It is well known that President Clinton's advisors on Northern Ireland, including Ambassador Val Martinez, cautioned him against issuing Adams a 48-hour visa in February 1994. Adams is indebted to President Clinton and needs his support, but in a sense, Adams has entrapped himself. He has made promises in America to take "the gun out of politics" and claimed that the cease-fire was "complete." He needs a platform if he is to be considered an international statesman. The British and Irish governments cannot give him one, but President Clinton can, but not if the cease-fire is broken beyond repair. At this writing, the PIRA has re-ignited its bombing campaign on the British mainland but has not, at least in a major way, returned to hostilities in Northern Ireland. If the cease-fire does breakdown completely, where does that leave Gerry Adams and Sinn Fein?

If those within the PIRA who want to return to violence are few in number, which probably is not the case, then Adams' supporters within the organization may attempt to eliminate them. If this happens Adams himself will then become a target of the dissidents. There may be a split in Sinn Fein/PIRA resulting in different factions going their own way. One only has to look at the history of splits in Irish paramilitary organizations to know what will happen to Adams if he goes on to lead a peace faction. No longer backed by military force and advocating extreme political change, he will lose his clout and fade into insignificance.

By May 1995 Sinn Fein was holding formal, but far from productive, talks with the British government. The PIRA leadership, however, appeared to be getting impatient with the peace process. Perhaps the Provos were never too enthusiastic about it in the first place. They were after all using the cessation of hostilities to continue to gather intelligence information on members of the security forces, train their "volunteers," and recruit new ones.

The British demanded that the PIRA decommission their weapons before being allowed to participate in all-party talks. The British position on decommissioning reportedly exasperated the Provos and drew an angry refusal from Sinn Fein. Many moderate Catholics also felt that the British government was being unreasonable. How could, they reasoned, one side in a conflict be expected to lay down their arms and practically give up before being allowed a seat at the peace table?

The International Body, a commission headed by former U.S. Senator George Mitchell, continued hearings on the decommissioning of arms. On January 24,1996, the International Body (the Mitchell Commission) concluded that paramilitary organizations would not have to disarm before all-party talks took place, but they should do so as the talks proceeded. While Unionists had reservations about that and other recommendations made by the Body and the Reverend Ian Paisley's DUP refused to meet with Mitchell and his colleagues, the other constitutional parties, as well as Sinn Fein and the loyalist paramilitary linked PUP and UDP gave at least limited support to the proposals. Prime Minister Major, ignoring the core proposals put forth by the Body, indicated his preference for "an elective process" (in which candidates would be elected to a negotiating body) that Sinn Fein/PIRA could either agree to or decommission its weapons before being granted a seat at the all-party talks. Major's reaction to the recommendations angered the Southern Irish government and caused John Hume, as well as others, to accuse him of attempting to "buy (Unionist) votes to keep himself in power."

In the meantime, punishment beatings carried out by the PIRA in Catholic neighborhoods, and to a lesser degree, those conducted in Protestant areas by loyalist paramilitaries, appeared to be getting out of hand. A provo front called Direct Action Against Drugs continued to kill so-called "drug dealers."

On February 9,1996, the PIRA ended its 17-month cease-fire by detonating a massive bomb near Canary Wharf in the London Docklands, killing two, and causing an estimated $150 million in damages. Adams was in trouble in America. Did he know about the PIRA's decision to resume the "armed struggle" and kept his mouth shut about it? If he did have prior knowledge of the bombing plans, did he attempt to stop it? If he did, does his failure to prevent it indicate that he can no longer influence the PIRA in any significant way? President Clinton wanted to know.

In February, Irish Taoiseach John Burton suspended all ministerial contact with Sinn Fein. Another PIRA bomb was diffused in London, and a PIRA "volunteer" died when a bomb he was carrying exploded on a London bus, injuring eight others. President Clinton renewed Adams' visa, but he was prohibited from fundraising in America. On May 30th, elections to all-party talks were held with Sinn Fein gaining 15.47 percent of the vote, making the party technically eligible to participate in the talks. On June 15th, a huge PIRA bomb exploded in Manchester, England, injuring more than 200 people and causing an estimated $150 million worth of damage. The Manchester bomb was followed by a mortar attack on a British military base in northwestern Germany. Security precautions were intensified in anticipation of the PIRA returning to violence in Northern Ireland.

Sinn Fein continues to be banned from all-party talks until the PIRA reestablishes its cease-fire. The accepted parties to the talks squabble over Senator Mitchell's role as the chairman to the International Body. In early July an interview with the PIRA GHQ spokesman made it clear that the Provisionals did not intend to call a cessation to violence, confirming the organization's earlier assertion that it would not consider renewing the cease-fire until preconditions on Sinn Fein's participation in all-party talks were removed.

More than a few American journalists surprisingly, to me anyway, angrily turned on Gerry Adams, pointing out that he refused to condemn the PIRA for the taking of life and the massive damage to property that it caused. Some journalists were, perhaps, wondering for the first time if they had been taken in by Adams' apparent sincerity during his U.S. visits, when he was promising to take the guns and bombs out of politics. To the Irish and English, however, this was the same old Gerry. Evidently the PIRA had not changed much either.

Even Sinn Fein voters, the ones who supposedly cast ballots for the gunmen in the past, seem to be sick and tired of the PIRA's terror war. A very close Catholic friend of mine, who was born and raised in Belfast's Catholic Andersontown neighborhood and personally opposes violence in any form, has tried to convince me that even Catholics who dislike the PIRA are not particularly disturbed by the recent bombings. Their feeling seems to be, according to my friend, that because nothing else seems to move the British government, perhaps a few warning bombs will result in some concessions.

I am glad to report that a *Coopers and Lybrand* opinion poll appears to prove him wrong. Over 80% of Sinn Fein voters in Northern Ireland expressed a desire for the PIRA to declare another cease-fire, as did 97% of the total population. When all the talking is done, public opinion overwhelmingly opposes the Provos' renewed bombing campaign. This of course does not mean that Sinn Fein voters or

Catholics in general agree with the British government's position that Sinn Fein should not be allowed at the bargaining table until the PIRA calls another cease-fire. In fact the vast majority of Catholic voters do feel that Sinn Fein should take part in the peace negotiations with the other political parties, even if the PIRA does not call a cease-fire.

Paul Clare *is a Professor of sociology and Criminal Justice at the State University of New York-Plattsburgh. He is a frequent contributor to the literature on terrorism and organized crime. His works include a monograph entitled Racketeering in Northern Ireland-- A New Version of the Patriot Game, published by OICJ Publications. Professor Clare's research on Northern Ireland represents the first attempt by an academic to conduct ground-level research into the racketeering activities of loyalist and republican terrorists. He is the Editor of Criminal Organizations and an Executive Board member of the International Association for the Study of Organized Crime (IASOC).*

NOTES AND REFERENCES

[1] The shift in UDA/UFF leadership was also facilitated by what transpired after one Loughlin Maginn was murdered by the UFF. In response to accusations that the UFF was killing Catholics who had no connections to the republican movement and the claim of the Maginn family that he was not involved in republican terrorism, the UDA produced official intelligence materials (police montages) that identified Maginn as a suspected member of the PIRA. The revelation that loyalist terrorists were able to obtain such information led to an investigation (the Stevens Inquiry in 1989) into alleged collusion between security forces employees and the loyalist organizations. As a result of the investigation, a number of older UDA/UFF leaders ended up in prison. It was also revealed that UDA intelligence officer Brian Nelson was serving as a spy for the British Army; at the same time he was involved in illegal activity for the UDA/UFF. When senior UDA/UFF men ended up in prison, as a result of the Stevens Inquiry, it became much easier for younger more aggressive activists, such as Johnny Adair, to step into positions of power. The security forces also lost an incredibly good source of intelligence on loyalist paramilitaries when Brian Nelson was taken out of circulation. Some ethical questions aside, it can be persuasively argued that many lives would have been saved if Nelson had been left in place.

[2] Ms. Devlin, as well as others, claims that the Big Man was part of the hit team that attempted to kill her and is said to live in fear of him. His alleged involvement in the attempt on Devlin's life is another possible reason why his name is said to be high on the PIRA's hit list.

[3] The Peace People was an organization that fostered peace and good relations between the two religious communities. Two of its founders, Mairead Corrigan and Betty Williams, were joint recipients of the Nobel Peace Prize in 1976.

[4] I found it to be surprisingly difficult to find out exactly how many Sinn Feiners were murdered by loyalists during this time period. I spent most of a day in Belfast visiting various government offices attempting to get information on the subject and met with little success. The RUC (police) people who collect statistics on terrorist activity explained to me that they were hesitant to label victims as members of Sinn Fein because they

risked violating libel laws by doing so. Therefore, I have relied on what is, from my perspective, probably the most unreliable source in Northern Ireland. Gerry Adams, President of Sinn Fein, stated on American television that 13 members of Sinn Fein were murdered by loyalist terrorists "in as many months."

[5] Paul Bew and Gordon Gillespie, *Northern Ireland: A Chronology of the Troubles--1968-1993* (Dublin: Gill and Macmillan, 1993, p. 293)

[6] This information was obtained from the RUC Press Office.

[7] Gerry Moriarty, "'King Rat' justifies atrocities as 'part of war,'" *The Irish Times,* July 20, 1996, p. 8.

[8] Some may argue that the PIRA was successful during this time period. They bombed the centers out of a number of Protestant towns (such as Bangor, Coleraine, Portadown, and Magerafelt) and destroyed a Protestant housing estate in Cookstown. Explosives in central Belfast and Newtownnards were part of the Provos' so-called economic campaign that left hundreds of displaced and/or injured Protestants in its wake. It is very true that the PIRA was frustrating and demoralizing Protestants to the point that many were questioning the ability of the security forces to protect them. However, I would argue that the UFF's direct assault on the Sinn Fein/PIRA leadership and, more importantly, its murder campaign directed against ordinary Catholics had the real potential for sending the social and political life of Northern Ireland into a state of complete chaos. For an excellent analysis of Protestant attitudes and concerns about these subjects see Steve Bruce, *The Edge of the Union: The Ulster Loyalist Political Vision* (Oxford: Oxford University Press, 1994)

[9] Two of these pictures can be found in Paul K. Clare, "Northern Ireland: Prospects for and Obstacles to Peace," *CJ Europe,* May-June, 1994, Vol. 4, No. 3, pp. pp. 4-7.

[10] Kevin Myers, "Irish Revolutionary Violence," *National Review,* July 15,1996, pp.25-27.

SINGLE-ISSUE GROUPS

Dr. G. David Smith

The term "single-issue terrorism" is broadly accepted as extremist militancy on the part of groups protesting a perceived grievance or wrong usually attributed to governmental action or inaction.[1] Generally, three principal issues are regarded as falling under that rubric: Animal Rights, Environmentalism, and Abortion. Those are the issues addressed in this chapter; the focus will rest on activities in the United States, Canada, and the United Kingdom.

Moderate, legitimate organizations such as traditional animal welfare societies have lobbied for years on behalf of their causes and have achieved some notable results. But over the past two decades radical elements have been attracted to some of the more popular issues, and have formed the militant core, which has resorted to extremist tactics involving threats, violence and destruction of property. Recently, in the case of the abortion issue, this has included murder.

For the most part, legitimate organizations disown the violent fringe, although some, especially in the realms of the environmental and abortion issues, accord tacit support to the extremists either openly or by a failure to condemn the activities. Following the November 1994 wounding of a prominent Vancouver, British Columbia gynecologist by a sniper, at least one activist condoned the incident, calling it "good shooting" and stating it would not have happened if the doctor had not been performing abortions.[2]

There is no archetypal issue group extremist, but there are some broad characteristics that apply. Animal Rights activists and Environmentalists tend to be on the left of the political spectrum extending as far as Anarchism. The founder of the Animal Liberation Front (ALF) in the United Kingdom, for example, is a self-confessed anarchist, as is a senior member of a similar group in Canada. The Abortion issue attracts both sides of the political divide, with "profilers" largely on the right. The abortion issue, however, has religious connotations that add a dimension not peculiar to Animal Rights or Environmentalism.

Extremists associated with any of these issues can and do come from all walks of life and social levels. For a time in England, participating in civil disobedience and militancy in support of Animal Rights campaigns was regarded as the "in-thing" amongst the trendy young crowd and considered an exciting diversion from their rather tame lifestyles. University students comprise a large number of Animal Rights supporters and Environmentalists. Extremists often are idealists who have become frustrated with the seemingly slow progress of moderate groups and seek to achieve their goals more rapidly by direct action. Paul Watson of Greenpeace fame is one such example.[3]

Although essentially domestic in their functioning, issue groups have an international scope. Animal Rights supporters claim to be active in more than 40 countries around the world and militant Environmentalists have carried out actions in a number of different regions. Both the Animal Rights and Environmentalist movements publish newsletters, such as *ARKANGEL*, a British-based newsletter for Animal-rights supporters, and *EARTH FIRST!*, a journal of the radical environmental movement. These newsletters contain a range of information, including descriptions of recent actions, techniques for conducting mischief, vandalism and sabotage, the addresses of targeted individuals and sites--doctors, scientists, research laboratories--and news about incarcerated activists.

All three movements use the Internet for publicity and communications purposes. The Militant Vegan, for example, provides a diary of Animal Liberation actions in Canada and the United States -- listing names and locations of targeted attacks and the tactics employed. This is very useful for statistical purposes.

Communication takes place to some degree between extremist groups within individual issues. This is not surprising in view of the availability of the Internet. Some similarities exist in terms of group names and operations, such as the Animal Liberation Front in Britain and North America. Not all linkages between groups are obvious. Nevertheless, cooperation, affiliations and crossovers do occur. A number of Animal Rights extremists are simultaneously members of several different organizations and movements, (Vegans, Feminists, Ecologists) and often use the guise of popular causes or legitimate organizations to pursue their own ideals. The Toronto Humane Society in Canada was captured by a stacked proxy vote on one occasion and large amounts of money and other resources were funneled to militants. Also, Animal Rights supporters and Earth First! activists are known to have integrated working relationships in Canada and the United States.

The extremist fringe of each movement has published some form of handbook or instructions on how to conduct mischief, civil disobedience, vandalism, and sabotage--ecotage, as it is known to Environmentalists. Some of their suggestions are extremely dangerous. Tree spiking has caused serious injury and has the potential to kill. The instructions often resemble those found in the *Anarchist's Cookbook* and include bomb-making details.

The level and scale of Issue Group Terrorism has lessened somewhat over the past two years. Certainly it is not comparable to the halcyon days of the 1980's and early years of this decade. But that is not to say that the threat has lessened. Extremist incidents continue to occur, especially ones associated with Animal Rights and Environmentalism, and particularly in England and Canada. Currently, the abortion issue has the potential to become more high profile and volatile in the United States as a consequence of the forthcoming elections, and also in Canada as a result of legislative controversy and several unfortunate incidents involving pregnant women.

The discussion of specific individual issues and groups will begin with Animal Rights. In fairness, one must divorce the traditional animal welfarists, who believe animals can be used by mankind if treated compassionately, from the animal-rights groups who insist animals are at a par with human rights and should be at liberty. Most Animal-rights activists do not advocate the use of violence but are not hesitant about resorting to civil disobedience as a ploy to gain attention. The extremist fringe of the animal rights movement, however believe that economic sabotage is one means to achieve their goal of protecting animals from harm by all human actions.

To reach that end, Animal rights activists use a variety of tactics designed to inflict economic loss with the intention that a targeted "offender" cannot afford to operate. They have achieved some success. Prohibitive insurance rates, the need for expensive security infrastructure, the costs of repairs to damaged buildings and equipment loss of revenue, negative publicity, and the destruction of research records representing years of work have forced the closure of many small businesses as well as scientific and commercial research facilities. Activists have boasted they could cause at least $60,000 damage in one week just from smashing windows.[4]

Research laboratories associated with medical and veterinary schools and clinics, and those testing cosmetics and food products, have been featured targets. Animals have been removed, equipment and records worth hundreds of thousands of dollars destroyed, and graffiti and hate mail directed toward the researchers sent. On at least one occasion in England, activists distributed derogatory leaflets at the school attended by the children of a scientist. In Canada, the home of a scientist was vandalized to commemorate the World Day for Lab Animals. The range of favored targets also encompasses butcher shops, fish markets, meat packing plants, chicken and egg producers, dog kennels and mink and fox farms, as well as furriers. Even fast-food outlets have been targets on occasion. In such cases, vandalism has usually been the tactic--graffiti spray-painted on buildings, glue poured in door-locks, windows etched with acid or smashed. Frequently attacks have gone beyond this stage. Vehicles have been stolen, damaged or burned, tires slashed, and fur-bearing animals have been set free. Several thousand expensive mink were released from two farms in Western Canada last Fall.[5]

Another effective and costly tactic has been the threat of product contamination, specifically targeting meat shops, drug stores, supermarkets and department stores. The Animal Liberation Front (ALF) in Great Britain can be credited with initiating this practice in 1984, when a butcher shop wag forced to close because of a threat of contaminated meat. Costly incidents have followed involving shampoo, candy bars, soft drinks, as well as Christmas time threats of poisoned turkeys, forcing the removal of literally millions of items from stores.[6] Similar incidents have occurred in Canada under the name of the Animal Rights Militia. Tens of thousands of Cold Buster candy bars were recalled in 1992 after claims of contamination with oven cleaner.[7] Prior to Christmas 1994, over one million dollars damage was caused by the threat of poisoned turkeys in Vancouver, British Columbia.[8]

Incendiary techniques and mail-bombs are included in the activists' tactical repertoire. In fact a string of firebombs in department stores in England led to the arrest of ALF leaders in 1987.[9] The bombing tactic took a deadly turn in 1989 when explosive devices were attached to the automobiles of a British veterinary surgeon and a university researcher. The vet barely escaped from her burning car; the researcher was saved when the bomb fell off his car, but a baby in a nearby carriage was injured[10]. Arson has also been a popular method of operation in

Britain, Canada and the United States. During the Christmas rush of 1993, the ALF placed nine firebombs in four department stores in Chicago.[11] In 1994 a series of letter bombs in Britain attributed to a group known as the Justice Department injured four persons.[12] In 1995 a letter bomb was sent to the British Minister of Agriculture, while in Canada a group known as the Militant Direct Action Task Force (MDATF) scattered four letter bombs among two white supremacists, a right-wing think-tank which supports the fur industry, and a genetics laboratory.[13]

A recently modified version of the mail bomb technique has featured razorblades allegedly dipped either in rat poison or AIDS-infected blood. This method, which included Prince Charles among the addressees, surfaced in Britain in 1995, claimed by the Justice Department. Similar letters also appeared in British Columbia in 1996 claimed by a Canadian group using the same name.[14] An intriguing twist is that the return address is of another targeted individual, thus if the original recipient refuses to accept the letter and returns it to the alleged sender, then another Animal Rights target is put at risk.

Probably the best-known and still very active extremist group in Europe and North America is the Animal Liberation Front (ALF), founded in 1976 in England by Ronnie Lee. The ALF appeared in Canada in 1981, quickly making a name for itself through break-ins involving vandalism, arson and the release of animals at several university and medical laboratories, followed by attacks on fur stores and meat-packers. First recognized in the United States in 1982, the ALF made the FBI's domestic terrorism list in 1987 with a multi-million dollar arson at a veterinary lab in California. Similar incidents in Arizona and Texas in 1989 were also classified as domestic terrorism.[15]

Among other notables are the Hunt Retribution Squad (HRS), a particularly vicious group in Britain; the Animal Rights Militia (ARM), an offshoot of the British ALF with namesakes in North America; and the relatively new Justice Department, which surfaced first in Britain and then appeared in Canada. The Justice Department, although small, has been an especially dangerous organization, claiming responsibility for a number of letter bombs.

When referring to the ALF in the United States, mention must be made of People for the Ethical Treatment of Animals (PETA). A powerful lobby group based in Virginia, its strength lies in its ability to attract prominent supporters and to raise large sums of money. PETA is alleged to be a support element for the ALF, much in the manner of the

Sinn Fein/PIRA relationship. PETA has frequently announced ALF actions and provided news releases almost immediately after events occurred, indicating at least foreknowledge if not some complicity. In recent years, PETA has also established branches in Canada and Europe.[16]

Professionalism is the operational hallmark of many extremist groups such as the ALF. Often organized on a cell structure similar to PIRA, they are difficult to identify and to penetrate. Security is relatively good. For instance, members are dissuaded from using telephone communications to avoid tracing and toll information. Activists carefully research each target, often spending days or months conducting surveillance on the targeted facility and staff members, including photographs and frequently lying in perimeter bushes overnight to establish the routines of security patrols. When possible activists will sign up for a tour of a target facility, recruit inside help or obtain employment in an attempt to gain information and to bypass security alarms. Occasionally, an attack will be videotaped to assist in obtaining media coverage or for use in later threat activity. Emphasis is placed on making every attack count because improved security arrangements will likely follow in the aftermath.

Dress and actions during raids often are intended to be intimidating. Hoods, camouflage jackets, and coveralls are worn. Pick handles and other hazardous items are used for breaking equipment and entering in a violent manner. Conscious efforts are made to destroy research material and to gather intelligence on suppliers or supporters of a research facility for purposes of follow-on targeting.

These tactics are terrorism. Animal rights activists use violence as a policy with the expressed intent of coercing government to act in a certain manner or to enact particular legislation. The fear engendered by claims of poisoned candy or other consumer goods, by obnoxious graffiti, by abusive and threatening telephone calls, by the mailing of letter bombs, and by the destruction of property is the outcome of terrorist methodology.

Turning more briefly to the Environmentalism and Abortion issues, they are not any less significant in terms of threat. The radical environmental movement comprises a broad spectrum of individuals and groups involved in an equally diverse assortment of issues and situations. It is estimated that as many as 2,000 environmental organizations are active in Canada alone. While resource exploitation and hydroelectric development are the most frequent targets, activists also are involved in opposition to such things as the nuclear power industry, chemical manufacturers, industrial polluters, urban sprawl, encroaching agriculture, and the modern industrial state in general.

Animal rights and anarchist groups have made common cause with environmentalists, and in some convenient cases alliances have been formed with native groups. However, the latter arrangements have not always been popular, especially in regard to fishing and hunting issues. Individuals who support extremist philosophies within the environmental movement, while small in number, have demonstrated the willingness and capability to use violence.

The most prominent group is Earth First!, whose followers have consistently advocated and employed sabotage as a tactic to defend the environment. Formed in 1980, Earth First! began to employ violence in 1984 with the introduction of tree spiking, a dangerous practice which continues even today.[17] Not only is spiking hazardous to loggers using chain-saws, but the spikes can cause saw blades at mills literally to explode, as occurred in 1987 when a mill worker was seriously injured. In 1985, Dave Foreman, one of Earth First!'s founders, wrote the ecotage manual *A Field Guide to Monkeywrenching*, detailing many of the sabotage techniques of the movement, including tree spiking.[18] In keeping with that vein, another ecotage volume, entitled *A Declaration of War*, appeared in North America, advocating the use of violence, including homicide, to stop animal and environmental abuses. This book calls for attacks against farms, animal research facilities, logging companies and hunters.

Greenpeace generally is credited as being the first environmental group to employ "direct action" in pursuit of its aims. But impatient with what he considered the slow pace of progress, Paul Watson formed the Sea Shepherd Conservation Society, with its offshoot, Orcaforce. Watson and his supporters have been involved in a number of militant actions against whale hunting, drift net fishing, seal hunting, and other related issues. Recently he has also undertaken activities against logging operations in Canada.

Extremist activity of late has been somewhat more prevalent in Canada than in the United States and Britain, although the latter has been the scene of growing activism over the past number of years. Scotland Yard's Special Branch made eco-terrorists a security priority during 1995, partly because of the concern that ecological activists involved with resisting new road-building schemes are turning toward the violent tactics of the ALF.[19] An Earth First! summer gathering was also held in Wales in mid-June of 1996.

Trip-wired booby traps have caused injuries to some construction workers, while others have been shot at with crossbows or have encountered VietCong-style man-traps filled with pungee stakes, and equipment has been damaged or subjected to arson. An "eco-terror" activist magazine published last year contained detailed plans on how to build a mortar, firebombs, grenades, and urged the use of buried explosives against the police.[20]

The FBI first listed an act of domestic terrorism attributed to the ecological movement in 1987, then again in 1988, in 1989, and in 1990. The 1980's incidents involving damage to power poles and ski lift equipment in Arizona and plans to destroy power lines leading to nuclear facilities in Arizona, Colorado and California. These acts were attributed to the Evan Mecham Eco-Terrorist International Conspiracy (EMETIC), although Dave Foreman of Earth First! was among those arrested. The Earth Night Action Group claimed the downing of power lines in Santa Cruz county, California in the 1990's. [21] Environmentalists are active across Canada, but extremists have tended to congregate on the West Coast where the full spectrum of activism has become increasingly militant. Extremists believe direct action is required to disrupt operations or projects that pose an immediate threat to the environment. Fundamental to the philosophy of direct action as espoused by extremists, and Earth First! in particular, is the belief in doing whatever necessary to disrupt, not merely oppose, any activity they consider detrimental to the environment.

The broader objective of sabotage is to draw attention and to sway legislation on behalf of environmental protection acts. The most immediate goal is to prevent or delay activities, such as logging, from going ahead by destroying equipment and infrastructure. Akin to the Animal Rights philosophy, sabotage also is an attempt to use economic damage to force companies to reconsider their operations. Repeated repairs to damaged equipment, production delays, higher insurance premiums, increased security requirements, and unfavorable publicity all contribute to the companies' expenses. In 1995, a logging bridge costing over $2 million was destroyed by fire in British Columbia.[22]

There are close links between Earth First! in Canada and the United States. Most actions have been associated with logging operations and have involved destruction of equipment and tree spiking. In what are seen as crossover actions with Animal Rights, taxidermy shops and hunting outfitters in Western Canada have been subjected to arson attacks and threatening letters, including the razor-blade version mentioned earlier, claimed variously by the Justice Department and a group calling itself The Earth Liberation Army.[23] On another occasion, under the name of The David Organization, supposedly noxious chemicals were spilled in the offices of government buildings and at the head office of a logging company.[24]

Environmental militancy has declined somewhat, in part due to successful lobby efforts. But logging operations in the West Coast regions of Canada and the United States combined with growing fishing and hunting controversies on both coasts will provide motivation for continued extremist response by Environmentalists and Animal Rights activists. And this may lead to serious confrontations between Environmentalists and those who believe their livelihood is being adversely affected.

Before concluding, some comments are provided on the third element of the single-issue triad, the Abortion movement (See Builta [25]). The abortion issue is emotive, particularly in relation to the pro-life movement and as a result, extremists sometimes capture this agenda. Currently, the fact that some of the more extreme right-wing groups include anti-abortion declarations in their rhetoric has raised serious concerns. Most people who oppose abortion do so lawfully. But others distinguish themselves as militants and test the limits of freedom of expression, as well as committing criminal acts in support of their cause. Damages associated with 42 incidents of vandalism and arson at abortion clinics in the United States totaled over $1 million during 1994 and 1995.[26]

The incidence of violence has been largely on the part of the pro-lifers, perhaps a result of frustration with unfavorable legislation. But religious connotations cannot be ignored. A worrisome development has been the fundamentalist antiabortion handbook, *"The Army Of God,"* which gives detailed instructions on the sabotage of clinics, silencers for guns and C4 explosive, and states, inter alia "We are forced to take aim against you… execution is rarely gentle." [27]

Abortion-issue violence largely has been confined to the United States and Canada. An attempt by a North American pro-life group to establish a branch in Great Britain in 1993 was thwarted when the government had the representative deported as being "a threat to the public good." In 1988 the Supreme Court of Canada struck down the law which had restricted the legal availability of abortion in Canada. Since then, the number of abortions sought by Canadian women has grown significantly and the vehemence of anti-abortion protesters has increased. Many pro-choice activists say they fear an escalation of violence such as the United States has experienced.

These fears may be well founded. Five people have been killed and 11 others wounded in the United States since 1993. Clinics have been subjected to graffiti, noxious gases, firebombs, and the staff threatened and harassed. Similar events have begun to occur in Canada. Sniper incidents a year apart, in 1994 and 1995, wounded two Canadian doctors. A clinic was burned down. And workers have been increasingly subjected to threats and harassment.[28]

Although the pro-life movement in Canada is generally poorly organized, it does include several large groups and prominent individuals with links to the movement across the border. American activists have visited Canada to address rallies and to encourage Canadians to adopt aggressive practices. The author of an anti-abortion publication, recognized and respected in extremist circles, has participated in demonstrations and picketing of clinics and doctors' homes in Canada.

American sociologist Dallas Blanchard noted that he has encountered members of the Canadian pro-life movement whom he considers as capable of violence and the pattern of activity in Canada is similar to that in the United States. An article in the May 1996 edition of *CHATELAINE* magazine depicts the current status of the abortion debate in Canada as a battlefield where the fear of violence rules. The atmosphere in clinics resembles a state of siege; with steel bars, security cameras, intercom systems, and workers trained to handle bomb threats.[29]

The issue will not go away. The potential for continued violence exists and may increase if the level of frustration on the part of the pro-lifers continues to grow, which it may do in the event of unfavorable legislation or legal judgments or the introduction of abortion drugs. In Canada, changes to government funding of abortions may encourage pro-life activists to indulge in more militant activity.

In conclusion, three observations deserve note. First, issue group militancy remains dangerous, despite lower levels of activity during the past few years. Each of the issues discussed remains controversial and will continue to attract individuals ready to use extremist tactics for selfish or believed-to-be-altruistic reasons. Many of those individuals are highly competent and capable of making effective use of modem technology to devise extremely dangerous devices. Second, there are real concerns about the risk of escalation of violence:

from vandalism, to arson, to bombs, to even more spectacular incidents, about the risk of copy-cat actions by inept individuals which could seriously endanger lives, and about the risk of vigilantism, which could create extraordinary problems for our law enforcement and criminal justice systems. Finally, the challenge is to provide a reasoned and reasonable response to the threat of issue-group terrorism, a response which is appropriate, avoids Draconian overreaction, and remains within the parameters of the rule of law.

Dr. G. David Smith *is the Deputy Director General-Strategic and Emerging Issues for the Canadian Security Intelligence Service (CSIS). He has been with the Ministry of the Solicitor General for Canada and the CSIS since 1987. Dr. Smith was the Chief of Staff for Canada's Federal Counter-Terrorism Task Force from 1988-1989. A career armored cavalry officer with service in North America, Europe, the Middle East, Cyprus, and Vietnam, Smith retired with the rank of Lieutenant Colonel*

NOTES

[1] G. Davidson Smith, *Combating Terrorism* (London: Routledge, 1990), p.7.

[2] *CHATELAINE,* May 1996.

[3] Sean P. Eagan, "From Spikes to Bombs: The Rise of Eco-Terrorism", *Studies in Conflict and Terrorism* 19:1-18 1996.

[4] G. Davidson Smith, "Militant Activism and the Issue of Animal Rights", *Commentary,* April 1992, No.21.

[5] Robin Brunet, "The cutting edge of animal rights", *Alberta Report,* Vol. 23, No. 8, 5 February 1996.

[6] G. Davidson Smith, "Political Violence in Animal Liberation", *Contemporary Review,* Vol. 247, No. 1434, July 1985.

[7] Smith, *Commentary*, April 1992.

[8] *The Militant Vegan,* Issue 8, 8 February 1995, Internet.

[9] Smith, *Commentary,* April 1992.

[10] *Chicago Tribune,* 6 August 1991.

[11] *Chicago Sun-Times,* 1 December 1983.

[12] *Independent,* 2 June 1994. See also: *PinkertonRisk* 24 August 1995.

[13] *Tronto Star,* 14 July, 1995,

[14] *Victoria Times Colonist,* 13 January 1996.

[15] *Terrorism in the United States,* U.S. Department of Justice, Federal Bureau of Investigation, 1989.

[16] Susan E. Paris, "Animal Rights terrorism Must Be Stopped", *Mass High Tech,* August 1995.

[17] Egan, "From Spikes.." p.6.

[18] Ibid., p. 8.

[19] *Independent,* 29 December 1994.

[20] *The Times of London,* 11 September 1994.

[21] *Terrorism in the United States,* U.S. Department of Justice, FBI, 1990.

[22] *The Vancouver Sun,* 21 October 199 1.

[23] *Globe and Mail,* Toronto, 12 July 1995. See also: Victoria Times Colonist, 13 January 1996.

[24] *Vancouver Province,* 17 October 1994.

[25] Jeff Builta, "Anti-Abortion Violence Movement Increases", *CJ The Americas On-Line,* Terrorism, Internet.

[26] *Summary of Extreme Violence Against Abortion Providers in 1994,* 1995, National Abortion Federation, Internet.

[27] *CHATELAINE,* May 1996. See also: *WASHINGTON POST,* 17 January 1995.

[28] *Toronto Sun,* 17 January 1995. See also: *The Abortion Rights Activist,* Internet.

[29] *CHATELAINE,* May 1996.

THE RETURN OF THE LEFT WING

Wendy Nicol

One of my responsibilities as a strategic analyst at the Royal Canadian Mounted Police headquarters is to try to identify emerging terrorist trends to inform senior managers and assist investigators. We do have a number of tools we use to determine our priorities but suffice it to say that no matter how carefully you watch, and no matter how much you read, something always comes to you from offside. The activity of the criminal left wing in Canada was just such an offside hit. The title of this chapter, the return of the left wing, is perhaps a little misleading. The left wing, like the right wing, and I stress here we are talking about the far edges of each ideology, is always there. Sometimes it has a little more prominence than at others and sometimes we have rhetoric, writings, and demonstrations. At other times, we have pipe bombs and booby-trapped packages in the mail.

When I discuss criminal cases that are ongoing I will be using information which is currently available in the open media. I am going to talk about the left wing, animal rights activists, environmental activists, and a number of other specifics based on wide group identifiers. I will be referring to the criminal activity of people who hold ideological views similar to those of members of those groups. Group membership, however, is of interest only to the extent it helps ascertain the likelihood of criminal activity, the access to weapons, the types of weapons we are likely to encounter, likely targets, and optimum level of violence.

As was mentioned in the chapter on single-issue groups, legitimate groups will often try to distance themselves from the more militant groups or to ostracize the more radical members. Paul Watson was kicked out of Greenpeace for radical criminal behavior, illustrating one of the best examples of mainstream groups trying to control credibility. There is even some argument, mostly developed by one of the founders of Earth First!, that radical groups give the mainstream groups more credibility and allow them to accomplish more than they would otherwise be able to.

Canada encourages socialist/left wing politics. There is one major active political party that is considered left-of-center and a number of fringe parties. The Marxist-Leninist Party fields a few candidates at every election. We also have a thriving right wing with a mainstream political party, some thriving right wing groups and criminal activity associated with some of the ideology. The criminal left wing in Canada is not likely very large but it is connected to the animal rights and environmental activist communities and cross border connections with limited connections internationally.

The attacks of the left wing may not immediately make sense to the uninvolved. But the meaning is clear to those intended to get the message, the violence is only seemingly meaningless, it is deliberately and carefully designed to convey a message. The radical left wing is generally well educated, although perhaps not formally, computer literate and pursues goals traditionally espoused by those in the left wing around the world. It is one of the few movements to make complete and equal use of women activists. Those with a developed left wing ideology have usually evolved from establishment politics. They decide the legitimate political process is too slow, ineffective or invalid. Therefore, they escalate to direct action, with some more interested in action than theory.

In Canada the loss of social programs, issues relating to the environment, genetic altering, native rights, racism, homophobia, and a myriad of other social issues have all sparked left wing protests. Early in the spring of 1995 the Anti-Fascist Militia sent letters armed with razorblades to extreme right wing targets in Canada and the United States, as well as sending a list of their names to local media outlets. The simple, straightforward letters warned of a 'boom' to follow. Shortly after, Nazi propagandist Ernst Zundel received a pipe bomb in the mail. The victim of recent firebombs and hate mail, Zundel was suspicious of the package. Finding it too heavy for its size, he called police. About a month later Charles Scott, an outspoken neo-Nazi from British Columbia was mailed another pipe bomb. His colleagues tried to disarm it with a coat hanger but contacted police when they spotted wires.

In a letter sent to the media, the Militant Direct Action Task Force (MDATF) claimed responsibility and showed intimate knowledge of the target and, in Scott's case, of who picked up the bomb. The letter claimed solidarity with a number of European and South American left wing groups, a usual tactic for the left wing, and dedicated the action to the memory of dead left wing martyrs in Europe. The logo at the top of the communications showed the letters MDATF superimposed over the silhouette of a Heckler and Koch MP5 with the letter A in the middle of a star. This mirrors the logo of the Red Army Faction in Germany.

The next MDATF target was the vice president of research and development for a cattle artificial insemination lab in Alberta. This was our first indication the targets would not be exclusively high-profile members of the Canadian right wing. The executive had been reading about the Unabomber and detonated the bomb as he hid behind his desk. He was not seriously hurt.

The final bomb was sent to a researcher at the Mackenzie Institute, a right wing think tank in Toronto that studies terrorism. The MDATF letters sent to various media indicated the reasons for the chosen targets; "The Mackenzie Institute bases its own existence on the spread of lies and hatred within this country and supports right wing hatred toward certain groups in our society. The Mackenzie Institute supports neo-Nazis, multinational corporations and is pro-American." Its members, the letter said, are xenophobic, blatantly homophobic, anti-feminist, and anti-choice. The letters went on to say that the institute regularly publishes academic papers to a wide audience including some which have been critical of Canada's immigration policy, aboriginal militancy, and some social programs.

The letters said that the cattle artificial insemination lab was targeted because it is a “fascist bio and geno-technology industry” and the work done by this specific lab was “a manipulation of nature simply so as to suit our ever-growing greedy appetites for bigger and better versions of unnecessary items.” They also described Scott, the second bomb recipient as “on the forefront of the racist right in Canada helping recruit, train and distribute hate literature to racists and Zundel is one of the largest suppliers of fascist literature and radio/video programs in the world.” The MDATF warned its actions would not be limited to fascists but also imperialists, military weapons producers, eco-destroyers and “all our oppressors.” Demonstrations are no longer enough, it said, and there was need for armed resistance.

Only Zundel is known to have received the AFM warning letter and the pipe bomb. Since those initial letters, there has been nothing from the AFM as well as nothing more from the MDATF since the Mackenzie Institute bomb. This remains under active investigation and there is a great deal about the left wing, and the surfacing ideological overlaps.

Those in the left wing believe democracies are set up as a business with the control of the production of wealth in the hands of a few and production the responsibility of man--the proletariat. He is alienated from his labor and so can never be realized. Crime is caused by the existence of the state and of private property. A revolution would result in more equitable sharing of wealth and of the means of production. Small-scale participatory groups run by consensus would make the decisions. The aim is to create the proper conditions for mass revolution so the masses can be led out of their oppression. The fact that this has seldom worked in the past has no impact. The basic belief is there should be no government and that people should be organized in collectives with decisions made by consensus. When people mention the similarities in basic goals between the left and the right, this is the center of it, although many of their goals may seem to be similar.

Historically the left has attached itself to current social issues as a means of unseating or discrediting the existing government. In Canada it has attached itself to issues as diverse as native sovereignty, the animal rights movement, and the very public fight to keep social programs. The organizations Anti-Racist Action and Skinheads Against Racial Prejudice in Canada have been engaging in attacks under the cover of popular demonstrations and have a developed demonstration style now well known to urban police forces. One of their particular venues is to participate, often violently, during right wing militant demonstrations. While they speak and act against the establishment they are willing to take assistance from these organizations in the form of welfare payments or student loans. They are sensitive to any indication of police infiltration or investigation and would love to have the opportunity to embarrass the government or the police. This enforces the need to investigate individual criminal activity and not allow investigations to stray.

Criminal activity is most likely to be conducted alone and in small cells. They may do reconnaissance for months, even years, and are not likely to know whom they acted with. A good example of this structure is Earth First! which has no leadership, no direction, and no central force. It is based on a left wing/anarchist model with the goal to stop capitalist/imperialist oppression of the ecology to the detriment of the masses.

Both the criminal and the legitimate activists in the left wing are making good use of the Internet and of other open-source vehicles that are relatively easy to get a hold of. Some is easy to read with well-developed arguments and thoughtful articles as well as good information on current and upcoming causes. As we move across the spectrum however, particularly into Internet communications, the prose is increasingly turgid, philosophical, and hard to read. They are set apart by their ability to work together. They get over their ideological differences to pursue a specific cause. They also have a sense of humor about attaining goals. All of this is a welcome change from much of the rhetoric we read.

The criminal anarchist community in Canada is small. We certainly do not have a national crisis on our hands. What we do have is a potentially deadly group of criminals who have come, so to speak, out of left field. Their activity has put a stress on the necessity of looking within, as well as, without when assessing criminal extremist threats. The importance of not overreacting and of not restricting the rights of the many, in order to control the activity of a few, must be stressed. This type of oppression is actually a left wing goal and they believe this popularizes the revolutionary goal and coerces the masses into their camp.

In Canada it is not illegal to belong to any group, regardless of its ideology, nor is it illegal to associate with known criminal extremists or for criminal extremists to raise money in Canada. It is frustrating from a law-enforcement perspective but it is the reality of what we do. This brief overview in no way represents a complete profile of the left wing or its political or criminal activity.

Wendy Nicol *joined the Royal Canadian Mounted Police five years ago and is currently a Strategic Intelligence Analyst in the Criminal Extremism Analysis Section of the Criminal Intelligence Directorate. Ms. Nicol has degrees in journalism and sociology, with a major in criminology. Before joining the RCMP, she was a reporter and editor at a number of major Canadian daily newspapers.*

ETHNO-RELIGIOUS VIOLENCE: ISLAMIC TERRORISM

Dr. Frank Tachau

A persistent American stereotype links terrorism with the Middle East and with Islam. This stereotype has been fed by a long history of hostility and conflict between Islam and the West. Before the rise of Communism, Islam represented the greatest danger to the West. In Spain from 750 to 1492 AD, Islam challenged the West militarily, in the form of the Ottoman Empire. They besieged Vienna first in 1529 and then in 1683. Islam also challenged the West materially. It was a world power during most of the time that Europe was grouping in the Dark Ages. Muslims were the middlemen in trade with the East. Finally, Islam challenged the West religiously. The Prophet Muhammad rejected the finality of Christianity. He accused both Judaism and Christianity of falsifying God's word. He appeared to the West to be the Anti-Christ.

In modern times, this relationship of relative strength and weakness was reversed. Europe became extremely powerful as a result of the voyages of discovery and the industrial revolution. Islam was supposedly the final word of God; Muslims were supposed to inherit the earth but reality contradicted this, producing deep frustration, thus leading to severe cognitive dissonance in Islam.

Terrorism is not the weapon of choice. It is the weapon of the politically and militarily weak. Given the political weakness of Islam in modern times, the association of Islam with terrorism should not be surprising. But this is not to say that this association is unique. Even the phenomenon of suicide attacks is not unique to Islam (e.g., World War II Kamikaze pilots). There are also many variations of Islam, non-violent as well as violent. The Iranian regime, for example, is rooted in the specifically Iranian Shi'I tradition, which is quite distinct. Furthermore, to the extent that Iran uses terror, it is an instrument of the state and a weapon to be deployed against external enemies, whether they be other Muslims (e.g., Saudi Arabia) or non-Muslim States. Almost all other

Islamic movements are Sunni, the Islamic Salvation Front, the Armed Islamic Group Algeria (the Islamic opposition in Egypt), and the Hamas in the West Bank Gaza.

For these groups, violence and terror are typically only one aspect of their activities. They also organize social welfare programs in competition with corrupt and inefficient government services. These activities, pioneered by the leftist National Liberation Front (FLN) during the war for Algerian independence from France, are designed to win hearts and minds of the masses, and alienate them from the regime of the day. These groups also broadcast propaganda emphasizing traditional Islamic values and excoriating opponents.

These movements have successfully taken power in three countries: Iran; Sudan; and, in September 1996, Afghanistan. While the ultimate outcome remains in question, other regimes that have confronted internal Islamic opposition (e.g., Egypt, Syria Jordan, Tunisia, Lebanon, Algeria, and the Palestinian Authority in the West Bank and Gaza) have managed to survive and ultimately put down such opposition.

In short, Islamic terrorism is an expression of political frustration. Hence, it is most likely to crop up under repressive and/or corrupt regimes (e.g., Egypt or Algeria), though some regimes are still efficient enough to nip all types of opposition in the bud (e.g., Syria and Iraq). It may also reassert itself in the Israeli-Palestinian conflict, if diplomatic negotiations for a final status agreement between the two sides get bogged down again or appear to become aimless and inconclusive. It remains to be seen whether a democratic society like Israel, or a quasi-state apparatus like the Palestinian Authority, are capable of, or willing to, engage in the kind of brutal repression which may be necessary to defeat violent Islamic militancy in the final analysis.

Dr. Frank Tachau *is a Professor Emeritus of Political Science at the University of Illinois-Chicago. He was Department Chairman from 1976 to 1982 and 1985 to 1987. He has been a Visiting Professor at the University of Chicago, the Hebrew University in Israel, and at Bilkent University and the Middle East Technical University in Ankara, Turkey. He was a Fulbright Fellow at the University of Ankara from 1963-64. Professor Tachau has published several books and many articles on the politics of Turkey and other countries in the Middle East. He has also edited an encyclopedia entitled Political Parties in the Middle East and North Africa. He is currently writing a book on the politics of the Middle East.*

ORGANIZED TERRORISM & MAFIA CRIMINALITY

Giacomo Barletta

Terrorism, Mafia, and organized crime are three sides of the same social disorder, a social disorder, which are first the effect and then the cause of a clear psychological disorder. Both these forms of "disorder" are of such a dimension as to represent a real illness, certainly, no less serious than other illnesses, with only one difference. With other illnesses, those who are ill are almost always victims of the illness. Those who are involved in terrorism, the Mafia, or organized crime do so out of free choice. For other illnesses, researchers are doing their best to discover microbes and viruses in scientific laboratories, as well as, predisposing therapies and pharmacological products. Legislators and the governments which should be the "doctors" of this social and psychological illness, skip from one temporary buffer provision to the next, overwhelmed by the last crime, and worried by the intolerance of public opinion and the scathing remarks made by the mass media.

The problem resides exactly in the individualization, almost always carried out hurriedly and emotionally of the modality of the event, of the number of victims, of the amount of laundering, and/or of the quantity of drugs seized. The politicians, pursued by the urgency of the routine case, do not have the time (or, maybe, do not understand) to put together a scientific research laboratory. A limited number of researchers, as well as an "intelligence" staff, rather than traditional police, study the therapies to be tried out to "try and try again" for what is defined as "successive approximation." This is nothing miraculous, but it is the only thing to do. Otherwise, we shall pass from one frustration to the other, waiting and holding our breaths for what will be the next crime or the next attack.

The second part of this paper is related to the need for parliamentarians and governments to establish a real criminal policy that covers individually, and all together, the three social phenomena:

terrorism, Mafia, and organized crime. Criminal policy constitutes the whole of the activities of the legislative, the executive, and the judiciary powers which moving from the study of the biological, environmental, and utilitarian causes of the crime, aim at the identification of the fitting instruments for restricting crime through elimination within the limits of what is possible, or, in any case, aim at its effectiveness.

Criminal policy is the result of the general vision of social and economic life which takes into account the periods of transition that have preceded in the country's life, which must not be forgotten. The periods of transition (political, social, and economic) are measured in years and decades; and it is possible to predict them with reasonable probability. The choice and the application of a criminal policy involve the simultaneous and coordinated intervention of all the components of the State at all levels.

The bodies of the State successively know or perceive, each within the sphere of its own competencies and functions, the foreseeable cultural socioeconomic modifications which function by frequently changing the basic picture of the criminal phenomena or of political criminality, which are not the same thing but which are grafted in the same sick social fabric. This makes analyses and diagnoses even more difficult.

In the presence of such objective situations, the legislative and executive powers must reexamine the choices that they had previously made, in light of the choices carried out, of the results obtained and of the changed situations. This allows for an even, partial modification of the diagnosis and for an adaptation of the therapy to the new realities. In other words, the same method adopted by researchers in medicine, physics, and chemistry laboratories would be used.

It is perhaps fitting to remember that the legislator intervenes only when the reality of the country has matured specific evolutions and involutions, by trying to step in line with the former and by trying to slow down the eventual process of the latter. In fact, the judicial norm does not generate itself. It is the result of the physiological process of society that the legislator has the duty to regulate. As a rule, social reality evolves much more rapidly than judicial norm.

History and chronicles teach us that a type of pursuit is set up between the customs of a country and the regulation of the customs of the same. Going back to the choice of a global criminal policy and not to a temporary one, it must be remembered that the responsible choice of the same presupposes the knowledge of humanist and social sciences such as biology, sociology, and political economy, for example. And at the same time, it presupposes the knowledge of the duties of an organized State, duties amongst which is found the one of guaranteeing a normal unfolding of social life which should be at the same time just, regulated, and safe.

So that having identified the germ of the crime after having individuated it, one can study the way of attacking it in the attempt to isolate it, eliminating if possible the cause of the difficulty. This is the moment when, having carried out the task of the research in the laboratory, the whole becomes a task of application of the general lines indicated.

The "handling of the collateral causes" comes into play here. These causes are at the basis of the difficulty, of the disorder, of the crisis of the principle of legality, of the crime. The moment when I speak of collateral causes, I must, however, specify a point. In order to avoid misunderstandings, cause and/or collateral cause do not mean taking away responsibility from man, as some sociologists wrote in the 1970's. Man always has a margin of psychic and intellectual freedom which allows and obliges him to choose between good and evil and thus to maneuver and direct his own behavior as he wishes, taking on himself however, all the ethical, moral and judicial consequences of the choice he has made.

An approach towards the complex and diversified problem of terrorism is the one witnessed by all those competent in the field, which substantially aims at tracing the history of the phenomenon, at individualizing its causes, at attempting to reach a definition of it, at outlining a psychological profile. This is a useful approach, but, in my opinion, it calls for further consideration on the "seriousness" of the agreements between governments, both on a bilateral level and on the level of international conventions and from the operative point of view. In such a perspective which I personally prefer to the historical and literacy approach. The Geneva Convention on the prevention and repression of terrorism on November 16, 1937, the Project of the "Code for international crimes" of the Commission for International Law of the UNO (6th Assembly, 1954), the international conventions on hijacking signed in Tokyo in 1962, Aja in 1970 and Montreal in 1971, nor the one of the International Convention of the Organism of the American States of 1971 and, to finish, I shall not talk to you about the European Convention on the repression of terrorism of 1977.

Well then, I shall not speak about aid, or these International Agreements on whose real validity I have some doubts. The real essence of terrorism is of a political nature, in all its implications, all well known to us and over which it is superfluous to draw our attention; Implications which are all political or, in any case, linked to politics. Whether it is of an anarchic or nationalistic nature, for or against the legitimate or illegitimate power, little matters as far as the repression of the phenomenon is concerned. And here we come upon the first banana skin over which the so-called good intentions of the interested countries slip. And this is because the same phenomenon is considered heroic or contemptible according to whether the reader of the phenomenon is interested in one diagnosis or the other. Or whether the reader is on the terrorists' or victims' side.

Such an attitude undermines both the ethical value of the behavior of States and the "seriousness" of the means adopted, or that are to be adopted, in order to attack the phenomenon. But there is a further circumstance that makes the commitment of some governments even less credible when they underwrite Conventions or proclaim faithfulness to anti-terrorism. Such a circumstance is represented by the sad reality that at times the very same governments mentioned above, gain an indirect advantage from terrorist action. The States, which in a more or less veiled manner cover terrorist groups, are blackmailed by such groups, which, whether through inertia or silence, guarantee peace to that country.

In the presence of such situations that are common to many, there is no government in the world that is not willing to mute any action of repression. Naturally, around these phenomena are constituted an infinity of interests which make the situation even more worrying. I am referring to the contacts between terrorist groups and legal or representative groups of the Mafia and/or of other organized criminality. It is evident, in fact, that terrorism needs money for moving from one place to the other and for buying firearms. So, the connivance is soon set up, with destabilizing consequences that are not easy to control.

The interests of the States, "the reason of the State", nationalist feelings, political hatred, and blackmailing are all the ingredients of a cocktail that few have the courage to analyze and report. I realize that through this hard analysis of mine I run the risk of being considered a defeatist without hope, but I would rather be defined in such a way than to serve you up with an odorless, tasteless and colorless cocktail.

But this hard analysis of mine, whether it be agreed with in whole or in part, can help us not to waste time in proposing lukewarm solutions which would leave us all happy, at least until the next attack. To plan a real operation of repression, it is first necessary to not deceive one another. And afterwards, having identified some points which are either more or less certain, to formulate some working hypotheses which take into consideration the weak points of the actual possibility of a battle to fight on tiptoe, at the level of Intelligence. Of course in a different world, in that world which man has been vainly pursuing for thousands of years until today, and which will continue to pursue tomorrow, in that world, we could hope for the loyalty of States, of politics and of morality.

Whilst sitting around a dinner table livened up by Sicilian music in Taormina, I said to a British scholar that a diagnostic and criminological error pertaining to the police is represented by putting together the two phenomena, both in analysis and in diagnosis, as well as in therapy. I am a philosopher, who practices law, but, like the scholars of ancient Greece, I believe that a philosopher-lawyer-mathematician must also be tuned in to the methodology of the medical laboratories. This is why in my activity as a scholar and in the practical one I often use laboratory methods, approaches, and terminology.

I said to my British colleague, that evening in Taormina, that if a man is caught stealing hens, the policeman, the journalist, the judge and the lawyer who all deal with the "case" are and remain unknown professionals. But if the journalist who gives the news says that the above mentioned thief is a Mafioso, immediately the journalist and the professionals who deal with him will rise immediately to the role of important persons. Maybe journalists from the press and from television will interview them. Maybe their photographs will be published and they will be gratified in their social circles. This is an important circumstance that leads to important sociological consequences. Exaggeration apart, I must say that I am of the opinion that all of us must resist the temptation to appear in the information media and to act as loudspeakers to events of a modest nature or lending ourselves to a harmful "deontological" interpretation of the same events.

Mafia and organized criminality are two different phenomena even though they at times have the same operative point of view and similar or same manifestations. This specification is neither terminological nor theoretical. The old Mafia was an illegal organization for the simple fact that it substituted itself for the State, which was more or less illegitimate, even though it was represented by an invading or tyrannical State. Anyway, for the laws of the time, Mafia was an illegal organization that was also, but not necessarily, and not always, an organization that had as its "statute" and its object criminal activities. So in the long run, Mafia penetrated the customs, mentality, and daily life, creating what was a Mafia culture.

It was possible that anybody, whether he was a peasant, a worker, or an illustrious professional, any honest, correct citizen of great morality, incapable of committing an illicit action, should follow with understanding that which, whether right or wrong, was a parallel justice carried out by the so-called Mafia justice. The Mafia was an illegal organization that committed abuses, homicides, extortion, gambling, and prostitution, was not only the commissioner and executor of such crimes, but was also an organization that aimed at a certain social justice, even if such a social justice was pursued with violence and crime.

This premise is indispensable to understand my approach, which implies operative repercussions that are by all means important. The moment when the illegal and criminal culture of the Mafia found itself at first meeting with, and afterwards clashing with organized criminality, a typical phenomenon of criminal culture was verified. Initially, the men of the Mafia tried to mediate to set up a dialogue, to believe, and then immediately after, to take back what had been conceded. In a second moment, faced by the activities of new groups and criminals that struck out, the Mafia took the hard line, even though it alternated successes with failures.

The 1939-1945 war represents the dividing line. At the end of the war, in fact, with what at times is a substantial change in life, in customs, in freedom and with a greater wealth for many and a greater poverty for others, the definitive clash between Mafia and organized criminality was inevitable. And so, one after the other, the leaders of the Mafia were struck down and this illegal and criminal organization was destroyed, all to the advantage of organized criminality which did not even need to cover up their crimes with social justifications as well.

From that moment, physiologically, (after the traumatic events mentioned above), the Mafia disappeared, substituted completely, by organized criminality which is not the new Mafia. It is not Mafia, (a mixture of arrogance, of romanticism, of Sicilian pride against the Spanish kings, of pride of the Sicilian and Neapolitan immigrants forced to live together and clash with the ex Irish or English immigrants), it is something else.

It is what I call organized criminality that does not need that vague hint of sympathy on the part of the inhabitants of the territory on which it operates, but rather it is completely against the inhabitants of that territory. It is an organization that does not create a "Mafia culture," which instead was necessary for the survival and rooting of the Mafia. The Mafia, in fact, without such rooting did not want to and could not progress, even if only within illegality. One of the proofs is that when criminals today speak about their organization, they prefer to define it as "Cosa Nostra" (our business) as if to mobilize themselves.

The diagnosis presented, which I am convinced of but which naturally I propose to you as a working hypothesis, inevitably implies a totally different therapy hypothesis with respect to the one put into practice till today. The "therapy" practiced by the politicians of the free government is, in my opinion, mistaken or at least inefficient both from a psychological profile, which is very important in this sector, and from an operative one.

It is wrong from the psychological point of view since the constant hammering carried out by the politicians who use the mass media and criminalize whole regions and/or sectors of civil society, obtains exactly the opposite effect. That is to put the "innocent" citizens (who are at times the almost total majority) against the State. Or at least it does not put them in a position to collaborate. And, here, the operative aspect comes into play, linked by cause and effects the psychological one. No choice of criminal policy that uses repressive measures can reach objectives in an adequate manner without the territorial support of the citizens.

These citizens - and so it becomes a vicious circle will deny, more or less aware, their support to a State which holds them in contempt, humiliates them, and marginalizes them, harms them even from an economic point of view. It is clear that the topics I was entrusted with have only been briefly mentioned. Each of the three topics deserves a degree course and perhaps even more.

***Giacomo Barletta** is a Founding Member and Delegated Counselor of the International Center of Sociological, Penal and Penitentiary Research and Studies (INTERCENTER) in Messina, Italy. He has been a consultant for narcotics, legal, and criminal justice matters to the United Nations, the European Community, and the International Association of Penal Law. Mr. Barletta was Director of INTERCENTER's International Courses for Senior Police Officers from 1982-87 and 1989-1995 and is the author of several studies and monographs.*

PART FOUR: RESPONSES

BIOLOGICAL TERRORISM: THE THREAT & THE RESPONSE

Frank McDonald

Germ warfare on the battlefield has long been a national security issue, especially during the build-up for Desert Storm. While chemical and biological warfare will remain a problem for the military, the greater threat is the criminal or terrorist use of these weapons against the civilian population of the United States. Around the world, especially in Asia and the Middle East, the deadliest chemical and biological weapons known to man are for sale to an ever-widening terrorist clientele. The supermarket for this technology has, and continues to come, from the laboratories of a secret Russian biological weapons program code-named "Biopreperat." Before and after the breakup of the Soviet Union, disgruntled military and poorly paid scientists with ties to the Russian Mafia funnel bio-weapons to eager buyers in Iraq, Syria, North Korea, and Iran. These weapons are then passed along to state-sponsored terrorist networks, which will confront the United States with nightmare scenarios counter-terrorist experts have quietly talked about for years.

Following the March 20, 1995 nerve gas attack on the innocent civilian riders of the Tokyo subway system that killed 12 and injured 5,500, high-tech terror became reality. For the past five years, BioMatrix has focused on the potential use of agents of biological origin (ABOs) as weapons, specifically their release within an urban setting in the United States. We have sought answers to the following questions: What characteristics of biological agents might attract terrorists? How likely is it that a terrorist or criminal group would be capable of "cultivating" such pathogens? What degree of expertise is required? What ABOs would most likely be used? How would they be cultured, vectored, and released? Is it possible to mitigate such use? How effective is the intergovernmental mitigation effort? In the event of a release of a germ weapon, how prepared are our public health and safety professionals?

Bioterrorism is the planned release of microorganisms or toxins to kill or cause disease to an unsuspecting civilian population. ABOs fall into one of three categories: bacteria, viruses or toxins.

- Bacteria (anthrax, plague, tularemia) have a long history as germ weapons. If diagnosed at an early stage, they can be treated with antibiotics such as penicillin and ciprofloxacin.
- Viruses (smallpox, flu, Marburg, Ebola) are much smaller organisms with a genetic core (DNA or RNA) encased by a protective protein which facilitates cell infection. Viruses require a receptive host in order to thrive and are far more difficult to treat than either toxins or bacteria.
- Toxins (botulism, Ricin) are poisons either made synthetically or by living organisms. Toxins are non-living organisms and therefore incapable of replication. They do not have a multiplier effect as some bacteria and most viruses do.

As with any terrorist threat, mitigating a bio-terror attack is primarily one of good intelligence. However, I believe that even with the vast resources of the FBI, CIA and other Intelligence agencies at its disposal, the United States will be unable to prevent the criminal or terrorist use of biological weapons in the near future.

This pessimistic conclusion is based not on a corollary of "Murphy's Law" that if something like a germ weapon exists, it will be used. I believe the horrific scene of a major city's hospitals engulfed with the sick and dying as a result of the deliberate release of a deadly ABO will appear on the nation's television screens because germ weapons are inexpensive to procure, relatively easy to produce, and very simple to vector and deliver.

Unlike radiological or explosive devices, metal detectors, trained dogs, or traditional anti-terrorist scanning equipment does not reveal ABOs. They can be transported in minuscule containers, with a tiny amount capable of doing great harm. They can also be designed with an elastic time lag between the agent's release and it's effect upon the population, thus providing the perpetrator a greater chance at avoiding detection.

Anonymity is the most salient characteristic of ABOs. Unlike chemicals, biologicals are odorless and tasteless. On the order of 1-5 microns, they are also invisible to the human eye. More worrisome, biologicals have a multiplier effect, the contagion factor makes them even more devastating.

ABOs can also be designed to defy identification. With technical expertise in bioengineering and a minimum of $10,000 of off-the-shelf equipment, a graduate student can produce a viral or toxic pathogen hitherto unknown. "Shaking and baking" a concoction of cultured anthrax, tularemia, botulism, plagues, smallpox, Ebola, Marburg, or Ricin is no more difficult than brewing beer. With a bit more application, the organisms could be freeze-dried, set to time-release, encapsulated, and be as portable as an Alka-Seltzer tablet. Then it is only a matter of dropping the agent into the housing of an air-conditioning system where it will aerosolize in air-ducts throughout, say, a federal building, cruise ship, sports-arena, transportation hub or terminal. Any facility where large numbers of people gather together in an enclosed space, especially space dependent on ventilation systems for air, is a high-risk and vulnerable target.

A threat assessment done by a security team for the World Trade Center calculated that one kilogram of dried botulism introduced into its air-conditioning system would circulate throughout the building's 10 billion liters of air-space within 72 minutes and cause a minimum of 30,000 casualties. Another study sponsored by the Department of Defense estimated that 50-kg of anthrax, sprayed in a two-kilometer line over metropolitan New York would incapacitate 700,000 and leave 400,000 dead.

In 1995, the Naval War College sponsored its annual war-game, "Global 95," which simulated a biological terrorist attack on Washington DC and Norfolk, Virginia. On that particular evening, because of favorable wind conditions, the attack on Norfolk resulted in few casualties. Washington was not so lucky. Specially rigged crop-dusting aircrafts sprayed anthrax over the city resulting in more than a million casualties. The United States retaliated with nuclear weapons against the "rogue" state that organized the attack.

A terrorist attack using an aerosolized agent will probably occur without warning. The first signs of attack will be hundreds or thousands of ill and dying patients flooding hospital emergency rooms. Since the pathogen can be time-released, there is no way of knowing whether symptoms of the attack would erupt within minutes, hours, or days.

By definition, a genetically engineered, bio-weapon is, until its release, an unidentified, unknown killer. There are bio-sensors which can identify the more common ABOs, such as anthrax and botulism, but for the bio-engineered variety of toxins and viruses, the medical emergency response will take shape only when the dead provide their tissue for analysis. Even if the intelligence community had fair warning and knew the genetic makeup of an ABO, to administer vaccinations to millions of potential victims would be impossible; nor is there any way to physically protect the civilian population with masks or decontamination centers.

At present, emergency medical teams could barely protect themselves in the event of a significant germ release. Masks or filtered respirator equipment are not available in sufficient quantities. The emergency chemical/biological responding units of all major U.S. cities could muster no more than three to four hundred decontamination suits in a national emergency. New York City has only twenty level-four, decon-suits for all of its EMS, Fire and hazard teams. The City's Public Safety officials acknowledge the seriousness of this problem, but they also admit to having few counter-proliferation assets at their disposal. When the Pope visited New York and world leaders gathered to celebrate the 50th Anniversary of the United Nations in 1996, Special Operations could deploy but five emergency decontamination stations around the city.

What can be done?

1. **Admit the "Germ Genie" is out of the bottle and increase public awareness of the threat of bio-terrorism.** Public officials have a real problem with this issue. Budget constraints, a reactive rather than proactive mind-set, and a general lack of knowledge about the problem results in an "I don't want to talk about that now" attitude. This is especially true of elected officials. Why frighten the people with something that might not happen?
2. **Increase funding for emergency responders**. The funding Congress has allocated for FY 1996 for an emergency response to a bio-terror attack is a paltry $9 million. These funds are meant to pay for national health advisories, agent identification, hazard reduction, vaccines, decontamination, clinical medical support, high risk training and last, but not least, mortuary support.

3. **Develop biological "smoke alarms."** Forget traditional counter-terrorist methods when it comes to bio-terror. To deal with high-tech terrorists we need to develop state-of-the-art bio-detection systems which, while they may not prevent a deadly germ release, would at least minimize our vulnerability. The DOD's Advanced Research Projects Agency is funding technology to detect in real-time the presence and identification of thousands of biological agents. The system can relay that information to a germ weapon library. This provides responders a significant advantage in coping with an emergency biological killing zone. FY 1994-96 the DOD allocated $172 million for a "Biological Weapons Monitoring And Detection Program," the most effective of the Pentagon's chemical threat research programs. The results of this research should be made available to civilian Public Health and Safety agencies.
4. **Prepare for the worst case scenario and stress post-incident, emergency medical disaster planning**. The lack of planning, resources, training, and equipment to cope with a bio-terrorist incident must be remedied. This will happen only when elected officials put significant resources behind that effort.
5. **Support a Chemical/Biological Rapid Deployment Strike Team (C/BRDST)**. Since it is likely that state and local resources will be overwhelmed in the aftermath of a terrorist attack, an integrated Federal, State and local response is required. The Office of Emergency Preparedness, together with the DOD, EPA, FEMA, DOE, and the CDC are in the process of organizing a Federal Strike Team with the necessary medical expertise, military support, and dedicated equipment to cope with a major terrorist attack. The Strike Team should be mobilized and on-site within three hours of notification. The C/BRDST is also a model for

Metro Strike Teams proposed for deployment in many major cities around the country.

One of the few public figures willing to go on record about bio-terrorism is Senator Sam Nunn, acknowledged as one of the Senate's leading expert on national security. Interviewed about the bio-terror threat in November 1995, his thoughts provide a sobering analysis.

> *"Would-be terrorists out there already know about these weapons. It's imperative the American people know about them..... I'd be very surprised if any U.S. city can be protected. If nothing is done about this threat, I can see us holding hearings about a biological disaster in this country..... In the end I think we will be very fortunate to avoid this kind of disaster at some point."*

The Massachusetts State of Emergency Management's (MENU) headquarters is located in a bombproof underground bunker thirty miles west of Boston. A seven-ton blast door that rotates on a mammoth wheelbase protects the entrance to the bunker. Beyond is a sloping walkway leading to the core of the complex. At the end of a long descent, there is a final security wall on which four words confront the visitor: "Not If, But When!" That caution symbolizes the essence of the NETWORK'S operative concern and purpose:

- To work with public safety officials, private corporations, scientific experts, and emergency medical personnel to better understand the threat of bio-terrorism.
- To further the public's awareness about that threat and the lack of federal, state, or local preparedness to cope with it.
- To research and evaluate biological monitoring systems, sensors, and other mitigating security technologies.
- To encourage greater funding for emergency management programs at all levels of government.

Frank McDonald *is the founder and Director of BioMatrix, a non-profit, public policy resource center consulting on biological terrorism and public safety issues. His career includes tenure with the U.S. Foreign Service and service with the United Nations Institute of Training and Research. He also served as Executive Administrator of the Caribbean Island of Anguilla. Mr. McDonald spent twenty years in England and Ireland consulting on art theft and tracking stolen or looted paintings, experience which contributed to his novel, **PROVENANCE,** an international best-seller, and a Book-of-the-Month selection. Mr. McDonald has lectured on national security issues at the New School for Social Research, Tufts School of Law and Diplomacy, the Inter-American Defense College (Ft. McNair), and the U.S. Air Force Academy.*

TACTICAL RESPONSES TO TERRORISM

Rod Paschall

We live in a period of political, racial and religious violence and because of that, we must know the best ways to respond to terrorism. Prevention appears to be the supreme single response to terrorism. Time, resources and effort put into anti-terrorist measures, barriers, guards, screening and identification stations, and other precautions will pay off--if nothing more than to decrease run-of-the-mill crimes such as theft.

But, we will never have the resources to protect everything and everybody. People will not tax themselves enough to hire all the guards necessary and they will not tolerate the degree of inconvenience or government intrusion essential to obtain a terror free society. There is no single cost-effective response to terrorism. Preventive measures will deter some terrorists, but defense does not have the potential to stop all that seek to gain their aims through violent, coercive intimidation. Terrorism will occur. We must consider the best ways to respond.

We have been responding to terrorists for about 30 years and there is enough experience to select responses likely to be reasonably effective. A sound first step is to put terrorism in perspective with other public hazards. Then, in considering our approaches to terrorists, we should acknowledge some general principles that apply to combating any particular terrorist group. In responding to a terrorist event, we should begin with a recognition that each incident is heavily shaped by its own peculiar circumstances and that specific successful response for one attack may not work for another.

However, by using available experience, we may be able to extrapolate some tactical principles, or failing that, at least identify the outstanding considerations that have applied in the past. Since appropriate counter-terrorist actions vary with each major category of terrorist incident, the principles are better considered in the context of each of the most common categories: bombing, assassination, kidnapping, and hostage barricade situations. And, since we have witnessed the first major terrorist attempt to employ nerve gas, we might explore chemical, biological and nuclear incidents.

Principles and considerations will include both proactive and reflexive actions, actions that may be effective just prior to, during, or immediately after an act of terrorism. Additionally, since terrorists are normally intensely interested in publicity, there are some principles of news media relations that should be examined.

Just how important is it to create an effective means of dealing with terrorism? Should we spend more or less fighting the terrorist than we do in defending against fire, theft, murder, flood, or tornadoes? The latter two, flood and tornadoes, are acts of nature so they are not comparable. But, most fires and all thefts and murders are acts of man and can presumably be controlled--if we use enough resources. Back in the 1970's, the government of Israel had 40,000 people, guards, investigators, analysts, and counter-terrorist specialists, whose everyday job was to defeat terrorism.[1] In proportional terms, that would translate in to 2.5 million Americans--more than all the uniformed members of today's entire U.S. Armed Forces. We can conclude from that experience that counter-terrorism can not only be very expensive, it is not likely to end terrorism. After all, Israel is still beset with terrorism and still paying a high cost in dealing with it.

How important is terrorism in the overall scheme of American risk? We can compare it with any number of human-caused public hazards. For example, back in the 1950's when we were not so concerned with terrorism, Americans had a one in twenty thousand chance of being murdered in any given year. Now, with about 24,000 U.S. homicides per year, an American has a one in ten thousand chance of being murdered.

Compare that with terrorism. For the last twenty years, we have averaged between 40 and 50 deaths per year due to terrorists incidents.[2] That computes to one chance in five million for any American to be killed by a terrorist in any given year. Murder is 500 times more hazardous to Americans than terrorism.

Is this comparison fair? The reasons for murder are so diverse and the phenomenon so wide spread and established in American society, that any form of government or any kind of program can not prevent it. Terrorism is more specific, can be targeted, and maybe, can be made less a hazard with the right application of resources and well-designed programs.

Then consider a hazard that can be eliminated: American deaths at grade-level railroad crossings. The United States has 280,000 places where a road used by cars and trucks is also crossed by rail road tracks--a grade-level rail crossing. Although the average number of people killed at grade level crossings has decreased from 1980 on, in 1995, 578 Americans were killed at these places.[3] Typically, we lose between 450 and 500 citizens per year at these spots. That translates into a one in a half million chance of being killed at a grade-level rail crossing, ten times greater than terrorism's lethality.

How do you eliminate this hazard? Build overpasses or underpasses at each of those places, or, more sensibly, build overpasses or underpasses beginning with those crossings associated with the highest mortality and keep building until grade-level rail crossing deaths become history.

Terrorism and rail crossings? Some will reject the comparison. They will argue that the unequal contest between motor vehicles and trains is not comparable to terrorism. There is no political component in traffic events. There is a political component in terrorism, that line of reasoning would have the state exert a stronger response to terrorism than to public transportation risks because there are not only lives, but political costs to consider. But, a skeptical American might counter with a question, what political costs? When did we cede a political benefit to terrorists?

According to the great bulk of terrorists who have used violent acts to intimidate the United States for the last 30 years, their argument with us was for: a) our support of Israel and/or b) our opposition to Marxism. We have never caved in on either policy. For the last three decades and for the foreseeable future, we have and will support Israel and are in steady opposition to communism. In fact, prospective American politicians who do not support these continuing policies have little or no chance to gain or keep office.

Terrorists have cost the United States lives and resources, but now, they are unlikely to be rewarded with significant political gains. In the past, there were some rewards. In 1968, North Korea forced President Lyndon Johnson into giving a false confession to obtain the release of the U.S.S. Pueblo's crew. Two years later, President Richard Nixon encouraged several European governments to release seven known or convicted terrorists in exchange for the release of 38 hostages being held in Jordan aboard a hijacked aircraft. In 1981, President Jimmy Carter released more than $8 billion in frozen Iranian assets for the 52

American hostages being held in Tehran. In 1985, President Ronald Reagan pressed Israel into releasing 766 Shiite prisoners in a swap for 39 Americans held hostage in Beirut. And, in 1985-1986, Reagan also made an arms deal with Iran for the safe return of three hostages.[4]

A 1983 truck bomb causing the deaths of 241 U.S. Marines in Lebanon had a definite role in the subsequent American withdrawal. But, the deployment of those Marines was controversial from the start within the Reagan administration. And, while the Marines withdrew, U.S. Special Forces remained, continuing to train those Lebanese forces friendly to the United States. For at least a decade, however, there have been no known deals with terrorists. It is reasonable to say that America has not suffered any significant political losses at the hands of terrorists for some time. In fact, any U.S. president who is seen yielding to a terrorist group may be well advised to seek other employment.

Today the costs of terrorism to America is lives lost and resources spent on anti- and counter-terrorist measures. That being so, then why not get to work on those rail crossings? After all, in cost-benefit terms, each dollar spent there is worth ten dollars spent on anti- or counter-terrorist measures. The logical inference is that we should transfer some counter-terrorism expenditures to traffic safety where public funds will do more good. Although, we will not do that because of the "Iron Pentagonal," five elements have an interest in seeing that a logical cost-benefit analysis does not intrude into the field of U.S. counter-terrorism.

The first element of the pentagonal is the American politician. Politicians are going to spend more of their time and our money on checking terrorism than on traffic safety. They will do that because they believe they must be seen as being tougher on terrorism than their domestic political rivals. They will maintain a considerable American counter-terrorist bureaucracy.

That bureaucracy, the second element in the pentagonal, will justify its own existence and growth through dire warnings about the terrorist threat and occasional pronouncements about what they are doing to counter it. That bureaucracy will provide tax dollars to the third group in the pentagonal. These are the American academic counter-terrorist experts who, not unsurprisingly, will solicit and present studies from and to the counter-terrorist bureaucracy proving beyond a doubt that terrorism is a menace. They will portray some rag-tag group of thugs in the Middle East in such bold terms that by comparison, Adolph Hitler would resemble a pale, harmless malcontent.

This, of course, is precisely what the fourth element of the pentagonal, the terrorists, want. Invariably, they have some shabby, impractical cause that ordinarily would not merit even mild interest. They will stage violent incidents to get publicity because they know they will be rewarded. The fifth and final group, the American news media, make the pay-off. This element will flock to any terrorist incident and spend an enormous amount of ink and airtime in covering every aspect of the event--including that shabby terrorist cause that needs the publicity.[5]

All that, of course, goads American politicians, the first pentagonal element, into a bidding war on who can spend the most on counter-terrorism. The iron pentagonal is strong. It feeds on itself. It has been around a long time. And it shows every prospect of having a prominent future. A rational perspective on terrorism, therefore, admits to an irrational American counter-terrorist response. A good rule of thumb is to calculate what resources make comparative sense for a response to terrorism, then multiply that calculation by ten. This is a fact of contemporary American life.

There are some general principles and considerations in opposing terrorism applicable in most every case. The first of these is to bring the right resources to bear at the earliest time. In the United States, that means getting the FBI into the case at the earliest possible minute. The Bureau's guidelines allow for the initiation of a federal investigation as soon as there is "an apparent intent to engage in crime, particularly crimes of violence." It is not necessary to await an actual act of violence.[6] The Bureau is the best choice for a case or intended case of terrorism because it is the lead agency for terrorism matters in the United States, it has the Hostage Rescue Team, it coordinates the domestic deployment of the federal Nuclear Search Team, and it has developed valuable contacts with foreign antiterrorist intelligence sources.

Additionally, the FBI monitors the more than 100 extradition treaties the United States has established with foreign governments and is the organ of government most likely to execute an extraterritorial seizure of a terrorist suspect in accordance with a 1984 law permitting such a broad power.[7] Also, the Bureau established a multi-agency to deal with possible terrorist attacks on the nation's vital telecommunications infrastructure in July 1996.[8]

Finally, the extraordinary resources and powers the FBI possesses in the field of counter-terrorism are likely to grow. The 1996 counter-terrorism legislation the Congress provides for one billion dollars in new hires, new organizations and new programs, to be spent over a five-year period. Much of this is targeted on the Bureau. This will be in addition to other openly published counter- and anti-terrorist expenditures, currently running at about $360 million per year. So, the FBI may be tapping an estimated $600 million per year.[9] It is the logical first stop for action against terrorists.

A second principle is penetration. It is of utmost importance to penetrate a terrorist group so as to not only preempt their planned actions, but to identify and incarcerate their membership. This has been particularly useful in the United States where the Federal Bureau of Investigation and the Bureau of Alcohol, Tobacco and Firearms, working with local law enforcement agencies, have been successful in placing informants within terrorist or would-be terrorist groups.[10]

On the other hand, this technique has been of little obvious assistance to the government of Israel or to the British government. Various terrorist groups operating in Israel, particularly the militant arm of Hamas, have largely been able to defy Jewish penetration attempts. The same situation, to an even higher degree, has prevailed in Northern Ireland for the past quarter century. Some terrorist organizations, such as the Italian Red Brigades, have required their new members to demonstrate their fidelity to the cause by killing a police officer or assassinating a subject chosen by the group's leadership. This requirement constitutes, as a minimum, a distinct limitation, if not an outright bar on a government's penetration attempts.[11] However, if penetration can be done, it is normally the most cost-effective means of dealing with a terrorist organization.

The third general principle is public awareness. It is essential to raise public concern about terrorism's dangers. A chief benefit of this action is to encourage citizens to support counter-terrorist efforts by reporting suspicious activity and assisting in the identification of a terrorist group's membership. Secondly, it can prepare the public to accept infringements on personal liberty and convenience--the inevitable product of passive, anti-terrorist measures. During periods of terrorist activity, this action is self-generating. A dramatic terrorist event, a lethal bomb blast, an assassination, or hostage barricade event engenders its own public awareness campaign. People readily accept screening procedures at airports, parking restrictions and the necessity to submit to entry identification procedures. So, there need not be pronouncements by high-ranking officials after a publicized terrorist incident.

There is the need for government officials to remind the public of past tragedies and the necessity for preventive measures during lulls of terrorist activity. Unfortunately, the imperatives of the iron pentagonal are usually at work. Terrorists normally act when they need the publicity. The news media magnifies their message and public officials make their warnings just when they are superfluous but likely to bring attention to a terrorist cause.

A fourth general principle is protection. This principle includes the passive antiterrorist measures: barriers that prevent automobiles or trucks from coming too close to sensitive buildings; guards and surveillance measures to prevent unauthorized access to areas that are likely terrorist targets; identification stations for screening people who are entering sensitive areas; and personal protection measures surrounding and used by an individual who is susceptible to assassination.

The fifth principle is effective information management. This principle includes intelligence on terrorist organizations but is more comprehensive. The principle encompasses the analysis of intelligence and open-source information on terrorist methods. For example, each message that comes from a terrorist organization should be closely scrutinized for not only content but also style. This kind of background knowledge is apt to come in handy when, for instance, one group stages an incident it hopes to blame on another terrorist organization.

The best intelligence is of no avail if it is not provided to the right official in a timely manner. It is of little use to anyone if it is presented in an ambiguous or broadly applicable manner so that a responsible official is unable to take specific action. Information which is used to counter terrorists must only be given to those personalities who are in a direct chain of action and responsive to a central authority. Otherwise, the information is likely to be compromised. For example, carelessly disseminated information is apt to find its way into the news media where once printed or broadcast, it will serve as an alert to terrorists who will, in turn, take precautions.

A "need-to-know" criterion is essential in handling terrorist-related information. For example, should a penetrator provide information that a terrorist organization is planning to strike a particular class of targets in a given time frame, that knowledge must be processed in such a way that prevents others from learning that the terrorist group has been penetrated by an informant. In this case, precautionary measures might be ordered for a wide array of potential targets for an expanded time frame so as to conceal the existence of the informant. It is also vital to recognize that terrorism is an international phenomenon. It is therefore essential to cultivate and maintain ties with foreign security services that are capable of providing knowledge about terrorists and their organizations.

The sixth and final general principle in dealing with terrorism is to actively preempt terrorist actions. This action bears the most risk of the general response principles. It involves taking action prior to an actual terrorist event and if it is performed abroad, it could constitute an unprovoked act of war.

President Ronald Reagan, however, initiated a preemptive counter-terrorist strike policy with his approval of the National Security Directive 138 on April 3, 1984.[12] The policy followed on the heels of two serious terrorist events: the April 18, 1983 van bomb at the U.S. Embassy in Lebanon that killed 62 people including 17 Americans, and the following October, 1983 truck bomb that took the previously mentioned 241 U.S. Marines' lives near the Beirut airport. The preemptive policy may not necessarily be followed by another U.S. administration. However, it is a precedent, and will probably be assumed by American opponents.

While observing the principles of penetration, protection awareness and information management might decrease the incidence of terrorism; such effort is unlikely to completely prevent terrorist strikes. But, if some experience-based principles surrounding tactical responses to terrorism are followed, a further decrease in the incidence of terrorism might be expected--even if these tactical principles are observed after a terrorist attack.

Because terrorist bombings, assassinations and hostage barricade events have been so common in the past 25 years, it is possible to extrapolate some techniques, procedures and considerations in dealing with these actions that have proven useful to counter-terrorist forces. Actions such as arson and vandalism are also well established in the terrorist's repertoire, but there is no indication that any reaction or response other than standard police procedures will be particularly useful. Since chemical, nuclear, and biological attacks might be anticipated, some protective considerations should be addressed.

For more than the last decade, terrorists have relied on the bomb for the majority of their outrages--and for good reason. In the decade from 1982-1992, there were 130 terrorist bombings in the United States, out of a total of 165 terrorist attacks of all types. Thus, nearly 79 percent of domestic terrorism was manifested with a bomb.[13] The June 1996 bombing of the U.S. barracks in Riyadh, Saudi Arabia that took 19

Americans, the 1995 Oklahoma City bombing that killed 168, the February 1993 bombing of the World Trade Center in New York City that resulted in 6 deaths, the 1994 bombing of the Jewish cultural center in Buenos Aires, Argentina that killed almost 100, and the March 1992 Hizballah car bomb at the Israeli Embassy in that killed 29--all these events simply followed a well-established pattern.

A large bomb can be unobtrusively transported to a target by a truck or van. The vehicle can be parked without drawing much attention. And, a simple timing device can trigger the bomb at a time, which permits the escape of the terrorist. Alternatively, the terrorist may plant the bomb on a conveyance such as the one that was placed aboard a French jetliner and killed 171 people in 1989. The technique appears to be foolproof and trying to deal with terrorist bombers may at first appear impossible. But some counter-terrorist techniques and procedures have not only led to the arrest of the bombers, they have, in special circumstances, prevented a bombing.

No aspect of the terrorist-counter-terrorist dynamic is so active as the cat-and-mouse game between would-be bombers and would-be defenders, a duel that shows to some extent in airliner bombings, but more vividly in Northern Ireland. A new phase in the airliner sector began in August 1982 when a bomb aboard a Pan Am Tokyo to Hawaii flight exploded, killing one passenger and wounding eleven more. A Palestinian who was later arrested by Greek authorities had placed the device on the flight.

The same technique was used against Pan Am Flight 103 over Lockerbie, Scotland in December 1988. That tragedy was due to a plastic explosive-filled radio in an unaccompanied bag. Essentially, the new phase was a dramatic decrease in airliner hijackings and a rise in plane bombings. For the terrorist, attacking airliners, often symbols of a particular country, became less suicidal.

Hopefully, the long-term decrease in the rate of terrorist-related incidents aboard airliners will continue, but the ease with which these acts are staged does not bode well for the future. From 1970 until 1980, there was an average of five such incidents per year. From 1980 until 1990, these incidents decreased to only half that figure, despite a considerable increase in the number of flights.

The problem is that not much progress has been made in discovering explosives in baggage or in small, powerful bombs left on an aircraft by a departing passenger. According to U.S. Attorney Michael J. Garcia, these acts can be committed against U.S. airlines by passengers who board and deplane at intermediate stops, thereby avoiding U.S. Government controlled passenger screening checks. And, explosives left behind may be in a very compact, easily overlooked package containing stabilized liquid nitroglycerin with a digital watch timer connected to a tiny detonator.[14]

By its very nature, bombing requires target proximity to be effective, so the first tactical principle in dealing with a bomb is to separate bomb and target. That, of course, is the aim of the protection principle cited as one of the general considerations above and certainly applies to the baggage inspection procedures at airports. However, separating bomb and target can also be a tactical move in a specific situation. For example, several U.S. Airmen were saved in the Dhahran bombing by alert guards racing through the barracks and shouting for the occupants to evacuate the building when the nearby suspicious truck was noticed. Separating bomb and target can also be accomplished by moving the bomb, a procedure that might require the use of a tow cable and grappling hook. That very move was being arranged by Air Force personnel when the explosion occurred.[15]

Perhaps the most sophisticated interactive dynamic between terrorist bombers and counter-terrorist authorities has been in progress for almost 25 years in the United Kingdom. Initially, in the late 1960's and early 1970's, the Provisional Irish Republican Army (PIRA) used crude, dynamite-type bombs with burning fuses. This practice was too obvious and risked identification of the bomber. So, electronic timing devices were created so as to facilitate discretely leaving a bomb in an innocuous package at the intended target. However, this too had its drawbacks. The primitive PIRA electronic fuses occasionally detonated the charge early, killing a number of would-be bombers. By the 1980's, PIRA bomb makers were skilled enough to fabricate radio-triggered explosives that utilized model airplane remote controls. This allowed for the safe placement of the bomb and detonation when the terrorist was satisfied conditions at the target was to his liking. This improvement in bomb technology proved vulnerable to counter-measures, which in turn, led to counter-counter-measures. The British Army discovered the nature of the triggers and created the mechanism and procedure to prevent detonation.

On an alert caused by a suspicious looking package or vehicle, counter-terrorist elements switched on a powerful jamming signal keyed to the model airplane frequencies. That blocked the detonation signal from reaching the bomb. Not to be deterred, the PIRA created a new triggering device using a speed-trap radar gun. This directional device was less likely to be detected and jammed by authorities. Later, the terrorist bomb makers even used light signals to set of a bomb rigged with a detonator keyed to a photographer's remote control photoflash device. At last report, the terrorists were ahead in this deadly cat-and-mouse game.[16]

So, it is possible to preempt some explosions and that constitutes a principle of counter-terrorist tactical response in bombing incidents. Obviously, preemption is a technique that is not apt to be effective unless very special conditions exist. However, it should not be overlooked.

The third counter-bombing tactical principle to consider is an action that occurs after the event, securing the evidence. While one deed has been done, the professional counter-terrorist must think of preventing a similar event at the hand of the same terrorist. Evidence discovered in the World Trade Center bombing investigation was not only instrumental in securing apprehension and incarceration of the bombers, it undoubtedly prevented the execution of a highway tunnel explosion the terrorists were planning. Then too, almost identical evidence, serial-numbered automotive parts, led to the apprehension, trial and execution of four Saudi terrorists who had killed seven people, including five Americans, with a truck bomb in November 1995.[17]

Bombing is not the terrorist's foolproof tool, in special cases it can be prevented and even when it does occur, there are techniques that will thwart the same bombers from repeating their act. When a bomb is found or suspected, the supreme tactical principle is to separate the bomb and the target either by evacuating the site or removing the bomb. If there is reason to suspect remote, electronically controlled detonation, jamming becomes a fundamental tactical counter measure. And, after the explosion of a terrorist's bomb, the skilled counter-terrorist officer will secure the evidence so that forensic work can preempt a similar future occurrence.

The oldest terrorist technique, assassination, is alive and well, and undoubtedly claiming more victims today than were claimed by the 13th-century Ismaili Order of Assassins. So, too, is another ancient technique, kidnapping. The United States Treasury Department's Secret Service is America's most expert repository of skills and techniques to counter terrorist assassins and kidnappers, but the cost of its services is so high that only a few personalities are professionally protected.

For the most part, government officials below the rank of state governor, businessmen and women and all others are left to fend for themselves. As the Unabomber has proven, we are all vulnerable to any terrorist who chooses murder or kidnapping to publicize his particular cause. In the United States, assassination is second only to bombing in terrorist incidents and, of course, many bombings have assassination as an aim.[18] Abroad, kidnapping is a favorite ploy, particularly in Latin America.

The first tactical principle to follow in personal protection is to avoid the questionable package or letter. Mail bombs are a favorite device of American terrorists for the same reason that bombing is the hands-down favorite of most terrorists worldwide. They offer the least exposure of the terrorist himself. So, if an unexpected package or suspicious letter arrives, it should be reported to the postal inspector or police, or it should be refused or returned. It is that simple.

While not as popular with terrorists as the bomb, the gun has been a staple tool for those Americans devoted to propaganda of the deed since John Wilkes Booth. Since assassins rarely if ever know their victims well enough to be alone with them, they must choose an interception point and time when their target is moving or find a spot where they will have a predictable, clear shot when the intended target is stationary. Normally, assassins will spend as much time and effort in selecting an escape route as they do in picking the interception point. So, they are apt to become inflexible as to time and place early in their planning. It is therefore vital to vary a subject's routes and schedule. Adding an element of unpredictability may be enough to deter some would-be killers.

A third principle is to ensure the person to be protected is not normally visible from an exterior location. Street-level offices can be hazardous, but higher ones might be just as bad if they are visible from an adjoining building.

A fourth principle of assassination avoidance is to keep the target away from crowds or unknown persons. That is virtually impossible with those who are voted into office. Because the numbers of democracies have grown dramatically since the early 1980's, assassination has become more likely as there are growing numbers of government officials who must expose themselves to voters. Personal protection has, therefore, become a rapidly growing, worldwide profession.

Kidnap avoidance involves the same techniques and principles associated with assassination avoidance. The chief difference is that American kidnap targets are likely to be businessmen rather than politicians or government officials. This facet of international terrorism is a murky one. No one knows just how many Americans are kidnapped each year since the incidents are often not reported and ransoms are usually negotiated and paid in secret. It is known that a large American insurance conglomerate, the Chubb Group, offers standard kidnap policies for U.S. commercial concerns operating abroad.

Growth in the numbers of American companies sending employees overseas has resulted in a two-tier kidnap coverage system. Typically, small companies usually take out policies that provide between one and five million-dollar ransom for an annual premium of between $750 and $1,500 depending on the location. Normally, U.S. companies buy coverage for all their employees sent to foreign sites. Larger companies may take out the maximum coverage, a $25,000,000 policy.[19]

The most dramatic terrorist technique is to openly take hostages, threaten their lives and make demands. Typically, hostage takers will promise the return of the hostages if they are given safe passage out of the country, a sum of money and the revision of some government policy or action. The hostages are sometimes the passengers aboard an airliner, ship, bus or train and sometimes the occupants of a building. An example of the latter type of incident occurred in 1977, when Hanafi Muslim terrorists seized several buildings in Washington, DC.

Hijackings come in several varieties. Thankfully, sky-jackings are not the massive problem they used to be. In a three-year span, 1968 to 1971, there were 200 passenger aircrafts taken over by some malcontent, one every nine days. Only ten of those seizures were judged political in nature, but the events of those days spawned the elaborate airport security procedures we are all still practicing and paying for.[20]

The next year, 1972, saw what was probably the single most influential event in the history of modem terrorism. The Arab terrorist group, Black September, killed two and took nine other Israelis hostages during the Olympic games in Munich, Germany. Subsequent rescue attempts by German authorities cost all of the hostages, five of the terrorists and one policeman their lives. Three surviving terrorists managed to return to their bloody careers.[21]

This incident caused European nations to recruit, organize, equip, and employ professionally trained counter-terrorist teams. Within a decade, the practice spread. By 1982, there were 41 nations that had produced such organizations, including the United States.[22]

The Western counter-terrorist teams kept in close contact and developed tactics to use in hostage barricade situations.[23] And, they learned from a number of terrorist incidents. In October 1977, the German team, GSG-9, rescued the passengers of a hijacked Lufthansa Boeing 727 at Mogadishu airport in Somalia. By the early 1990's, GSG-9 had grown to some 35 members. In June 1993, it tracked down and killed a Red Army Faction terrorist, Wolfgang Grams. In August of the same year, the German team staged another storming of a hijacked KLM aircraft on the ground at Dusseldorf. The team subdued the lone Egyptian gunman without firing a shot.[24]

From the very beginning, the most active of the European counter-terrorist teams has been the French Gendarmerie unit Groupe Intervention Gendarmerie Nationale (GIGN). Rarely numbering more than 60 members, the unit has participated in a number of counter-terrorist actions in France and abroad beginning with a dramatic rescue of thirty kidnapped French school children in Djibouti in February 1976.

In December 1994, GIGN performed its most widely publicized feat, the liberation of 170 hostages aboard Air France Flight 8969. The counter-terrorist organization killed four members of the Armed Islamic Group, a particularly murderous terrorist band that had been responsible for the deaths of 80 foreigners in Algeria prior to their seizure of the Airbus A300.[25]

The most celebrated counter-terrorist operation of the British team occurred in May 1980. The hostage-taking at Princes Gate and the Iranian Embassy by Iraqi-inspired terrorists lasted for six days and ended when a contingent from the Special Air Service Regiment stormed the building, freed 20 hostages, and killed all but one of the terrorists.[26] Studying these and other rescue operations, Western counter-terrorist teams gradually developed a set of procedures for dealing with hostage barricade situations.

The first tactical principle derived from this experience is to establish and maintain a double security ring. The outer-ring prevents anyone from entering or communicating with those in the hostage holding site. Those who man the inner-ring maintain surveillance of the hostage site.

Secondly, the rescue element must develop an emergency action plan. The plan may not be a good one and might just be a rush into the hostage holding site, but it is essential to have an action scheme should terrorists begin execution of the hostages.

The third principle has to do with gaining control. It is vital that the counter-terrorist elements have as much control of the event as possible. If possible, officials should handle all communications going into and out of the site. This will usually be difficult to achieve if the incident is in a populated region, particularly one in the United States. Typically, the terrorists will attempt to establish communications with the news media, a situation highly desirable to those reporters who seek the notoriety of becoming a part of the story they report. The terrorist has a message to publicize, and if his only communication is with police authorities, that message is apt to go unheralded.

If telephone service is available at the hostage holding site, it should be routed exclusively to the counter-terrorist command post. If television or commercial radio reception is possible at the site, it should be jammed. If necessary, terrorists should be given secure radio communication equipment to converse with negotiators.

A fourth principle is to exploit every entry and information access point to the site. This includes audio, visual, and physical entry positions. The one thing that there is never enough of at a hostage barricade site is information. And, a rescue plan should present the terrorists with overwhelming force from every conceivable direction. This coincides with the fifth principle, to develop and rehearse a deliberate rescue plan, and if possible, gradually abandon or revise the emergency plan.

There are two principles to observe after the execution of a rescue operation: preservation of evidence and immediate debriefings of hostages and rescuers. Of immediate concern to the counter-terrorist force is the possibility that a terrorist has concealed himself among the hostages after the rescue has been effected. This actually happened during the Princes Gate operation. So, everyone at the site has to tell his or her story and that is best done, one-on-one, in private. And, every hostage holding site is a crime scene and should be treated as such.

The foremost consideration in the mind of a counter-terrorist official facing a nuclear, chemical, or biological threat or incident is evacuation. The potential for mass murder is so stark that all other priorities pale in comparison. This condition will exist as long as the public has no protective masks or protective clothing, a situation that is expected to last into the foreseeable future. In order to direct evacuation or deal with a chemical, radiological, or biological event, law enforcement officials must be given protective clothing and masks. Special consideration must be given to wind direction. There are, however, some preventative measures to think about.

The most likely type of organization to use chemical, nuclear, or biological weapons is the single most rapidly growing type of terrorist band, radical religious groups. If surveillance is to be prioritized, these organizations bear the closest examination. In 1968, when terrorist organizations first began to be listed internationally, none of the eleven original groups were predominantly of a religious character. In 1980, there were only two such bands out of a total of 64. But by 1992, there were eleven such organizations.

These groups have been the most willing terrorist organizations to use or threaten to use weapons of mass murder, often believing in the sacrifice of themselves, their enemies, and innocents can be a divine act blessed by the deity.[27] The March 1995 use of the nerve gas, sarin, in a Japanese subway that killed 12 and injured over 5,000, was the act of the religious cult Aum Shinrikyo. And, there is little doubt about the nature of a related group attempting to mix enough sodium cyanide and sulfuric acid to create sufficient cyanide gas to kill between 10,000 and 20,000 commuters.[28] Religious terrorists constitute a special and potentially powerful threat.

The United States is poorly prepared for a domestic chemical weapons incident. It has only been since late 1995 that a limited number of law enforcement officers have been attending the Army's Chemical Defense Training facility at Fort McClellan, Alabama.[29] And, the lack of detection equipment in the hands of civil authorities ensures that there will be great confusion and a delay in applying the correct type of antidote to victims.

Preventive considerations for nuclear terrorism is the special province of the Department of Energy's Nuclear Emergency Search Team (NEST). This organization, whose domestic deployments are coordinated by the FBI, has a limited capability to detect gamma rays and neurons, both of which may indicate that a nuclear weapon is within a hundred feet or a couple of hundred yards. The team is skilled in disablement as well as detection. NEST has been in operation since a 1974 incident in Boston where the FBI was informed of a nuclear threat and a demand for $200,000. Since that time it has responded to over 80 incidents, all of which have turned out like that first one, a hoax.[30]

The counter-terrorist official who treats the news media with contempt jeopardizes his mission. It is essential to put terrorists, reporters, news publications, and news broadcasts into perspective. One of the standard, but nonetheless valid, cliches used to describe a terrorist hijacking is that the terrorist's aim was to hijack the media. More often than not, the entire idea of an act of political or religious terrorism is to gain publicity for an otherwise unworthy cause.

Whether or not news media professionals want to be a part of the story, they are likely to influence the terrorism story they cover because they possess the keys to what the terrorist wants. Indeed a rough, but usually reliable, test of whether a terrorist is acting on political rather than criminal motives is his demand for access to the news media. If that demand is not present, as was the case in many Latin American kidnappings, the act is likely born of criminal, not political, intent.

Nothing about this news media "hijacking" is new. In 1907, the famous novelist Joseph Conrad had his title character in *The Secret Agent* give-up his professorial career and move to a small, secluded house where he began to build bombs. He constructs an explosive device to destroy the Greenwich Observatory as a dramatic, widely heralded demonstration against science. Conrad's work was a successful effort to capitalize on the spate of anarchist terrorist bombings of the era. The Unabomber, Theodore J. Kaczynski, was an avid reader of Conrad and used the alias of "Konrad" or "Conrad" for many of his mail bombs. Kaczynski was obviously attempting to replicate a violence-publicity-anti-technology sequence that was almost a century old.[31]

As Joseph Conrad knew, reporters will flock to the scene of a terrorist incident and they can contribute to murder and jeopardize the success of rescue attempts. It has happened before. In the 1977 Hanafi Muslim hostage taking in Washington, DC, a local TV cameraman caught the lifting of a basket of food to an upper floor of a building in his camera lens. There, eleven people who had escaped the terrorists' attention were hiding. Through a broadcast, the terrorists discovered their oversight. Fortunately, the eleven were rescued before they, too, joined the hostages. The Hanafi leader, Khaalis, communicated with a reporter by telephone that, because of his publication deadline, pressed the terrorist for a decision. And yet another reporter, through ignorance, linked Khaalis with a terrorist group the Hanafi hated, creating an outburst where a hostage was threatened with death.

In the same year, during the hijacking of Lufthansa Flight 181, a German reporter discovered the dispatch of Bonn's counter-terrorist team, GSG-9 and announced their imminent arrival at the hostage holding site. German media reports also compromised the fact that the airplane's captain was secretly communicating information about the terrorists, an action that resulted in the murder of the pilot by the leader of the terrorists, Zuhaair Akache.

During the 40-plus days of U.S. Brigadier General James Dozier's capture in 1982, the most complete information the Red Brigade kidnappers obtained on the general and his family was provided by the U.S. news media.[32] And during the 1980's, former American hostage David Jacobsen, being held in Lebanon, revealed he was given beatings when the U.S. news media reported he was delivering "hidden messages" while reciting the speeches he had been given by his terrorist captors.

Not all news media is so destructive or careless with the information they discover or assume. For example, during the lengthy Teheran hostage crisis of 1979-1980, several news organizations discovered Canadian diplomats were hiding six American employees of the U.S. Embassy. These news media companies refused to publish or broadcast that information.[33]

U.S. news media coverage of terrorism got bad marks from the American people during the 1980's, but this attitude did not result in much change. The Gallup polling organization reported 51% of respondents stated terrorists were getting too much coverage, 60% believed that coverage was increasing the chances of future terrorist acts, and most believed media treatment of terrorism lengthened captivity time for hostages. Furthermore, the majority of the public believed terrorists were manipulating the news media. Regardless of public sentiment, Americans continue to watch TV stories dealing with terrorism and eagerly buy print media to get more details on the same events.[34]

Since there is no profit in condemning news media and no legal possibility of halting reporting of terrorist activities, counter-terrorist officials have to find ways to work with journalists and broadcasters. The first principle is to provide as much information as possible to the news media--and do it as often as possible. The theory behind this tenet is that the more time reporters spend with officials and the more they become dependent on the government for information, the less time they will have to develop other sources of information.

Secondly, the problem news media personalities have created in past terrorist events should be openly discussed with news media editors, producers, and journalists. And, law enforcement officials should not wait for a terrorist event to hold these discussions. While reporters and broadcasters will undoubtedly reject advice about how they conduct themselves, most will want to avoid certain public ridicule if they were to repeat some of the errors mentioned above. Finally, terrorists should win nothing, as they surely will if we begin to abandon our notions of a free press.

In responding to terrorism, we should be prepared to use ten times the resources we would ordinarily spend on another type of crime. The interaction between politicians, terrorists, the counter-terrorist bureaucracy, terrorist analysts, and the news media causes this distortion. There are some general responses to terrorism that should be followed. The right resources and right counter-terrorist organization should be brought to bear as soon as possible. Every effort should be made to penetrate a terrorist organization, create public awareness of the problem, protect us against the terrorist, and effectively manage information dealing with terrorism. Finally, if at all possible, preemptive action should at least be recommended.

Tactical responses to bombing include the obvious separation of bomb and target, blocking the trigger, and securing the evidence. Avoiding the suspicious package or letter, varying a subject's routine, blocking exterior views, and avoiding crowds can on occasion prevent assassinations and kidnappings.

Hostage barricade situations are the most complex of terrorist events. The first order of business is to establish inner and outer security rings. Second, an emergency rescue plan must be established. Every effort to gain control of the situation and exploit every access and vantagepoint must be made. A deliberate rescue plan has to be created and rehearsed. After the plan is executed, evidence must be preserved and all people who were at the site have to be carefully debriefed.

The first consideration of a suspected chemical, biological, or nuclear terrorist event is evacuation. In these cases, terrorist groups with religious motivations should be placed under surveillance before all others. However, we should recognize that the country is poorly prepared for this type of attack.

The first principle in dealing with terrorist related news media affairs is to provide as much information as often as possible to journalists and broadcasters. Secondly, past terrorist-related news media problems should be discussed with news media editors, producers, and journalists. Finally, we must cede as little as possible to terrorists including any of our freedoms. Any victory for them is a defeat for us—it is a zero sum game.

***Rod Paschall**, a free-lance consultant and writer, is a 1959 graduate of West Point and first joined U.S. Army Special Forces in 1961. Commands include an "A" detachment in Vietnam, a battalion of the 5th Special Forces Group, and Delta Force. Staff assignments included the Special Operations Division of the Joint Chiefs of Staff. He is the author of Critical Incident Management (1992), LIC 2010: Special Operations & Unconventional Warfare (1990), and The Defeat of Imperial Germany (1989).*

NOTES AND REFERENCES

[1] Hanan, Alon. *Countering Palestinian-Terrorism in Israel: Toward A Policy Analysis of Countermeasures* (Santa Monica: Rand Corporation, 1980).

[2] Clifford Krauss, "Now, How Low Can Crime Go?" *The New York Times* (January 28, 1996), p. E5. Figures taken from Department of State, *Patterns of Global Terrorism, 1995* (Washington, DC, 1996), p. 74, and additions of the figures on domestic terrorism taken from news reports.

[3] Penny Loeb, "Running Off the Rails," *U.S. News and World Report (May27, 1996), p.51.*

[4] Former CIA Director Stansfield Turner. "Let's Deal for our Hostages," *Christian Science Monitor* (October 26, 1988), p. 13.

[5] Of all the elements in the iron pentagonal, the news media has been the only element to occasionally subject itself to self-criticism. This most forcibly happened in a reaction of some members of that media to the excesses of their fellow journalists during and briefly after the 1986 hijacking of TWA 847. See the commentary of Mortimer B. Zuckerman, editor *of U.S. News and World Report*, "Playing the Terrorists' Game" *U.S. News and World Report (June 9, 1986), p.* 86; the full page Times Mirror infomercial *The New York Times (October* 9, 1986), p. A36 and the news media observations of Ambassador Paul Bremer, "Terrorism and the Media," lecture given at the U.S. Army War College, Carlisle Barracks, Pennsylvania, November 6, 1987.

[6] FBI Director J. Freeh, "FBI Hasn't Tried to Change the Rules in Bombing Aftermath," *The New York Times* (May 14,1995), p. E14.

[7] Christopher S. Wren, "Long Arm of U.S. Law Gets Longer," *The New York Times* (July 7, 1996), p. E4.

[8] *Associated Press* news release, "Clinton orders anti-terrorist task force," (July 16, 1996).

[9] Tim Weiner, "Clinton Endorses Anti-Terrorism Measure," *The New York Times* (May 9, 1996), p. A18. Jerry Gray, "F.B.I. Chief Pleads for Anti-Terror Firepower," *The New York Times* (August 2, 1996), p. A12. It is estimated by the author that classified spending by the federal government on anti and counter-terrorist programs amount to about $600 million per year. If that estimate is correct, the United States government will be spending about $1.2 billion per year on terrorism-related programs. This, of course, does not include the amount airlines are spending on inspection procedures or any such commercial or private security spending.

[10] A good example of infiltration was in the 1996 case of Arizona's Viper Militia. An informant penetrated the group despite its initiation oath that required members to kill infiltrators. James Brooke, "Agents Seize Arsenal of Rifles and Bomb-Making Material in Arizona Militia Inquiry" *The New York Times* (July 3, 1996), p. A18.

[11] Author's experience during the early 1980's as the commander of Delta Force and engaged in response to an anti-U.S. terrorist event in Italy.

[12] James Berry Motley, "Terrorism," *National Defense (January, l985) pp. 41.*

[13] Department of Justice, Federal Bureau of Investigation, *Terrorism in the United States, 1982-1992* (Washington, D.C, 1993), p. 10. While the Department of State, in its yearly calculation of international terrorism, makes a distinction between firebombs and bombs designed for blast effects, the FBI made no such separate categories in its 1993 publication. The 1995 international figures for both firebombing and blast bombing constitute about 70 percent of all terrorist incidents. See *Patterns of Global Terrorism, 1995,* p. 70.

[14] Jeffery Smith, "Passenger Departs, Nightmare Begins," *The Washington Post* (July 21,1996), p. 1.

[15] Steven Erlanger, "U.S. Commanders at Saudi Base Defend Efforts to Avoid Attack," *The New York Times* (June 28, 1996), p. 1. Philip Shenon, "FBI Finds Clues to the Truck Used in Saudi Bombing," *The New York Times* (June 30, 1996), p. 1.

[16] Rand Corporation analyst, Bruce Hoffman, "Responding to Terrorism Across the Technological Spectrum," lecture given at the U.S. Army War College, Carlisle Barracks, Pennsylvania, July 15, 1994.

[17] Philip Shenon, "Saudis Rebuffed U.S. Efforts to Interrogate 1995 Bombers" *The New York Times* (June 28, 1996), p. 1.

[18] Department of Justice, Federal Bureau of Investigation, *Terrorism in the United States 1982-1992* (Washington, DC, 1993), p. 10.

[19] Edwin McDowell, "Business Travel," *The New York Times* (September 13, 1995), p. D8.

[20] Richard Clutterbuck, *Protest and the Urban Guerrilla* (New York: Abelard-Schuman, 1974), pp. 256-258.

[21] Francis M. Watson, *Political Terrorism: The Threat and the Response (Washington, DC:* Robert B. Luce Co., 1976), pp. 5-6.

[22] Author's personal experience as the commander of the U.S. Delta Force.

[23] Claire Sterling, *The Terror Network: The Secret War of International Terrorism* (New York: Rinehart and Winston, 198 1), pp. 287-289.

[24] Samuel M. Katz, "The Best of the Best," *Armed Forces Journal* (January 1995), p. 42.

[25] GIGN's adventure in Djibouti is detailed in Gilbert Defiez, *La Brigade des Mission Impossibles* (Paris: Jacques Grancher, 1979), pp. 39-50. A detailed description of the Air France Flight 8969 hijacking and rescue is found in Thomas Sancton, "Anatomy of a Hijack," *Time* (January 9, 1995), pp. 54-57.

[26] The Princes Gate action, Operation Nimrod, is detailed in Tony Geraghty, *Inside the S.A.S.* (New York: Ballantine Books, 1980), pp. 187-210.

[27] Bruce Hoffman, "Responding to Terrorism Across the Technological Spectrum," lecture given at the U.S. Army War College, Carlisle Barracks, Pennsylvania, July 15, 1994.

[28] Nicholas D. Kristof, "Japanese Police Foil Gas Attack in Subway," *New York Times* (May 7, 1995), p. 10.

[29] Douglas Pasternak, "Planning for the Worst," *News and World Report* (June 24, 1996), p. 61.

[30] William J. Broad, "Preparing to Meet Terrorists Bearing Plutonium," *The New York Times* (August 1, 1993), p. E3.

[31] Terry Teachout, "Mad Loner Builds Perfect Bomb," *The New York Times* (July 13, 1996), p. 19.

[32] U.S. Army intelligence analyst, Dr. Rudolf Levy, "Terrorism and the Mass Media," *Military Intelligence* (October-December, 1985), pp. 34-37.

[33] Ambassador Paul Bremer III, "Terrorism and the Media," lecture given at the U.S. Army War College, Carlisle Barracks, Pennsylvania, November 6, 1987.

[34] *The New York Times* (October 9, 1986), p. A36.

TERRORISM AND LOCAL LAW ENFORCEMENT: NEW COMPLEXITY, NEW FEARS

Matt L. Rodriguez

There was a time when international terrorism was international terrorism and local law enforcement was local law enforcement. And, seldom did the two converge. Traditionally, the people in our country who were concerned with international terrorism were for the most part unconcerned with local law enforcement matters. And local law enforcement personnel, already overwhelmed with problems such as street gangs, domestic violence, handguns, and the like, were largely insulated from matters of international terrorism and all the foreign policy machinations and geopolitical intrigue involved in this complex issue.

Most local law enforcement executives, and especially our police officers out on the street, had the luxury of "not" having to make room for terrorism on the already ample platter of problems that we were dealing with. Events of recent years and months and weeks have changed all that, of course. If the bombing of the World Trade Center was a grim reminder that our major cities are not immune from international terrorism, the attack on the Murrah Federal Building in Oklahoma City shocked us into the reality that we face serious threats from within our own borders, as well from any number of single-issue and extremist groups. These two incidents demonstrate that the traditional tactics of international terrorists, tactics such as car bombings and attacks on air travel and other forms of public transportation, can increasingly be used against targets in our own country as well. If nothing else, today's terrorists have shown that they can, and will, strike anytime, anywhere. For local law enforcement, the impact has been immediate, profound, and above all, permanent.

Although we cannot know the precise, long-term implications on law enforcement, one thing is clear: Local law enforcement will never again have the luxury of being able to insulate ourselves from the issue of terrorism, whether domestic or international in scope. All of the serious problems we have traditionally dealt with, the street crime, the gangs, the drugs, the guns, are only compounded now by the gnawing threat of terrorism and the spontaneous, irrational, desperate, and ultimately deadly forms it can take.

Terrorism has forever added a new layer and a new level of complexity to the already complex job of local law enforcement. And we must begin preparing now for the challenges that lie ahead. For example, local law enforcement will need additional training in understanding terrorism and appreciating its subtleties and complexities. We will need help in responding to current threats and preparing for future trends. We will need technical assistance in recognizing and implementing new technologies to battle terrorism. And we will need help in building new partnerships with federal counter-terrorism officials, with members of the national security and diplomatic corps, with behavioral scientists, and with all the others who have traditionally been involved in fighting terrorism on an international level.

Of course, this new environment of truly global terrorism, this "New World disorder," will mean dramatic changes for more than just local law enforcement. Just as recent events have forever changed the perspective of municipal police officials, so too have they changed the outlook of international counter-terrorism experts.

Just as local law enforcement can no longer insulate themselves from the international aspects of terrorism, neither can this "Cloak and Dagger" set remain isolated from local law enforcement. And just as local law enforcement officials desperately need to learn more about terrorism from a global and foreign policy perspective, so too must the international counter-terrorism community learn more about this issue from a domestic and localized perspective.

In the future, locally gathered intelligence information will be critically important, on everything from sophisticated drug-dealing street gangs, to antigovernment extremist groups, to trafficking patterns in firearms and other weapons. Everyday, police officers in Chicago and other cities across the country gather information on local crime conditions and patterns, information that may have important national and international implications.

We need to develop not only the partnerships, but also the policies and the information systems that will allow us to collect and share this type of information more quickly and analyze and process it more effectively. We need to look toward developing new and secure networks for sharing operational and intelligence information, whether that information originates in Iraq or Illinois, Dhahran or Dade County, Florida.

In closing, let me point out that the challenges facing those of us dealing with international terrorism are not unlike the challenges of those of us who are dealing with homicide, gang warfare, and other problems of urban America. In both instances, we are forced to confront not just the problem itself, but also the public's "perceptions" of the problem of what we, as public officials, are doing to address it. One of the best-kept "secrets" in our country today is that serious crime is down, and down dramatically in our major urban areas, over the last few years. But the public's perception of crime, its fear of crime, is "up." It almost seems in inverse proportion to the actual decline in the official crime statistics. We can expect a similar pattern with respect to terrorism.

While the State Department reports that the number of international terrorism incidents has generally declined since the late 1980's, the public's fear of terrorism has not subsided and in fact is likely to increase in the future, especially as terrorism hits closer and closer to home. For local law enforcement officials, managing the public's perceptions of crime, and reducing their level of fear, have become integral parts of managing and solving the problem itself. From a community policing standpoint in particular, we have learned that helping residents address their fears is often a necessary first step to helping them address their actual crime problems and improve the quality of life in their neighborhoods. Managing public perceptions will be equally crucial from a counter-terrorism perspective as well. As we work to root out and prevent terrorism itself, here at home and abroad, we must also work to reduce the public's fears and, thus, help maintain the freedoms an quality of life we enjoy. This will be achieved, not through slick public relations campaigns or some sleight-of-hand marketing techniques, but through real and sincere demonstrations that we understand peoples' fears and are taking concrete steps to address those fears. I am confident that by working together (local law enforcement, the research community, and international terrorism experts), we can work through the new complexity of truly global terrorism.

***Matt L. Rodriguez** is the former Superintendent of the Chicago Police Department. In his thirty-six years of professional service with the department, Rodriguez has risen through the ranks, including service in Patrol, Criminal Investigation, Organized Crime, Vice Control, Gambling, Training, Youth Crime, and Technical Services. Superintendent Rodriguez developed "Together We Can: A Strategic Plan for Reinventing the Chicago Police Department," which outlined the Chicago Alternative Policing Strategy, or Chicago's now nationally renowned implementation of Community Policing. He is an adjunct professor at the University of Illinois at Chicago, teaching Criminal Justice Administration and Organized Crime Enforcement. Rodriguez is the author of numerous articles in publications, such as the FBI Law Enforcement Bulletin and The Police Chief, on topics ranging from innovative technical programs to organized crime trends and investigations.*

INDEX

Abortion, 151-153, 156, 159-160
    Damages, 159
Achille Lauro, 113
Active Service Unit, 132
Adair, Johnny, 132, 133, 136, 138, 139, 149
Adams, Gerry, 134, 136, 137, 141-142, 144, 145, 147, 150
Afghanistan, 27, 172
Africa, 7, 21, 28, 97
    North, 180
    South, 21
    West, 31
Airlines – see Aviation
Air France Flight 8969, 204, 212
Air Traffic, 6, 43
    Control, 16, 18, 29, 45
Akache, Zuhaair, 208
Algeria, 105, 172, 204
Anarchist's Cookbook, 153
Anglo-Irish Agreement, 138
Animal Liberation Front (ALF), 151-152, 154-156, 158
    Founded, 155
    FBI Terrorism List, 155
Animal Rights, 151, 152-153, 155-159, 165, 166, 168
    Groups
        Animal Rights Militia (ARM), 154, 155
        ARKANGEL, 152
        "Justice Department," 155, 159
    Sabotage, 152, 153, 157-159
    Tactics, 156-157
    Types of Attacks, 154-155
Animal Rights Militia (ARM), 154, 155
Anthrax, 29, 184, 185, 186
Anti-Fascist Militia, 166
Anti-Racist Action, 168
Argentina, 199
ARKANGEL, 152
Armed Islamic Group, 172, 204
Arms, 5, 26, 107, 146, 176, 194
    Trafficking, 3, 26, 216
        Northern Ireland, 139
Arson, 67, 103, 154, 155, 158, 159, 161, 198
Aruba, 33
Asia, and, 9, 183
    Latin America, 119
    Middle East, 119, 183
    Narco-Terrorism, 119
    Southwest, 26

Assassination, 121, 130, 131, 132, 135, 139, 191, 196, 197, 198, 201, 202, 203, 209
Asset Forfeiture, 22
ATF - see Bureau of Alcohol, Tobacco and Firearms
Aum Shinrikyo, 29, 30, 37, 206
Australia, 7, 29, 54
Aviation Security, 113-116
Aviation Security and Antiterrorism Act of 1996, 113
Ayoob, Massod, 87

Bacteria – see also Bioterrorism, 184
Baghdad, 43, 105
Bahamas, 6
Balkan, 26
Banking, 10-12, 15, 22, 32, 48, 51
Barletta, Giacomo, 173, 180
Basque ETA, 27
Begley, Thomas, 136, 137
Beirut, 57, 59, 194, 198
Biological, 174, 184-189, 192, 205
    Agents, 183, 187
        Availability of, 183
        From Russia, 183
    Attacks, 13, 185, 198, 209
    Warfare, 121, 124, 183
    Weapons, 29, 30, 105, 126, 183-184, 187, 206
        Anthrax, 29, 184, 185, 186
        Botulism, 29, 184-186
Bioterrorism, 184-188
    Bacteria, 184
    Prevention/Preparedness, 186-188
    Toxins, 30, 184, 186
    Viruses, 29, 30, 173, 184, 186
Black September, 203
Black Tigers of Eelam, 52
Bolivia, 32
Bomb – see Explosives
    Manchester, England, 147
Botulism, 29, 184-186
Branch Davidian, 109, 110
Bratty, Joe, 131
Bremer, Paul, 210, 213
Britain – see Great Britain
British Columbia, 151, 154, 155, 158, 166
Broad, William J., 213
Brooke, James, 211
Bruce, Steve, 150
Brunet, Robin, 162
Builta, Jeff, 159, 163
Bureau of Alcohol, Tobacco and Firearms (ATF), 66, 110, 196
Burglary, 79
Burma, 27
Burton, John, 146

Camp, Jeff, 92-94
Canada
    Abortion, 151, 156, 159-160
    Animal Rights, 151, 153, 155, 159, 166, 168
    Canadian Security Intelligence Act, 61
    Canadian Security Intelligence Service (CSIS), 61-63, 71, 72, 161
    EARTH FIRST! Activists, 152, 153, 157, 158, 165, 168

Environmental Crime, 151, 152, 153, 156, 157, 158, 159, 165, 166, 174
Ecotage, 153, 157
Eco-Terrorism, 157, 158
Left-Wing Groups, 165-170
Montreal, 175
Royal Canadian Mounted Police (RCMP), 61-63, 71, 73, 165, 169
Security Intelligence Review Committee (SIRC), 62
Toronto Humane Society, 152
Vancouver, British Columbia, 72, 151, 154
Canadian Security Intelligence Act, 61
Canadian Security Intelligence Service (CSIS), 61-63, 71, 72, 161
Carter, President Jimmy, 193
Center for Disease Control (CDC), 37, 187
Central Intelligence Agency (CIA), 43, 61, 79, 184
Chemical Weapons, 29-30, 105, 123, 126, 159, 183, 184, 186, 187, 192, 198, 206
Sarin, 29, 206
Phosgene, 29
Sodium Cyanide, 29, 206
Chicago Terrorist Task Force (CTTF), 65-69
Chicago Police Department (CPD), 65-69, 218
China, 7, 8, 19, 54
Clare, Paul K., 129, 148, 150
Clinton, President William, 51, 80, 115, 142, 143, 145, 146
U.S. Peace initiative, 146
Clutterbuck, Richard, 212
COHORT Program, 96-98, 103
Cold War, 1, 2, 7, 25, 26, 35, 43, 51
Colen, Marc Steven, 119, 126, 127
Collins, Barry C., 127
Colombia, and, 2, 132, 149
FARC, 2
M-19, 2, 120
Mafia, 2, 122
Palace of Justice takeover, 120
Samper, Ernesto, 123
Shining Path, 2, 26
Commission on Global Governance, 21
Communist Party, 35
Conrad, Joseph, 207
Contract Killers, 5, 8
Cooper, Jeff, 79, 87
Corruption, 3, 13, 20, 24, 25, 27, 32, 34, 35
Counterfeiting, 2
Craig, Colin "Crazy," 131
Craig, Jim, 130
Criminal Intelligence Directorate, 72, 73, 169
Cruise O'Brien, Conor, 144
Cuba, 114
Cult, 28, 102, 206
Cyber-terrorism, 18, 52, 121, 125
Cyprus, 63, 161

Dallas Morning News, 84
Darlack, Dave, 94
David Organization, 159

Democratic Unionist Party, 131
Department of Defense, 15, 96, 117, 125, 127, 185
  Bioterrorism climate, 185
  Military Operations in U.S., 125
Desert Storm, 45, 46, 107, 183
Deutch, John, 43
Devlin, Bernadette, 131, 149
Djibouti, 204, 212
Dominican Republic, 6
Donahue, Frank J., 113, 117
Drug
  Cartels, 2, 119, 120, 122, 124, 127
  Control, 123-124
  Interdiction, 123-124
  Laboratories in U.S, 124.
  Trafficking, 1, 2, 6, 11, 22, 26-27, 31, 33, 38, 39, 119-120, 122, 123
    Colombia, 122
    Middle East, 119
Dublin, 135, 136, 138, 139

EARTH FIRST!, 152, 153, 157, 158, 165, 168
  Foreman, Dave, 157-158
Earth Liberation Army, 159
Earth Night Action Group, 158
Ebola, 29, 30, 184, 185
Ecotage, 153, 157
Eco-Terror, 157, 158
  Tactics, 156
Egypt, 172, 204
El Rukn, 68
Elder, Ray, 131
Electric, 15, 43, 48, 51, 52, 92, 110
Electronic, 10, 15, 45, 123, 200
  Mailboxes, 20
  Networks, 13
  Surveillance, 22, 66, 68
Ellistadt, Edward, 127
Embezzlement, 17
England, 6, 18, 31, 54, 121, 139, 141, 142, 152, 154, 189
  Abortion, 159
  Animal Rights, 152-155, 158
  Environmental Crime, 157-159
  Manchester Bombing, 147
Environmental Crime, 157
  Ecotage, 153, 157
  Tree Spiking, 153, 157, 158
Environmentalists, see also Eco-Terror, 151, 152, 153, 157, 158, 159
  David Organization, 159
  EARTH FIRST!, 152, 153, 157, 158, 165, 168
  Earth Liberation Army, 159
  Earth Night Action Group, 158
  Greenpeace, 152, 157, 165
Erlanger, Steven, 212
Escobar, Pablo, 23
Espionage, 52, 62
Europe, 26, 63, 55, 156, 161, 166, 167, 171, 175, 180, 193, 203, 204
  Eastern, 7, 22, 119, 120
  Western, 6, 7, 9, 14, 26, 85, 101
Evan Mecham Eco-Terrorist International Conspiracy (EMETIC), 158
Explosives, 28, 30, 52, 67, 78, 79, 94, 101, 110-112, 114, 116,

124, 139, 150, 154, 158, 159, 184, 199, 200, 207
Airliner, 29, 121, 199
Bombs, Bombing, 28, 42,44, 51, 57, 58, 65, 67, 68, 77-79, 83, 94, 96, 102, 105, 107, 108, 111-113, 121, 132, 133, 135-142, 145-147, 150, 153-156, 160-161, 165-166, 188, 191, 194, 196, 198, 199-202, 207, 209, 211, 215
Kingman, 79, 109
Letter Bomb, 155-156
Extortion, 17, 18, 31, 34, 36, 131, 178

FALN- see Fuerzas Armadas de Liberacion Nacional Puertorriquena
Fax, 20
Federal Aviation Administration (FAA), 113-117
Office of Civil Aviation Security, 114
Federal Bureau of Investigation (FBI), 36, 65, 68, 69, 82, 85, 89, 94, 102, 106, 108, 158, 184, 195, 196, 206, 211, 218
Capabilities Against Terrorism, 65-66
Eco-Terrorism, 157, 158
Terrorism List, 155
Feeney, Brian, 137
Finance, 26, 48, 51, 68
Fire Walls, 17
Flu, 184
Foreman, Dave, 157-158
Fortier, Michael, 97, 101, 102, 109, 111
France, 6, 172, 204, 212
Fraud, 9, 17, 31
Freeh, Louis J., 210
Fuerzas Armadas de Liberacion Nacional Puertorriquena (FALN), 65, 68

Garcia, Michael J., 199
Gas, 15, 43, 44, 48, 51, 160
General Accounting Office, 15
Germ Warfare, 183
Germany, 6, 7, 167, 203, 210
East, 119
IRA Bombing, 147
West, 102
Ghana, 31
Gibney, Damien, 135
Gibney, Jim, 135
GIGN- see Groupe Intervention Gendarmerie Nationale
Global Information Infrastructure (GII), 15, 17
Gompert, David, 15
Grams, Wolfgang, 204
Grancher, Jacques, 212
Gray, Jerry, 211
Great Britain – see also England
Greenpeace, 152, 157, 165
Watson, Paul, 152, 157, 165
Greysteel Massacre, 129, 137-140
Gritz, Bo, 85, 110
Groupe Intervention Gendarmerie Nationale (GIGN), 204, 212
GSG-9, 204, 207

Hacker, 16, 17, 32, 42, 52, 92
Hamas, 172, 196
Hamelton, David, 131
Hanafi Muslim Terrorist, 203, 207
Hanan, Alon, 210

Harder, Chuck, 84, 110
Hashish, 120
Hendron, Joe, 137
Heroin, 26, 35, 120
Hersley, John R., 108
Hijacking, 113, 114, 175, 193, 199, 203, 204, 207, 210, 212
Hill, Sean, 51, 54
Hillard, Terry, 65, 69
Hizballah, 120, 199
Hostages, 120, 193, 194, 203, 204, 205, 207, 208
 Barricade Situations, 192, 196, 198, 204, 205, 209
Hoffman, Bruce, 29, 212, 213
Hume, John, 141, 143, 144, 146
Hunt Retribution Squad (HRS), 155

Iacocca, Lee, 36
ICBM, 42
Illegal Aliens, 5
Illinois State Police (ISP), 65-68
Immigration and Naturalization Service, 68
Information, 6, 14, 20, 36, 41, 53, 59, 65, 69, 71
 Infrastructure, 15, 16, 17, 29, 30, 34, 36
 Management, 58, 197, 198
 Systems, 16, 17, 18, 19, 30
 Technology, 9, 15, 16, 33, 42, 43
 Warfare, 17, 41, 42, 44, 45
Intellectual Property, 17
INTERCENTER, 180
IRA – see Irish Republican Army
Iran, 171, 172, 183, 193, 194
 Embassy, 204
Iraq, 85, 105-107, 172, 183, 204, 217
Ireland, 129, 130, 134-139, 142-145, 147, 148, 150, 189, 196, 199
 Dublin, 135, 136, 138, 139
 Irish National Liberation Army, 130
Irish Republican Army (IRA), see also Provisional Irish Republican Army
 27, 129, 130, 140, 142, 147
Islam, 28, 44, 171-172, 204
Islamic Salvation Front, 172
Israel, 8, 27, 121, 172, 192-194, 196, 199, 203
 Terrorism Prevention, 192
Italy, 7, 36, 180, 211
 Mafia, 2, 8
 Red Brigade, 196, 208

Jacobsen, David, 208
Jamaica, 6
Japan, 14, 23, 29, 113, 206
John Birch Society, 84
Jordan, 172, 193
"Justice Department," 155, 159

Kaczynski, Theodore J., 207
Katz, Samuel M., 212
Khartoum, 59
Kidnapping, 28, 121, 192, 201, 202, 203, 204, 207, 208, 209
King, Larry, 143
Kingman Bombing, 79
Korea, 39, 67
 North, 183, 193
Kraus, Clifford, 210
Kristof, Nicholas D., 213

La Cosa Nostra – see Mafia
Lansky, Meyer, 12
Latin America, and, 8, 21, 202, 207
  Asia, 119
  Middle East, 119
  Narco-terrorism, 119
Lebanon, 120, 172, 194, 198, 208
Letter Bomb, 155-156
Libya, 68
Levy, Dr. Rudolf, 213
Loeb, Penny, 210
Loyalist, 129-140, 142, 143, 146, 148, 149, 150
  Billy "King Rat" Wright, 135
Luciano, Lucky, 36
Lufthansa Flight 181, 204, 207
Lipsha, Peter, 37

M-19, 2, 120
Mackenzie Institute, 167
Mafia, 173-176, 178
  Colombian, 2, 122
  History, 27, 36
  La Cosa Nostra, 2, 8, 177
  Russian, 33
Mail, 98, 154
  Bomb, 154-155, 165-166, 202, 207
  Cover, 77
Major, John, 141, 142
Manchester, 147
Manson, Charles, 28
Marburg, 184, 185
Marijuana, 120
Marxism, 28, 166, 193
Maskey, Alex, 134
Maurer, Keith, 91
McCrea, Reverend William, 131
McDonald, Frank, 183, 188, 189
McDowell, Edwin, 212
McGuinness, Martin, 135
McHugh, Scott, 57, 59
McLamb, Jack, 85, 110
McMichael, Gary, 130, 131
McMichael, John, 130, 131
McVeigh, Ed, 87
McVeigh, Timothy James, 77-112
  Action in Iraq and Medal, 107
  Assigned to Ft. Riley, KS, 100
  Assigned to West Germany, 103
  Assigned to Saudi Arabia, 104
  Experiments with Pipe Bombs, Explosives, 94-95
  Drug Experimentation, 111
  Graduated High School, 92
  Joins Army, 95
  Joins National Guard, 109
  Law Enforcement Contacts, 110-111
  Meets Terry Nichols, 99
  Promoted to Sergeant, 105
  Special Forces Assignment, 103
  Tim Tuttle Alias, 96
  Work at Burger King, 89, 91
  Work for Armored Car Company, 92-93
MDATF – see Militant Direct Action Task Force
Mercenaries, 27, 33
Mexico, 6, 47
Meyers, Kevin, 142

Middle East, and, 7, 27, 54, 63, 72, 120, 122, 161, 171, 172, 183
Asia, 119
Narco-Terrorism, 119
Migration, 6, 7, 8
Militant Direct Action Task Force (MDATF), 155, 166, 167
Militant Vegan, 152, 162
Military Assistance, 35
In U.S., 125
Militia, 4, 166, 211
Molander, Roger, 41
Money-Laundering, 9, 11, 12, 23, 32, 33, 34
Montreal, 72, 175
Morrison, Danny, 134
Morrison, Tommy, 132
Moscow, 59
Motley, James Berry, 211
Munich, 203
Olympics, 21
Murphy, Lenny, 137
Murrah Federal Building, 121, 215
Myers, Kevin, 150
Myers, Lawrence W., 77, 112

Narco-Terrorism, 119, 124, 125
Definition, 127
National Information Infrastructure (NII), 15, 16, 49
National Infrastructure Assurance Council, 53
National Liberation Front (FLN), 172
Naval War College, 185
Nelson, Brian, 149
Neo-Nazi, 166, 167
Netherlands Antilles, 33
New York Police Department, 65
New York Police Academy, 65
New York Times, 91, 210-213
News Media Coverage, 156, 208
Nichols, James, 79, 88
Nichols, Robert, 85
Nichols, Terry Lynn, 85, 88, 97, 99, 101, 102, 109, 110
Nicol, Wendy, 62, 71, 73, 165, 169
Nigeria, 7, 31
North America, 26, 63, 152, 155, 157, 159, 161
Northern Ireland, 130, 135-138, 142-145, 147, 148, 150, 196, 199
Arms Trafficking, 139
Gangsters, 131
Irish Republican Army, 27, 129, 130, 140, 142, 147
Ulster Defense Association, 130, 131, 133, 136-138, 149
Ulster Freedom Fighter, 130, 131, 133, 136-138, 149
Nuclear, 2, 157, 158, 195
Materials, 23, 25, 121, 205
War, 42, 192, 198, 206, 209
Weapons, 185
Nuclear Emergency Search Team (NEST), 206
Nunn, Sam, 49, 188

Office of Civil Aviation Security, 114
Oil, 9, 15, 43, 48, 51
Oklahoma City, 51, 57, 77, 79, 83, 84, 102, 108, 111, 112, 199, 215

Olypmic
Bombing, 57
Munich, 21, 203
Operation Nimrod, 213
Opium, 27, 35
Orcaforce, 157

Palestine, 21, 172, 199
Palestinian Authority, 172
Pan Am 103, 57, 103, 113, 115, 116, 199
Paris, Susan E., 162
Paschall, Rod, 191, 209, 210
Pasternak, Douglas, 213
Peace People, 132, 149
Pentagon, 3, 7, 96, 104, 187
People for the Ethical Treatment of Animals (PETA), 155, 156
Peru, , 26
PIRA, see Provisional IRA
Plague, 184, 185
PLO, 120
Posse Comitatus Act, 125
Private Industry, 48, 49, 53
President's Commission on Critical Infrastructure Protection (PCCIP), 51
Product Contamination, 154
Protestant Action Force, 137
Provisional IRA (PIRA) - see also Irish Republican Army, Sinn Fein, 131-150, 200
Active Service Unit, 132
Bombings, 133, 135, 136, 147
Sinn Fein, 132, 134, 143, 145, 146, 156
PROVOS, see Provisional IRA
Puerto Rico, 65, 68

Radical Religious Groups, 206
Radioactive, 30
Rand Corporation, 15, 16, 41, 126, 210, 212
Reagan, President Ronald, 50, 194, 198
Red Army Faction, 167, 204
Red Brigades, 196, 208
Red Hand Commando, 137
Refugees, 6, 7
Reynolds, Albert, 142
Ricin, 184, 185
Riddile, Andrew S., 41, 50
Rio de Janeiro, 14, 23
Robbery, 65, 67, 111
Rodriguez, Matt L., 215, 218
Rome, 59
Airport Massacre, 113
Royal Canadian Mounted Police (RCMP), 61-63, 71, 73, 165, 169
Royal Ulster Constabulary, 137, 138
Rule of Law, 14, 32, 161
Russia, 7, 8, 11, 12, 23, 29, 30, 31, 32, 33, 35, 36, 101, 119, 120, 122, 123, 183

Sabotage, 34, 46, 62
Animal Rights, 152, 153, 157-159
Sancton, Thomas, 212
Samper, Ernesto, 123
Saudi Arabia, 51, 57, 104, 171, 198
Schwarzkopf, Norman, 107
Scotland Yard, 157
Scott, Charles, 166
Sea Shepherd Conservation Society, 157

Secret Service, 66, 201
Security Intelligence Review Committee (SIRC), 62
Senate Permanent Committee on
 Investigations, 29
Shankill
 Bombing, 133, 135-136, 138, 140
 Butchers, 137
Shenon, Philip, 212
Shining Path, 2, 26
Sicily, 7, 177, 178
Sinn Fein, 129, 132-135, 139-148, 149, 150, 159
 Adams, Gerry, 134, 136, 137, 141-142, 144, 145, 147, 150
 Members Killed, 150
Skinheads Against Racial, 168
Smallpox, 184, 185
Smallwoods, Ray, 131
Smith, G. David, 61, 63, 151, 161
Smith, Jeffery, 211
Soldier of Fortune, 85, 100
Somalia, 204
South America, 166
Soviet Union, 6, 8, 11, 21, 22, 25, 31, 183
 Biological/Chemical Warfare, 183
Special Air Service Regiment (SAS), 204
Special Forces, 84, 85, 98, 101, 103, 104, 107, 108, 194, 210
Special Operations, 83, 108, 186, 210
Sterling, Claire, 212
Stickney, Brandon, 90, 95
Strom, Kevin, 110
Sudan, 172
Suicide Attacks, 171
Synthetic Drugs, 35

Tachau, Frank, 171, 172
Tajikistan, 38
Tamils, 26
Teachout, Terry, 213
Teheran Hostage Crisis, 208
Telecommunications, 13, 20, 48, 195
Terrorism, 2, 4, 13, 14, 21, 27, 30, 31, 34, 35, 36, 38, 41, 41, 44, 45, 46, 47, 52, 54, 57, 58, 59, 66, 67, 68, 71, 78, 111, 113, 119, 121, 122, 125, 127, 149, 151, 153, 155, 156, 158, 161, 167, 171, 172, 173, 174, 175, 176, 191, 192, 193, 194, 195, 196, 197, 198, 203, 206, 207, 208, 209, 215, 216, 217
 Bombings, 28, 42,44, 51, 57, 58, 65, 67, 68, 77-79, 83, 94, 96, 102, 105, 107, 108, 111-113, 121, 132, 133, 135-142, 145-147, 150, 153-156, 160-161, 165-166, 188, 191, 194, 196, 198, 199-202, 207, 209, 211, 215
 Cyber-terrorism, 18, 52, 121, 125
 Politics of, 193-194
Texas, 109, 122, 124, 155
Toronto Humane Society, 152
Toxins, 30, 184, 186
Transportation, 5, 13, 14, 15, 23, 48, 52, 113, 116, 117, 185, 193, 215
Tree Spiking, 153, 157, 158
Tularemia, 184, 185

Tunisia, 172
Turner, Stansfield, 210
Turner Diaries, 80, 97
Tuttle, Tim, 96
TWA 847, 113, 210

UDA – see Ulster Defense Association
UFF – see Ulster Defense Association
Ulster Defense Association (UDA), 130, 131, 133, 136-138, 149
Ulster Democratic Party, 131
Ulster Freedom Fighters (UFF), 130, 131, 133, 136-138, 149
Ulster Volunteer Force (UVF), 131, 132, 135, 136, 137, 139
Unabomber, 137, 202, 207
Unemployment, 7, 23
United Kingdom – see England
United States
  Abortion, 153
  Animal Rights, 153, 158-159
  Attorney, 67, 83, 199
  Department of Defense, 15, 96, 117, 125, 127, 185
  Department of State, 59, 210, 211
  Environmental Crime, 157
  Secret Service, 66, 201
UVF – see Ulster Volunteer Force
Uzbekistan, 38

Vancouver, British Columbia, 72, 151, 154
Venezuela, 7, 8
Vienna Massacre, 113, 171
Vietnam, 54, 63, 96, 99, 100, 161, 210
Viper Militia, 211
Virus, 29, 30, 173, 184, 186

Waco, Texas, 79, 109, 110, 122
Washington Times, 84
Water Supply, 48
Watson, Francis M., 212
Watson, Paul, 152, 157, 165
Weapons of Mass Destruction (WMD), 9, 29, 30, 31, 34, 206
  Biological, 29, 30, 105, 126, 183-184, 187, 206
  Chemical, 29-30, 105, 123, 126, 159, 183, 184, 186, 187, 192, 198, 206
  Nuclear, 2, 23, 25, 42, 121, 157, 158, 185, 192, 195, 198, 205, 206, 209
Weiner, Tim, 211
White Supremacist, 122, 155
Williams, Phil, 1, 39
Wilson, Peter, 41
Wisconsin, 84
Witness Protection, 22
WMD – see Weapons of Mass Destruction
World Bank, 21
World Trade Center, 51, 57, 121, 185, 199, 201, 215
World Wide Web, 15
Wren, Christopher S., 211
Wright, Billy "King Rat," 135

Yakuza, 23
Yugoslavia, 26

Zapitistas, 47
Zuckerman, Mortimer B., 210
Zundel, Ernst, 166, 167